BUYING A HOUSE IN NEW ZEALAND

By Alison Ripley Cubitt

Dedication

For Paige and Augustine,
my great-nieces. Love and hugs.

CONTENTS

Foreword 1

PART I LIVING IN NEW ZEALAND **3**
Living In New Zealand 5
Residence And Entry 72

PART II LOCATION, LOCATION **89**
Where To Find Your Ideal Home 91

PART III THE PURCHASING PROCESS **179**
Finance 181
Finding Properties For Sale 197
What Type Of Property To Buy 207
Renting A Home In New Zealand 230
Fees, Contracts And Conveyancing 245

PART IV WHAT HAPPENS NEXT **261**
Services 263
Making The Move 275
Building Or Renovating 285
Making Money From Your Property 299

Bibliography 322
About The Author 331
Also by Alison Ripley Cubitt 332
Acknowledgements 333

FOREWORD

New Zealand's stunning landscape is known throughout the world, but neither man nor woman can survive on scenery alone. For those of us privileged to call New Zealand home, we do so, not just because it's a beautiful country, but a very liveable one too.

It is ten years since the first edition of this book, and while much has changed, this little country in the South Pacific still continues to punch above its weight on the world stage — in agriculture, in film and on the sports field.

You may have already formed an opinion of what life in New Zealand might be like by going there on holiday, or from friends or relatives who moved out and made a new life.

But I can guarantee that when you experience New Zealand first hand, it will be so different from the one in your imagination. Crave the city life, but one with a South Pacific flavour? Auckland might be for you. Prefer a more urban lifestyle of galleries and theatre? Then give Wellington a try. If cities don't appeal, there's plenty on offer for families in the regional centres.

New Zealand has enjoyed many triumphs these past ten years but has also suffered its share of tragedy, the most notable of which devastated the people and city of Christchurch in February 2011, when an earthquake of a magnitude of 6.3 struck at a shallow depth of 3 miles/5km. Being so close to the surface and only 6 miles/10km from the city centre made it one of the deadliest of New Zealand's natural disasters. It killed 185 and 164 people were seriously injured. In the months following the first quake, the seismic activity didn't let up, and the residents of Christchurch endured aftershocks, some of which were even stronger than the first major quake.

But South Islanders are stoic and community-minded and they were determined to restore the city. Five years on, those brave enough to stay can take pride in the city they have rebuilt.

One of the most heartwarming stories of community spirit to come out of New Zealand was a social media crowdfunding campaign to buy a South Island beach and gift it to the nation. In just a few weeks the NZ two million dollars needed was raised, and in 2016 the beach was incorporated into the Abel Tasman National Park.

Whether it's a holiday house or a complete change of lifestyle that you crave, I hope this book will help you find it. Wherever in the world you come from, I'm sure it won't take long to call New Zealand 'home'.

PART I

LIVING IN NEW ZEALAND

LIVING IN NEW ZEALAND
RESIDENCY & ENTRY

LIVING IN NEW ZEALAND

CHAPTER SUMMARY

The standard of living is still good enough to persuade high-fliers from London and Los Angeles that it's worth taking a cut in salary to move there.

History. The 1840 Treaty of Waitangi is regarded as New Zealand's founding document.

Mythology. Maori mythology is as evocative and powerful as the stories of ancient Greece and Rome.

Getting There. Competition between the airlines that fly the route allows travellers a wider choice of stop-overs than ever before.

Geography. Packed within this one small country is a diversity of landscapes that is generally found only in entire continents. Nobody is more than a couple of hours drive from a beach.

Politics. The 'first past the post' voting system was abandoned in the mid 1990s for a version of proportional representation called MMP.

Crime. It is a safe destination where violent crime inflicted upon strangers is rare.

Food and Drink. The first person to make wine in

New Zealand was a Scot.

Communications. Broadband upload speed is faster than in the UK but download speed is slower.

There is still only one telephone area code for all of the South Island.

Media. Only on satellite television can you watch films or sports without advertisements.

Education. Schools are of a good standard with a number offering either Cambridge A Levels or the International Baccalaureate.

* * *

INTRODUCTION – FRIENDS IN COMMON

The last landfall before Antarctica, New Zealand is the ultimate destination to 'get away from it all'. While this geographical isolation might deter some, for those of you reading this book, New Zealand's perceived remoteness only adds to the allure. After that marathon plane journey, you might never want to leave. New Zealand offers a way of life with access to the outdoors that is unsurpassed, and with a population of just 4.7 million, you're sure to find an isolated beach somewhere.

For anyone coming from Australia, India, the UK or the USA, one of the attractions of moving to New Zealand is that you don't have to learn a new language to live the Kiwi lifestyle. And although you're bound to miss family and friends back home, staying in touch with loved ones has never been cheaper or easier, now that phone and video calls can be made over the internet.

Even though the strong ties between the UK and New Zealand have started to unravel in recent years, the two still have much in common. They compete in many of the same sports, including rugby. The forthcoming 2017 British and Irish Lions rugby tour will encourage thousands of sports fans to visit. As the Lions fans found out on their last tour in 2005, New Zealanders are easy going – except during a rugby tournament.

Rugby isn't just a sport – it's a national obsession, with the mood of the nation reflected by how well the All Blacks are playing. But despite the rivalry amongst the supporters and the teams during the tour; off the pitch, the thousands of fans who will travel half way round the world to watch their team play will be given a very hospitable welcome.

But New Zealand maintains important ties with other countries too, including its closest neighbour, Australia. Despite the occasional silly public digs that the media on both sides of the Tasman like to indulge in – it's Australia that continues to be New Zealand's closest trading partner, favourite holiday destination, and sporting rival. And although some New Zealanders like to heckle from the sidelines when their bigger and more powerful neighbour flexes its muscles, the rest of the country know that even good friends squabble occasionally. When it matters, the ties that bind them are just too strong.

The film industry is an important cultural link between New Zealand and the USA. In recent times the two nations have engaged in quiet diplomacy to heal their political rift, since New Zealand took its anti-nuclear stance, preventing nuclear-powered or nuclear-armed vessels from entering New Zealand territorial waters. Politics aside, visitors from the USA have always been well received.

The lure of Australia, the UK and the USA has proved too much to resist for the thousands of young (and some not so young) New Zealanders who go abroad to seek opportunities that are denied them in a country with such a small population. In the 20th century, many of the brightest had no option but to leave. Katherine Mansfield went in search of a literary peer group and Earnest Rutherford left for Britain as he was unable to find a suitable academic post. There he founded the discipline of nuclear physics.

In the 21st century, film director and local hero Peter Jackson stayed put and is admired as much by New Zealanders for persuading Hollywood to come to him, as he is for his *Lord of the Rings* and *Hobbit* films. Being able to make commercially successful work on home turf, without the need to export intellectual capital to Australia, the USA or the UK has brought a new energy to the creative industries. The once dreary capital of Wellington, or Wellywood, as some wags call it, is now a vibrant place to live and work.

As much as there are similarities between the United Kingdom and New Zealand, there are some important differences. As historian Michael King describes it, many came to New Zealand, looking to 'create a better Britain'. Although New Zealand may have been a 'better Britain' in the boom years of the 1960s, it was a dull one, with everything but the beach and church closed on Sundays. The lingering perception of the country as Britain's dairy farm, (now under the stewardship of a few hobbits) still exists. Some migrants are surprised at what a Pacific feel the city of Auckland has, and that British heritage is but one small part of a diverse, modern city.

New Zealand once had one of the highest standards of living in the developed world. That changed when the United Kingdom joined what was then the Common Market, (now the EU) and New Zealand had to find new places to sell its dairy products. Although the standard of living might not be as high as it once was, there are immeasurable qualities about New Zealand life that remain. Nobody is more than a couple of hours drive from a beach. Children attend schools that have green space and playing fields. Universities have pleasant campuses. There is little heavy industry. People who need a helping hand from the state aren't forced to live in depressing high-rise housing estates. The most modest home will generally have some outside space.

The wages might be better in neighbouring Australia, but the downside is that there are much greater divisions between rich and poor and social problems on a scale not yet seen in New Zealand. And despite the continued rumblings over the Treaty of Waitangi, New Zealand is much further along the path of reconciliation with its indigenous people. Not only has the country apologised for the wrongs of the past, but it continues to pay compensation for seized land.

The stunning scenery is there for everyone to visit and enjoy, and there are still remote rural areas where doors are left unlocked. But for the majority of New Zealanders who have to work for a living, most live an urban or suburban lifestyle, far removed from that rural idyll.

Cities though are much smaller than those in other countries. Even if you live in Auckland, the largest, with 1.57 million people, you can be out walking in a wilderness or sailing on the sparkling waters of the Hauraki Gulf within forty minutes of leaving work. That same evening, you could go to a concert of classical music, or the theatre, attend a cultural performance by a Pacific Island group, dine out at a top restaurant, or eat your fish and chips at a local beach.

Whether you want to spend a few months of the year escaping the northern hemisphere winter or are planning to make New Zealand your permanent base, there are many more options available to house hunters than there would be back home. You can buy a plot of land and commission an architect to design your forever home. Or how about a house and land package? If it's a case of best house, worst street, then the house can be relocated to somewhere better. You can renovate a church, build an earth house, or buy a good old Kiwi holiday house or *bach* (pronounced batch).

The median house price in Auckland, the most expensive city to buy a house, according to REINZ (Real Estate Institute of New Zealand) in September 2016, was NZ$825,000 (UK£464,000). Trophy property, waterfront or cliff-top goes for considerably more. But Auckland isn't representative of the rest of the country and there are still plenty of places with an excellent quality of life, where house prices are much lower. In September 2016, median house prices were NZ$450,000 in Nelson/Marlborough, the sunniest place in the country.

Houses or plots of land in remote rural areas, especially in pockets of the North Island, although a bargain, may be far away from shops, schools and medical services. Overseas buyers attracted to the Far North because of its subtropical climate don't realise that away from the main towns of Kerikeri, and Russell, there are few services. An unoccupied house in an isolated area is as vulnerable to theft as it is in any other country, unless you have a property management system in place. Alarms are of limited use if it is a 45-minute drive for the alarm monitoring company to get there.

Warm climate. Kerikeri, Napier, Nelson and Whangarei offer a great outdoor lifestyle and accessible facilities that attracts city dwellers from Auckland as well as new arrivals.

North of Auckland. Warkworth, just north of Auckland is worth considering, as it is less than an hour's drive to the city, retains a sense of community but one with great beaches and a number of wineries.

Opportunities in Christchurch. Five years on since the earthquake, the ongoing rebuild has created a number of job vacancies. It offers a great lifestyle for families willing to relocate there. The schools are excellent and family homes

20% to 40% cheaper than Wellington or Auckland. The climate is dry and although colder in winter, the Canterbury region has long, hot summers. The Mount Hutt ski field is a 90-minute drive from Christchurch, and it has the longest season of any ski resort in the country.

* * *

THE CREATION MYTH – MAUI LANDS A FISH

The creation myth of Maori mythology is one of many wonderful stories in a culture that celebrates an oral storytelling tradition. When *Ranginui* (Sky Father) and *Papatuanuku* (Earth Mother) got together, their union created powerful offspring: *Tu Matauenga*, the God of War, *Tawhirimatea* the God of Winds and Storms, *Tangaroa*, the god of the Oceans, and *Tane Mahuta*, the God of the Forests.

Rangi and Papa were so tightly joined that no light was visible between sky and earth. But Rangi and Papa's children were no different to any others. They wanted to do things their way. Tired of living in perpetual darkness, they demanded that there be light. Their only option was to separate their parents. Tawhirimatea stood up to his brothers and opposed the plan. He was so angry that he flew up into the sky and threw down great bolts of thunder and lightning.

The other siblings tried but failed to prise Earth from Sky. And then it was Tane Mahuta's turn. The giant kauri tree placed his shoulders against his mother, the Earth and his feet against his father, the Sky and with all his might he finally forced his parents apart. At last the world was awash with light, but Ranginui cried tears enough to fill the oceans. And even now the grief of their parting manifests itself as rain and mist.

But Tane's work wasn't over. Creatures and gods weren't

enough to inhabit the world. A woman had to be created. Made from the red earth found at Kurakawa, *Hinetitama*, the Dawn Maiden went on to form a union with Tane. And from this union came the human race. But when Hineti-tama found that her husband and father were one and the same, she escaped to the spirit world. Because of her the dawn rises in the east and sets in the west. Not far behind her is Tane, and like all of mankind, must follow her for eternity down her chosen path.

Maui Goes Fishing and Comes Back with the North Island. The exploits of the half-human demi-god, *Maui* are known in myths right across the Pacific, from Hawaii to the Solomon Islands and across to New Zealand. Even before Maui went fishing, he did man a favour, slowing the sun's journey through the sky so the days were longer and the nights were shorter.

Out fishing with his brothers, Maui slung his enchanted fish-hook (made from the jawbone of a female ancestor) over the side. The water started to froth and foam as Maui chanted. His brothers could scarcely believe that Maui had fished up a great tract of land. They called it *Te Ika a Maui* (the fish of Maui). Maui asked his brothers to look after his find while he went and made an offering to the gods. But they disobeyed him and started to scale this fish and hack pieces off it. The gods became angry at this insult. They hadn't even been offered their promised fish.

Te Ika a Maui started to move and writhe about, and that's why much of the land of *Aotearoa* (New Zealand) is mountainous and uncultivated. Had the brothers done as Maui told them it would have been smooth and flat.

The dry land fished up by Maui, which had lain beneath the sea, became the North Island of Aotearoa. And when you look at a map you can see that it's fish-shaped. The mouth is Wellington Harbour, the East Coast and Taranaki are the two fins; Lake Taupo is the heart and Northland is the tail. And the hook (*Te matau a Maui* – Maui's Fishhook) is the cape at Heretaunga (Cape Kidnappers).

According to some tribes the South Island is the canoe *Te Waka o Maui* from which Maui went fishing. To steady himself, Maui placed his foot on the Kaikoura Peninsula, and Stewart Island was the anchor stone that kept the canoe steady while he hauled up his enormous catch.

A Voyage of Mythic Proportions. Like the creation myth, the story of New Zealand's settlement was written down, not by Maori but by Europeans. A version of the story is told by both cultures. In 950 AD the great Polynesian navigator, *Kupe* came to a land filled with only birds, which he named Aotearoa 'the land of the long white cloud'. On his return to Hawaiki, the ancestral home of all Polynesians, he gave instructions on how to retrace his voyage. Where Hawaiki is exactly, no one knows. The Society Islands (one of which is Tahiti) or the Cook Islands are the two contenders.

Kupe's voyage was retraced in 1350AD when a 'Great Fleet' of seven canoes arrived simultaneously to settle, staying together, establishing a tribal structure that formed the basis of the seven main tribal groups found today. One theory is that they followed the migratory route of whales or birds. Generations of school children were told this tale, but the real story of how New Zealand came to be settled may never be known. From the air, the Pacific Ocean seems vast and empty, so it's hard to imagine what kind of extraordinary courage, strength and navigational skills it took to set out on such a voyage.

* * *

HISTORY

The First Settlers

Scientific evidence suggests that New Zealand was first settled within a 100 years of the 'Great Fleet' myth, around the thirteenth century AD. An initial population of between 100 to 200 was needed for the numbers to grow to the 100,000 reached by the 18th century and although Aotearoa has since been adopted as the Maori name for New Zealand, it wasn't known as this when the first Europeans arrived.

The social structure of Maori society was established long before the white man set foot on this land. It was an agricultural society where food crops, (all of which had to be brought by canoe on those early voyages) of *taro*, (yams) and *kumara* (sweet potato) were cultivated. Maori lived in villages centred around a *marae* (meeting house) and strict protocols had been established about encounters between social groups meeting for the first time.

Moriori and Maori. A tribe settled on the Chatham Islands who called themselves *Moriori*. Now regarded as just a different term for the word Maori, the story went that this group were settlers from West Polynesia who had arrived before Maori. These peaceful people, it was alleged, had got there first and were therefore the rightful indigenous inhabitants of New Zealand and Maori were the colonisers who behaved as badly to the Moriori as the white man did to Maori.

Although the Moriori were unable to fend off repeated attack and did suffer at the hands of other Maori tribes, they were one and the same people. The theory that they arrived before Maori was disproved as early as the 1920s, but even as late as the 1980s, the story was promoted for political gain as a way of justifying the seizure of Maori land, without having to pay financial compensation.

The First Europeans

In the 17th century, an era of remarkable scientific and technological advancement, visitors from one of the world's richest trading nations ventured further south than any earlier expedition had done. Abel Tasman had strayed that far south, in his search for *terra australis incognito*, the elusive southern continent. On behalf of the Dutch East India Company, he was seeking further opportunities for trade in precious metals, minerals and spices. Tasman managed to miss the continent of Australia on his voyage and brushed past a much smaller landmass, which was named *Van Diemen's Land* – Tasmania as we know it today.

Catching sight of the South Island he anchored in a bay that must have looked idyllic. But when a group of Maori in a canoe challenged the occupants of a rowing boat, the lack of any understanding of Polynesian protocol led to the deaths of four of Tasman's crewmen. When another canoe got too close to Tasman's ships, one of the Dutch vessels fired upon it, killing one of its occupants. This deadly encounter marked the first killing of a Maori by a European. To the First People the force of the firepower unleashed by these visitors must have been terrifying. Tasman had not so much as set foot on the land before he had to flee. He called the new land 'Staten Land' later to be renamed *Nieuw Zeeland*. That idyllic spot was known as Murderer's Bay although now locals prefer the name Golden Bay. The visitors may have been from one of the world's richest and sophisticated trading nations, but their failure to comprehend the local social customs meant that Tasman was unable to claim the territory for Holland. The First People were left alone by outsiders for another 125 years.

In 1769 Captain Cook was in the Pacific completing his observations of the transit of Venus across the sun, a very rare event. Under the command of the Royal Navy he was instructed to sail south, either to find the elusive terra australis incognito or, failing that, to continue to 'the land discover'd by Tasman'. Cook was far better prepared than Tasman as he had on board the *Endeavour* a translator from Tahiti who could not only act as an interpreter but more importantly understood custom and protocol. Cook aimed to ensure cordial relations with any native peoples he encountered.

Despite his best intentions, misunderstandings were inevitable, particularly among the frightened crew who fired on and killed indigenous people when they mistook bravado for aggression. But Cook was able to observe social customs, and although initial social contact appeared hostile, he believed that much of it was for show. Careful to avoid any confrontation, he was able to barter goods in exchange for fresh food for his crew.

On that first voyage, Cook spent six months circumnavigating both islands. His charts were so accurate that he was able to determine that the mythical southern continent that Tasman had tried in vain to find had never existed. Where Tasman had seen one landmass, Cook discovered that there were two main islands of New Zealand.

He noted that this land had a plentiful supply of timber and flax and that there were seals and whales offshore that could be commercially harvested. Cook made two further voyages in 1773 and 1774 and again in 1777 before he was killed in a disastrous skirmish in Hawaii. Closely followed by Cook were two French expeditions one of which ended in calamity for crew and locals alike. A breach of protocol resulted in most of the remaining French sailors being killed then eaten. Firepower from what crew that was left caused the deaths of up to 300 Maori.

By the 1790s the barbaric practice of transportation to the penal colonies in what is now Australian territory brought many ships off New Zealand's coast. These ships needed to take shelter from storms and sailors needed somewhere to rest. But as many New Zealanders will tell you, the prosperity of the early settlers wasn't built on the convict trade. Nor are they the descendants of those who survived the misery of transportation. Europeans had already learned from the deaths on the Dutch, British and French voyages that Maori wouldn't hesitate to fight back if anyone tried to subdue them. They would no doubt have fiercely contested any such attempt to use their land in such a way. Norfolk Island was selected as a penal colony instead.

Although sealers and whalers were the first to harvest the natural resources in New Zealand's oceans, it wasn't until the 1820s that the land was exploited. A supply of tall, straight, top quality native hardwoods was needed to build more ships, necessary to expand Britain's naval fleet. With the assistance of Cook's artists, who had so meticulously recorded the flora of New Zealand, shipbuilders knew exactly where such a plentiful supply existed.

By the 1820s the first major European settlement was in the Bay of Islands, considered to be a rough and lawless place. Missionaries had no difficulty imposing their Christian values on the indigenous population: it was the sealers and whalers who were the problem. As well as drunkenness and loose morals these visitors brought something far worse. With no immunity to any European diseases Maori were unable to withstand the onslaught on their health and many died.

Despite Cook's painstaking efforts in charting and circumnavigating the coastline on his three voyages, New Zealand had never formally become a British possession. Britain was having enough trouble with its two major colonies of America and Canada, so there was little enthusiasm for adding this small South Pacific outpost to its empire. A compromise was made over governance, and it was decided that the nearest neighbour, New South Wales should extend its laws to include New Zealand. Separated by the Tasman Sea, the distance made it impossible to administer laws from afar.

By the early 1830s a group of northern Maori chiefs, concerned at the lawlessness of the colonists, decided to approach the British government for formal protection. Maori were concerned at the growing number of European settlers who were trying to buy land in one-sided deals that were highly unfavourable to the indigenous people. Regulation was needed to protect Maori interests. *Ngai Tahu* of the South Island, in particular, was anxious about their established and lucrative trade with New South Wales.

As well as their problems with the British, Maori were worried about French imperial ambitions in the region. France had set up a Catholic mission station in the Hokianga, which brought their ships and traders to the area. As the retaliation for the killing of Marion de Fresne had been so brutal, Maori had no desire to enter into negotiations with France. If they were forced to make a choice, Britain seemed the better option.

The Treaty of Waitangi

The British government responded in half-hearted fashion by sending an inexperienced and under qualified James Busby as British Resident. Busby was sent to live in a modest cottage at Waitangi, since preserved for the nation as the site where the historic treaty was signed. Appointed as a civilian administrator, he had no real powers of governance. Busby's assertion that Maori were unable to govern themselves led to the British government proposing the 1840 Treaty of Waitangi. The Maori translation of the Treaty, signed by 500 of the 539 Maori chiefs was at odds with the English version. The Treaty that Maori signed stated that the British Crown would preserve law and order between Maori and the Europeans, would protect Maori trade and ensure that Maori controlled land and other resources that they wished to keep. The English version gave full sovereignty to the British Crown.

Maori were asked to concede sovereignty, but the word in Maori was translated as governorship. It is unlikely that Maori would have signed away their right to sovereignty had they understood what exactly it was. In the Maori text, the Crown guaranteed to the *tangata whenua* (people of the land) the right to possess their properties as long as they wished to keep them. In perhaps the worst mistranslation of all, the English version expressed this as individual property rights, something that didn't exist in a culture based on collective ownership.

The English version stated that the Crown had exclusive right to buy Maori land, something that has caused considerable disagreement as Maori were unable to sell any land to a third party, even if the Crown rejected it. Another significant part of the Treaty that wasn't understood by Maori was that they were now under the jurisdiction of British law and what citizenship meant in practice. In international law it is the indigenous text that should have been agreed to, instead of the Crown's version. These important discrepancies have ensured that there continues to be on-going debate around the Treaty.

The New Zealand Wars

Almost as soon as the Treaty was signed, there were allegations of breaches. Hone Heke, who was a supporter of the Treaty, believing that it would bring more opportunities for trade was so frustrated by these transgressions that he chopped down the flagstaff at Russell in protest. Frustrations with British incursion into territory deemed to be under the authority of Maori erupted into what is now known as the New Zealand Wars in 1845, which lasted until 1872. According to the historian James Belich, these were not mere skirmishes but involved 18,000 armed troops against 60,000 Maori, including women and children. That Maori were able to hold out against colonial expansion was remarkable, given the uneven odds. Belich's view is that the New Zealand Wars marked a turning point in the country's race relations.

In the late 1950s, conservative Maori groups chose to work within the system to champion Maori rights. Younger activists accused them of being part of the establishment and unrepresentative of urban Maori. In the 1970s, younger activists demanded to have their voices heard. Through a series of well-publicised marches and demonstrations, they became noticeably more politicised.

Land Marches and Treaty Settlements

In 1975 30,000 protestors marched to Parliament under the slogan, 'Not One More Acre of Maori Land'. The onus was on government and other New Zealanders to address issues around the treaty that had been forgotten in the ensuing years. One of the most high profile demonstrations occurred at *Takaparawha* or Bastion Point in Auckland.

The Waitangi Tribunal was established, but a government bill sought to restrict the amount that could be paid in reparations in total as a billion dollars. Through the Office of Treaty Settlements some of the first claims began. The settlements were neither perfect nor fair, but the participating tribes saw them as a way to move forward and a chance to rebuild their assets.

To illustrate the limits of compensation, the Waikato settlement of 170 million dollars was a fraction of the estimated 21 billion dollars estimated loss to the tribe. And to many Maori the payments ignores the issue of sovereignty altogether.

To those coming to New Zealand now it can seem that the problems with the treaty are about looking to the past rather than to the future. Although the treaty is far from perfect it's still New Zealand's founding document, and some New Zealanders regard it the way Americans see their Constitution.

One contemporary issue that has highlighted the grievances of the past is the ownership and access to the seabed and foreshore. In 2003 a court decision stated that Maori could claim customary title over this coastal land, but the government contradicted that saying that the Crown owned it. Protests over this move forced a compromise and the government sought to defuse the situation by putting the land in question into the public domain for all New Zealanders.

European Settlement

At Te Papa, New Zealand's national museum, an exhibition traced the origins of European settlement. Between 1840 and 1850 over 22,000 immigrants arrived from England through the New Zealand Company. Part of a social experiment instigated by Edward Gibbon Wakefield, the concept was to ensure that many of the settlers were middle-class so that they would have a 'civilising' effect on the country. But like so many attempts at social engineering, this one failed as uncontrolled immigration came from the rest of the British Isles including Scotland and Northern Ireland. And despite conflicts with the indigenous people, life for the settlers prospered, thanks to wool, gold and timber.

In 1893, New Zealand gave women the vote, the first country in the world to do so. New Zealand suffered as much as any country did during the Depression in 1929, with food queues and riots. In World War 1 out of a population of one million people, New Zealand sent 100,000 men to fight for Britain in a war 12,000 miles away. And in World War II troops from the dominion were sent in the same numbers to fight in Europe, the Middle East and in South East Asia.

An Enviable Lifestyle

For a country still suffering from rationing, the attraction of New Zealand was a strong one and from the late 1940s until the 1970s over 75,000 Britons moved there with the assistance of the government. These 'ten pound poms' who came over on an assisted passage were brought in to make up numbers in the rapidly expanding work force. The marketing campaign promised them a life they could only dream about in urban industrial Britain – fresh air, a detached house, good weather and a beach lifestyle.

In the 1950s and 1960s, New Zealand prospered and had one of the highest standards of living in the world. Britain's joining of the Common Market was inevitable, but New Zealand didn't have any long-term strategy in place and was unprepared when it did happen. Although other markets had been found for exports, the morale of the nation was gloomy.

End of the Boom Years

In 1975 the Prime Minister of the National government was the blustering Robert 'Piggy' Muldoon who perfected the art of the 'sound bite' media comment. When asked if he was worried about the country's brightest and best moving to Australia, Muldoon in typical fashion, managed to put a sarcastic spin on it, claiming that, 'New Zealanders who leave for Australia raise the IQ of both countries'. Muldoon was quick to blame the outgoing Labour government for the country's woes, but National's spending habits under

Muldoon put Labour's in the shade. As unemployment rose and New Zealand's famed standard of living began to drop, thousands left to seek a better life overseas.

The 1970s saw the formation of bike gangs in South Auckland. At the same time, Polynesian immigrants arrived in large numbers causing tensions not only with white society, but with some Maori, concerned that the immigrants would compete with them for housing and social welfare. Muldoon responded by instructing police to conduct spot identity checks to ensure none were in the country illegally. Those that were found to be were deported with little or no right to appeal.

During the Muldoon era, African nations boycotted the Montreal Olympics because New Zealand had sent an All Black team to South Africa during the boycott. In 1981 the New Zealand Rugby Union chose to ignore public opinion by planning a Springbok tour of the country. It caused serious civil unrest with marches and demonstrations and even caused divisions within families between those that believed that the tour should go ahead and those that passionately opposed it.

Muldoon's reign although full of grandiose schemes such as his 'Think Big' economic strategy, was largely ineffectual. By 1984 the country was tired of Muldoon and his over-spending and returned a Labour government to power, headed by David Lange. But once voted in, Labour abandoned its traditional left-wing policies to solve the country's considerable economic problems. Under the stewardship of Finance Minister Roger Douglas, the government embarked on a range of free market economic reforms that went further than even those of Margaret Thatcher's.

Standing Tall

In 1985 all nuclear-armed and nuclear-propelled vessels were banned from New Zealand waters. New Zealand's allies in the ANZUS treaty, Australia and the USA didn't much like this move. Nor did France, which was busy conducting nuclear tests in the Pacific. That same year, the Greenpeace vessel, *Rainbow Warrior*, was bombed by French intelligence agents, while docked in Auckland harbour. A member of the ship's crew died in the explosion. This cowardly act hardened New Zealand's resolve to maintain a firm anti-nuclear policy, and the country was much admired by many in the developed world. Smaller nations saw New Zealand as a role model that dared to stand up to its much bigger and more powerful allies.

In 1987 those investors who had embraced free market reforms found out the hard way that there was a downside to their speculation. The economic crash hit New Zealand hard and a period of economic recession ensued. There was one event during the era of all that belt-tightening that gave the whole country the morale boost it needed. In 1995 Team New Zealand won that most prestigious yachting title, the America's Cup.

By the end of the 1990s recession was over and New Zealand had much to look forward to. In 2000 it was the first country to see the sun rise on the new millennium and later that year Team New Zealand successfully defended its America's Cup title, only to lose it in 2004 after a disappointing race series. But the mood of the nation was buoyed by the total domination of the 2004 Academy Awards by Peter Jackson and his crew. If only Gollum could have got his hands on 'the precious' – the biggest haul of gold statuettes that New Zealand has ever seen. A triumphant Return of the King indeed.

* * *

THE POLITICS OF POWERSHARING

New Zealand's system of government is a parliamentary democracy with Queen Elizabeth II as the head of state. The Governor-General is appointed as her representative. There is only one legislative chamber, the House of Representatives. The Prime Minister and Members of Parliament are elected by New Zealanders. The two main political parties are the centre-right National and Labour on the centre-left. Up until 1996 elections were won or lost using the 'first past the post system', but when New Zealand's version of proportional representation (Mixed Member Proportional – referred to as MMP), was introduced, the situation became more complex.

With MMP voters have two votes, one to elect their MP and the other to choose a party. Proportional representation is a much fairer system but problems arise when the majority party has to form a coalition with a minor party that may be at odds with them on certain key issues. It was the National government in the mid 1990s that introduced MMP and they were in coalition with the right-wing New Zealand First. But the two parties fell out over key policy and the situation became so bad that the coalition was dissolved and National struggled to govern alone.

In 1999 a Labour-led coalition headed up by Helen Clark ousted National. In 2002 Labour was returned to power for a second term. National had lost its way in the worst election defeat in 70 years. Labour found aspects of MMP to be equally as challenging as National. Either the relationships soured over the three-year term or their preferred coalition partner didn't pass the crucial 5% vote threshold. The paradox of MMP is that power sharing can only work where the parties share a common ideology. But even natural allies like Labour and the left-leaning Greens had a major dispute over the issue of genetic modification.

Life for the minor parties is perilous as every three years not only does the individual risk losing their seat in parliament, but if the party doesn't manage to retain 5% of the vote, it risks political oblivion. In a small country like New Zealand, career politicians have a habit of re-inventing themselves and returning to power either in local government or as representatives of a minor party.

The September 2005 Labour-led election victory was won by such a narrow margin that the results weren't declared for another month, after the special votes had been counted.

In 2008 National won, ending Labour's nine years in power. But National under Prime Minister John Key found that they too couldn't win outright and had to form a minority government. National won again in 2011 and 2014, still unable to govern without support from the minor parties. The next general election will be held in 2017.

* * *

GEOGRAPHY

Physical Features

The size of the United Kingdom, Italy, or the US state of Colorado, but spread across two main islands, the total land mass of New Zealand is 104,454 sq miles (270,534 sq km). A body of water as wide as the English Channel, the Cook Strait separates the two islands. Stewart Island, the third largest of all the off-shore islands, lies at the southern tip of the South Island. Lake Taupo in the central North Island is the country's biggest lake at 235 sq miles (607 sq km) and is the source of the longest river, the Waikato, which runs for 264 miles (425 km). Packed within this one small country is a diversity of landscape that is only found in entire continents, with lakes, mountains, volcanoes, sub-tropical beaches and rainforest.

Geological Features

New Zealand is a geological upstart as its present shape was formed barely 10,000 years ago. But rocks found dating back 500 million years that originated in Australia and Antarctica suggest that New Zealand was once part of that supercontinent, *Gondwanaland*. After the land had broken away a combination of continental drift, volcanic and seismic activity formed more land and over the centuries the country gradually began to take shape.

Earthquakes and Volcanoes. New Zealand sits on top of two tectonic plates, the Indo-Australian and the Pacific plate. Seismic activity occurs when the two overlap, ensuring that this restless land never sleeps. From the Bay of Plenty, a fault line runs diagonally through New Plymouth and down through Wellington. Across Cook Strait, the fault line passes through Marlborough, Nelson and then on a diagonal to join the Alpine fault on the west coast of the South Island.

Most of the 400 earthquakes recorded every year pass unnoticed, although earthquakes have caused damage and fatalities. Until 2011, New Zealand's most devastating earthquake was in 1931 when a quake measuring 7.8 hit Napier in the Hawke's Bay. Out of the rubble of the 1931 Napier earthquake a new city was built in the Art Deco style.

In May 1968 a recently emigrated British family living near Nelson, recall shattered glassware and their newly surfaced tennis court developing a large crack running down its length. Measuring 7.1 on the Richter scale the epicentre was over 100km away at Inangahua Junction, on the South Island's west coast.

The February 2011 earthquake that hit the city of Christchurch measured 6.3. There were 185 deaths and 164 people were injured. Much of the downtown area was reduced to rubble, including the iconic Christchurch Cathedral. It was the quake's shallow depth – only 5km from the earth's surface and 10km from the city centre that made it one of New Zealand's worst natural disasters. In the months following the first quake, the seismic activity didn't let up, and the residents of Christchurch endured aftershocks, some of which were even stronger than the first major quake.

In September 2016 a powerful quake of 7.1 was recorded off the coast of Gisborne. It could be felt as far away as Auckland, but locally the only consequence was some minor damage to property. In November that same year, two quakes of 7.5 hit close to the coastal town of Kaikoura and inland near Hamner Springs in north Canterbury. This quake killed two people and caused significant damage to roads and the railway line between Picton and Christchurch.

But tectonic plates crashing against each other cause more than earthquakes. The Southern Alps, the icy spine that runs 300 miles (500km) along the South Island was a direct result of this geological disturbance. Here you will find Aoraki Mount Cook (the Cloud Piercer), the country's tallest mountain at 12,316 feet (3754m).

As well as earthquakes and mountains, volcanoes form in the gap between plates. And in the central North Island, the atmosphere can get a little heated. The volcanic heartland is the Taupo Volcanic Zone, part of the Pacific Ring of Fire that links the mountains around Lake Taupo (in fact, an enormous crater lake), beyond the coast of the Bay of Plenty to White Island. White Island is the country's most active volcano and can be visited on a day trip. While the volcanic cones that dot Auckland, especially the sleeping giant Rangitoto out in the Hauraki Gulf, have lain dormant for the past 500 years, in the Taupo Volcanic Zone, seismologists carefully monitor the crater lakes for signs of potential eruptions.

Close to Rotorua, partial excavations have unearthed a village on the shores of Lake Tarawera, where in the 19th century a catastrophic eruption not only buried a village but destroyed the famous Pink and White Terraces. In 1995 and 1996, Mount Ruapehu erupted, forcing the closure of the ski fields. In 2012, Mount Tongariro did the same, diverting New Zealand's most spectacular day walk, the Tongariro Crossing.

But all this geological and geothermal activity has meant that visitors and locals alike have plenty of opportunity for recreational escapes. You can relax in a hot pool after a day's skiing, or, at Hot Water Beach on the Coromandel Peninsula, you can lie on a beach and soak in a hot pool at the same time.

* * *

CLIMATE

Surrounded by the Pacific Ocean to the north and east and the Tasman Sea to the west, all that water gives New Zealand a maritime climate where temperatures at sea level never get too hot or too cold. But as more than 75% of the country is over 200 metres high, variations in temperature, amount of rainfall, and wind vary significantly. In all, there are nine climate zones, ranging from subtropical in the north, to cool and temperate in the far south, to alpine conditions in the Southern Alps. These microclimates occur because of proximity to the west or east coasts, their situation near mountains, whether sheltered from winds, such as Nelson and Marlborough, or exposed in coastal areas buffeted by gales, like Wellington. Mean annual temperatures in the north are as high as 16 degrees and as low as 10 degrees Celsius in the south. Midsummer temperatures can reach the 30s.

The seasons in the Southern Hemisphere are an exact reversal of those in the northern, with winter from June to August, spring from September to November, summer from December to February and the autumn months March, April and May. Seasonal variations are more marked in the South Island, while in the subtropical north, temperatures are more evenly spread throughout the year.

Weather systems forming in the Tasman Sea and the Southern Alps protect the east coast of the South Island from the full force of the prevailing westerlies. The west coast experiences some of the wettest weather while the east coast remains the driest, due to the protective barrier created by the mountain ranges.

In the north and the central North Island winter is the season for the highest rainfall whereas in the southern areas winters are generally drier. Most of New Zealand has more than 2000 hours of sunshine a year, the sunniest place being Nelson at the top of the South Island. But the sun brings with it a very high and potentially damaging UV level to those with fair skin, especially in summer, autumn and spring. It's particularly high in mountainous areas.

* * *

GETTING THERE

New Zealand is a long haul destination from almost anywhere except Australia. Sydney, Melbourne and Brisbane are a mere three hours away by plane. Although some cruise ships include Auckland on their itineraries, the only realistic way to get there is by air. While the tyranny of distance might deter some, others are attracted by the peaceful isolation in the South Pacific, far away from the world's trouble spots. The discomfort of the journey is soon forgotten as visitors start to experience a lifestyle that is the envy of many.

Tourism is a major industry, which means that travellers have a choice of a number of airlines that fly the route. Since Emirates added Australasia to its itinerary, travellers from Britain have the additional option of flying via the Middle East, as well as via North America or South East Asia. It is also possible to travel through South America. On a direct route, the trip can be made in around 24 hours. From North America, there are a number of stopover options in the South Pacific.

The airlines listed below fly directly to New Zealand or work with a partner airline that operates the service. The airline alliances that serve this route are One World and Star Alliance. Use the list below to check schedules and timetables. The intense competition between airlines means that routes can be axed at short notice. While airlines like Air New Zealand and Singapore Airlines have daily services, other airlines may only fly three or four times a week. Contact the airline or your travel agent for current information.

Airlines

From Australia:

The competition amongst airlines that fly across the Tasman between Australia and New Zealand is intense. Customers have benefited from even cheaper prices since the no-frills operators have entered the market.

Air New Zealand: Brisbane Travel Centre 07 3334 2036; Melbourne Travel Centre 03 9251 5036; Perth Travel Centre 08 9442 6077; Sydney Travel Centre 02 8248 0030; www.airnz.com.au

Emirates: 1300 303 777; www.emirates.com.au

Jetstar: 03 9645 5999; www.jetstar.com

Qantas: 13 11 31; www.qantas.com

Virgin Australia: 13 67 89; www.virginaustralia.com

From the UK:

Air New Zealand: 0800 737 000; www.airnz.co.nz from London Heathrow to Auckland via LA or San Francisco, or various Pacific Island destinations.

British Airways: 08750 850 9850; www.britishairways.com from London Heathrow to Auckland and Christchurch via America and Australia.

Cathay Pacific: 020 8834 8800; www.cathaypacific.com from London Heathrow to Auckland via Hong Kong.

Emirates: 0870 243 2222; www.emirates.com from London Heathrow to Auckland and Christchurch.

Auckland via Dubai or major centres in South East Asia. Christchurch is via Dubai and Melbourne.

Garuda Indonesia: 0807 1 GARUDA427832; www. garuda-indonesia.com from London Gatwick to Auckland via Jakarta, Bali and Brisbane.

Korean Air: 0800 413 000; www.koreanair.com from London Heathrow to Auckland and Christchurch via Seoul.

Jal: 0845 7747700; www.jal.co.jp from London Heathrow via Tokyo connecting with a codeshare partner to Christchurch and Auckland.

Latam Airlines: 0800 917 0572 www.lan.com from London Heathrow to Madrid then via Santiago to Auckland.

Malaysia Airlines: (MAS) 0161 835 3020; www. malaysiaairlines.com from London Heathrow to Auckland via Kuala Lumpur.

Qantas: 020 8846 0466; www.qantas.com from London Heathrow to Auckland and Christchurch via Bangkok, Singapore, Sydney or Melbourne.

Singapore Airlines: 01784 266122; www.singaporeair. com from Manchester and London Heathrow to Auckland and Christchurch via Singapore.

Thai Air: 0870 606 0911; www.thaiair.com fly from London Heath- row via Bangkok.

United Airlines: 0800 0656 2001; www.united.com fly from London Heathrow connecting into various destinations in the US with a code-share partner to Auckland.

From Canada and the USA:

Air New Zealand: 1 800 262 1234; www.airnewzealand.com

Air Tahiti Nui: Toll Free 877 824 4846

From South Africa:

Qantas: 11 441 8550; www.qantas.com.au to New Zealand from Johannesburg via Australia.

South African Airways: 0861 359 722; www.flysaa. com from Johannesburg as far as Australia, where you can connect to New Zealand with code share partner Qantas.

Travel Advice

In low season, some of the deals can be incredibly good value, given the distance. Low season is generally from April to June in the UK. Avoid Christmas, if you can, as not only do you have to book months in advance, but the flights cost significantly more.

Direct flights with the shortest refuelling stops are always the first to be booked out, no matter when you travel. Dates for low, shoulder and high season vary between airlines. For those with more time, a round-the-world ticket may be the best option for travellers keen to see as much as they can on the way. The ticket may not be much more expensive than a standard return, although the cost of the stopovers should be taken into account.

Travel Agents and Online Booking

Austravel: 0808 115 5218; www.austravel.com

Bridge the World: 0800 988 6884;
www.bridgetheworld.com

Cresta World Travel: 0161 927 7177;
www.crestaworldtravel.co.uk

Expedia: www.expedia.co.uk

Flight Centre: 0808 260 9779;
www.flightcentre.co.uk

Lastminute.com: 0800 083 4000;
www.lastminute.com

STA Travel: 0333 321 0099 www.statravel.co.uk

Trailfinders: 020 7368 1400; www.trailfinders.com

Travel Bag: 0871 402 1644; www.travelbag.co.uk

Airports. Auckland and Christchurch are the two major international airports. Wellington Airport's runway is too short to handle wide-bodied aircraft. Regional airports such as Dunedin, Rotorua and Queenstown operate flights to and from Australia.

* * *

GETTING AROUND

Domestic Air Travel. The major domestic airline is Air New Zealand, which through the Link service, offers connections to many of the smaller centres. Jetstar, the low-cost airline owned by Qantas, flies a domestic route in New Zealand and is the national airline's main competitor.

Car hire. The best option for house hunters to get around the country is to fly and then hire a car, as there's no long distance train service. Global companies such as Budget, Hertz and Avis all have offices or agents in most of the bigger cities and towns. The larger firms may also offer one-way rentals. Some don't allow you to take their car on the ferry across the Cook Strait, or else they charge a premium to do this. A car will normally be dropped off in either Picton or Wellington and another vehicle will be ready for collection after you've crossed the strait.

Local car hire companies offer much better rates than the big firms, but without a network of countrywide branches, if a car breaks down there could be delays in finding a replacement vehicle. Smaller firms may not provide Collision Damage Waiver Insurance.

On the Road

Negotiating the sometimes narrow and twisty roads can be a challenge for international visitors. There is no long distance motorway network and the only real motorway is in Auckland.

State Highway One, the main road between Auckland and Wellington would be considered an A road in the UK. Mainly single or dual carriageway, the further south you travel, the highway detours through town centres, which can add to the journey time. Roads can be rough, with uneven camber, so exercise care when overtaking.

Speed limits. The speed limit on the open road is 100 kph (62 mph) and 50kph (31 mph) in most built-up areas. The Limited Speed Zone or LSZ sign requires drivers to make their own assessment on when it is safe to travel at 100 kph or when to slow down to 50 kph.

Driving Standards

The standard of driving is lower compared with the UK or Europe. New Zealanders are courteous until they get behind the wheel. When two lanes become one, instead of merging 'like a zip', drivers often barge in front, with no consideration for the person behind them. On the urban motorway network each lane is treated as a separate entity, so that the principle of keeping left doesn't apply. Slow drivers can hog the outside lane, holding up all the traffic, exacerbating urban congestion. Impatient drivers will overtake on the inside lane and weave in and out of the traffic. Tailgating and an aversion to indicators are another factor of driving on New Zealand roads. Stop signs are treated like Give Way signs and Give Way generally means go, if you can sneak in.

Traffic Management. Getting caught speeding can result in a hefty fine and police make good use of hidden speed cameras. Be careful on the straight, empty roads in Canterbury. None other than Helen Clark, the then Prime Minister, travelling in a motorcade, was caught speeding, resulting in an embarrassing court case. As drink driving is a contributory factor in many road accidents, a rigorous system of random breath testing is enforced.

Driving Hazards. When approaching large logging trucks and slow camper vans on country roads, be aware of reckless overtaking by impatient drivers. Driving too close to the edge on rural roads can be hazardous because of loose stones. The rule, as it is driving anywhere, is to drive to the conditions. In winter, icy roads can be a problem in more remote areas. Driving at night can be challenging on rural roads. Marker posts at the side of rural roads can be difficult to adjust to, if you are used to the 'cats eyes' system. Rural bridges may have weight restrictions and are often single lane only. Even when it is your right of way, slow right down and pull to the side if necessary.

The use of hand-held mobile phones in cars is not yet banned, even though their use has contributed to many road fatalities. In the cities, it pays not to be hard up against the intersection when turning right, in case a careless driver fails to take the corner correctly and clips the right wing of your car. SUV drivers who steer with one hand and look down at their phones to send or receive a text message are particularly frightening.

Road Accident Statistics. New Zealanders love their cars. There were 3.2 million cars registered on the road in May 2016, according to the NZ Transport Agency, out of a population of 4.7 million. Unfortunately, the country rates poorly in the fatal accident league table with 0.9 people dying per 10,000 vehicles. Out of every 100,000, there are 6.9 deaths. Only the USA at 10.2, is worse, in a selective table of countries known for safer driving. Australia has 4.9 fatalities per 100,000, United Kingdom 2.9 and Sweden is the safest at 2.8. Excessive speed is to blame for 29 percent of the fatal accidents, with drink driving blamed for 28 percent, despite the introduction in 2014 of one of the lowest alcohol limits in the world.

Safety Belts and Child Restraints. Safety belts must be worn by the driver and the passengers, unless you have a doctor's certificate. Children under the age of five should be properly restrained in an approved child restraint, unless travelling in a taxi. Five to seven-year-olds should use a child restraint, if available, or use a safety belt.

Driving Licences. Overseas drivers are permitted to drive up to one year with their current licence, before they have to pass the driving theory test, a series of multi-choice questions. Sample question and answers sheets can be purchased prior to the test. Anyone who has sat the demanding British driving test should sail through.

* * *

COMMUNICATIONS

Postal Services

New Zealand Post, through its network of Post Shops, operates postal services, bill payment and banking services through their subsidiary, Kiwibank. Standard post can take up to three days within New Zealand and FastPost has a target of next day delivery between the larger centres. Standard post costs start at $1 and FastPost $1.80. Stamps can be bought at supermarkets, dairies, petrol stations and stationers, as well as at Post Shops. They are open five days a week, keeping the standard office hours of 9am-5pm. Some affiliate shops stay open on weekends.

Posties deliver to letterboxes, situated in front of each house rather than direct to the front door, like they do in the UK. A box made of metal, rather than wood provides the greatest protection from the elements.

In rural areas, each house has a collection as well as a delivery. A red flag indicates you have letters to post. In towns and cities, official New Zealand Post mailing boxes tend to be in suburban shopping areas.

General Delivery (Poste Restante). Poste Restante is available in the main post shop in each large town. A passport or another form of photo identification is required. The post is held for up to three months and then returned to sender. Redirection is available at a cost.

Telephones, Mobile Phones and Broadband Internet

Spark New Zealand is one of the largest companies on the New Zealand Exchange (NZX). It provides fixed line telephone services, a mobile network and internet services. Other companies that offer some, but not all of the same services are Black + White, CallPlus, Clear Mobitel, Compass, Gemalto, Orcon, TelstraClear and Vodafone New Zealand.

Calling via the Internet. VOIP or Voice over Internet Protocol. SkypeOut allows users to call standard phones and cell phones via a pre-paid account. The drawback is that users can't receive calls from either landlines or mobile phones and are unable to dial the emergency services. And some analysts say, that although Skype rates are very competitive, they are, in some instances, beaten by the easy to use low-cost calling cards, available from local shops. Anyone with an Apple iPhone device can use FaceTime (iPhone 4 or later, a fourth generation iPod Touch, an iPad 2 or a computer with OS X) to make internet calls.

Making and Receiving International Calls. To call New Zealand dial the international access code 00 from the UK, 011 from the USA, and 0011 from Australia then 64, the area code, minus the initial zero and then the number. To call the UK dial 00 followed by the country code 44, then the number, omitting the first zero in the area code. If dialling the USA the country code is 1, for Ireland it is 353.

Keeping Track of the Time Difference. New Zealand Standard Time is 12 hours ahead of Greenwich Mean Time. The clocks go forward on the first Sunday in October for Daylight Saving, until the third Sunday in March. In summer time the clocks will be 13 hours ahead of GMT and in winter the time difference will be 11 hours. If you don't own a smartphone with a world clock, to check the time difference, go to timeanddate.com.

Dialling Within New Zealand. There are only five area codes throughout the country and the South Island only has one. They are: Auckland and Northland **09**; Hamilton, Napier and Tauranga, **07**; New Plymouth and Wanganui, **06**; Wellington **04**, Christchurch, Nelson and the South Island, **03**.

Emergency & Useful Numbers

Emergency Services – ambulance, fire and police **111**

National Poisons Centre 24 hours 7 days a week **0800 764 766**

* * *

FOOD AND DRINK

Food

Food cooked at home, rather than served in restaurants, reflects how the nation eats. New Zealanders have adventurous tastes and like to embrace the best of other food cultures. The *kumara* (sweet potato) was brought by Maori, the lamb came from Britain, but how that North American staple, the pumpkin came to be served with roast lamb – is anyone's guess. Where once lamb would have been so overcooked that it had the texture of an Ugg boot, now it is as likely to be served rare as lamb racks, or baked slowly as meltingly moist lamb shanks.

In an emerging nation, where there are no ancient food traditions to have to live up to, cooks have the freedom to create without fear of breaking inflexible food rules.

Just as the best meal of the day in the UK was supposed to be breakfast; in New Zealand, in the 1950s and 1960s, it was morning or afternoon tea. Club sandwiches, pinwheels, pikelets (drop scones), ginger crunch, Anzac biscuits, cream sponge and copious cups of tea were served up in village halls up and down the country. And which side of the Tasman Sea the first pavlova was made, matters less than the fact that New Zealanders (and Australians) still care enough to continue baking them at home.

The Dutch, who emigrated in large numbers in the middle of the last century, brought with them the taste for freshly ground coffee. Dutch coffee houses sprang up around the country, bringing a touch of European flair to the culinary scene. Set up so that homesick new arrivals could meet and speak their first language, the friendly atmosphere and delicious strudel soon found favour with the locals.

With the arrival of a new group of migrants in the 1980s, this time from South East Asia, the emphasis shifted from meat and dairy products towards a healthier style of eating and cooking. The innovative and talented chef and restaurateur Peter Gordon has gone much further than merely copying imported trends, by showcasing the best local ingredients and combining them to create a distinct and exciting style of fusion food, which has found favour in London and beyond. In the wrong hands, fusion food can lead to confusion, such as the confectionary manufacturer that developed green tea flavoured chocolate wafer biscuits. Food fashions come and go but for people who love to cook, New Zealand offers some of the world's freshest produce.

While lamb and beef have always been staples, what most New Zealanders take for granted is that the animals are free range and fed a natural diet of grass, producing delicious and succulent meat. Thanks to the market garden-ing skills of recent immigrants from Asia, you never need to eat another boring Brussels sprout again.

Even though supermarkets are where most New

Zealanders shop for food, the key to eating well and cheaply is to buy in season. While the 'upside down' seasons can take a while to get used to, it's worth persevering. You can still find tomatoes in winter, but they'll be grown in a greenhouse, and twice the price of the outdoor ones available in summer.

Freshly caught, delicately flavoured fish and seafood is a treat. While the different Southern Hemisphere fish species may have unfamiliar names, for firm white fish try *snapper*, *hapuka*, *tarakihi* and blue cod. Try serving *pipis* – a clam-like shellfish, with spaghetti to create an Italian style pasta dish. New Zealand's green-lipped mussels are tender and sweet when fresh. Crayfish (rock lobster), although expensive, is a winner for special occasions. Bluff oysters from the South Island are a gourmet treat. Whitebait, a tiny sweet-tasting fish, is usually served in a light pancake batter, called a fritter.

Tamarillos (tree tomatoes) taste great poached in a vanilla-infused syrup, while you will either love or loathe the perfumy *feijoas* or pineapple guava. Originally from South America, these fruits are as much part of Kiwi food culture as the new season's cherries from Central Otago at Christmas, or the first succulent apricots from Hawke's Bay. With those delicious stone fruits, you'll want to add a scoop of creamy ice cream. For those with a sweet tooth the hokey pokey (butterscotch), boysenberry or plain old vanilla flavours still maintain their hold over the nation's taste buds.

Cheese has been another dairy success story, with a great many more locally made European-style cheeses available now. Thirty years ago the three varieties were tasty cheddar, medium cheddar and mild. Bread has always been good, with Swiss-style mixed grain bread a favourite. Hand-finished Italian style bread is becoming increasingly popular.

New Zealanders (and Australians) like to think they

were at the forefront of the coffee revolution. The terms long black and flat white may have originated Down Under, but Italy can still lay claim to latte, machiatto and capucchino. Despite the availability of sushi at lunch-counters, Kiwis still consume around 66 million pies a year. For the past few years, the Supreme Pie Award has been dominated by bakers that hail from Asia, cooking up such fillings as mince and cheese, steak and vegetable or bacon and egg.

Generations of Kiwis have enjoyed cooking simple food on their summer holidays at their *bach* (holiday house) or crib, as it's known in the South Island. For anyone arriving here now the high price of coastal property puts owning a beach house out of reach for most people, but they can still rent one. Even for city families, who don't have much outdoor living space, cooking a meal outdoors is still possible as many local parks provide gas barbecues. In summer the different generations get together for an impromptu weekend lunch.

Markets. It might seem to visitors that New Zealand is just one big farmers' market and up until thirty years ago, there was some truth in this. Supermarkets were still a novelty and most people had access to a patch of garden where they could grow lettuces and tomatoes. Today, many urban dwellers don't have access to outdoor space. But now artisan producers bring their delicious organic produce direct to the city consumer in weekly or monthly markets up and down the country.

The monthly glossy *Cuisine* will help you make the best of the local produce. It's an award-winning publication dedicated to New Zealand food and wine. It features the latest food trends, one of which has been the cultivation of avocados for oil.

Drink

Wine. From the oldest established vineyards west of Auckland, to the newly planted vines in Canterbury, there are over fourteen wine regions in New Zealand. A Scot, the British Resident, James Busby made the first wine in Northland, in the 1840s. With its high humidity and rainfall, the region wasn't suitable for mass cultivation and is now only home to a handful of commercial vineyards. Out east in the Hauraki Gulf, Waiheke Island has a microclimate, perfect for growing full-bodied red wines. New vineyards have sprung up on the island attracting regular visitors from Auckland.

An hour's drive north of Auckland, the Matakana Valley is the perfect place for a leisurely lunch amongst the vines. Further down on the east coast, chardonnay grapes have been grown commercially in and around Gisborne for many years. The first place in New Zealand to see the sun, the drier climate makes it perfect for viticulture.

Hawke's Bay is New Zealand's premier area for wine and food tourism. With over 40 vineyards, some of the names to watch out for are Black Barn, Sileni Estates, Te Mata and Kim Crawford. Hawke's Bay even has its own appellation – 'Gimblett Gravels', named after the unique local soil. Just as the wine and food regions of France and Italy are inextricably linked, so too in Hawke's Bay where you have a choice between a casual way of enjoying the food or a more formal fine dining experience.

There are standout white wines in the Wairarapa and in the top half of the South Island from Siegfried in Nelson and Cloudy Bay in Marlborough. But it is in Central Otago and now Canterbury where really exciting developments have been taking place. For a country known for its first class sauvignon blanc, making a success of the much more fickle and labour-intensive pinot noir grapes proved an irresistible challenge to ambitious pioneering wine-makers.

Along the Waitaki River in Canterbury, pinot noir is still the favourite grape to plant. What's all the excitement about? Canterbury is sunnier during the crucial summer fruit ripening months and so has the edge on its Central Otago neighbour. You might want to raise a glass to that.

Beers. New Zealand has come a long way since the days of the 'six o'clock swill' – when it was a race to down as much beer, between the time you finished work and when the pubs shut at six. Boutique breweries have sprung up in the hop-growing regions in the South Island. Look out for brands such as Speights, Macs and Monteith all of whom offer a range of pilsners, white beer, ales, lager and seasonal specials.

Spirits. 42 Below is the brand to watch out for, producing a highly rated vodka and gin. Locally made whisky or kiwifruit liqueur is to be avoided.

* * *

SCHOOLS AND EDUCATION

School attendance is compulsory for children aged from six until sixteen, although most children start school at five. Parents and caregivers have the choice of a range of schooling options from private and integrated (religious schools integrated into the state system or schools of special character). The majority of children are educated at state schools.

Early years. Primary schools take children from the age of five – Year 0 to the end of Year 6.

Imtermediate. Children in Years 7 and 8 may go to a separate intermediate school, if there is one in the area, or continue at their primary school.

Secondary. Secondary schools take students from Year 9 to the end of Year 13.

There is no school meal service at either primary or secondary school and children take a packed lunch. Classroom sizes vary and in some cases may be larger in the state schools compared with the home country. Even in the cities, schools have a grassed area or playing fields for children to enjoy. And many of the universities are situated in the older, established areas, or on a green field site just out of town. The campus at the University of Waikato is particularly pleasant, with a lake, trees and extensive landscaping.

Zoning

For parents with school age children, the decision about where to send your child to school, can have a strong influence on where to buy a house. Around 25% of the state schools in New Zealand are zoned. Zoned schools are situated in the areas of highest population density. If you live at an address in the zone, then the school is legally obliged to enrol your child. The system was designed to prevent overcrowding, but if housing density in the central city areas continues at the pace it has been running at in recent years, then zone boundaries may have to be looked at again. In some outer suburbs, rolls are falling, as parents, fed up with the long commute move closer into town, thus putting further pressure on schools closer to the CBD (central business district).

Zoning and house prices. The zoning system has a marked effect on house prices with houses in zone having a higher premium than those just out. Parents who want the best education for their children will move house, just so that they can get into the top school in the area. There are many other factors to take into account when choosing a school. Just because a school in your area isn't zoned, doesn't mean that you should avoid it.

Ranking System

An informal ranking system operates in New Zealand schools, where the income of the parents, rather than the quality of the education is measured. Decile 10 is the highest, with Decile 1 reflecting the lowest socio-economic ranking. Low decile schools receive more funding from the government, while the higher decile schools rely more on parents to fundraise. In their desire to do the best for their children, parents can sometimes forget that dedicated and gifted teachers may not want to work in the top decile schools, but may choose more challenging environments. Some parents mistakenly believe the system allows them to compare one school with another. It is far more important to read the detailed school review report, which highlights where the school is doing well and where improvements need to be made. The Education Review Office, part of The Ministry of Education, reports on schools on a regular basis. The findings are published at www.ero.govt.nz.

NCEA

In 2002 a new standards-based qualification system, The National Certification of Educational Achievement (NCEA) was introduced. The NCEA breaks down subjects into units with grades of Excellence, Merit, Credit or Incomplete given. In a subject like English, individual grades could be given for comprehension, formal writing and oral skills.

When the new qualification was first introduced, critics claimed that while marking against standards might be beneficial for the average student, this holistic approach doesn't prepare high achievers. There was concern that once students leave the cocoon of school, they will have been ill-prepared to compete against their peers for places on sought-after courses at university and eventually for jobs. Another downside of NCEA is that the new assessment system no longer allows schools to be compared.

The New Zealand Qualifications Authority (NZQA), who run NCEA, was criticised for a poorly tested system as pupils suffered from wild fluctuations in exam results up until 2004. But twelve years on, students have since gone on to study overseas, graduate from university, and take up jobs across the globe, without being disadvantaged by their qualification. But NCEA isn't the only qualification offered in New Zealand secondary schools.

CIE and IB

Many schools offer alternative qualifications like the Cambridge (CIE) system or the International Baccalaureate (IB), where the results can be measured. The advantages of the IB course is that it is a highly portable and rigorous qualification.

Critics of Cambridge question the relevance of a qualification with no New Zealand content. But elitist or not, as competition for jobs across the globe increases, anyone who strives to attain an internationally recognised qualification and is capable of doing so deserves to be encouraged.

State schools can only offer Cambridge alongside NCEA, so the lack of New Zealand content argument doesn't really stack up. Expatriates who don't plan to remain in New Zealand, or who wish to give their child the option of being educated in their home country, may prefer the Cambridge or IB route. The schools listed below are registered to offer the Cambridge (CIE) international qualifications, although some may only offer a limited selection.

ACSNZ Association of Cambridge Schools in New Zealand

The number of schools offering the Cambridge exams has grown to approximately 50. Some of the schools listed offer a limited choice of subjects but may be planning to add new subjects in the future, so check with the individual school.

For the full list of schools go to: https://www.newzealandnow.govt.nz/living-in-nz/education/school-system.

The Academic College Group (ACG) is the umbrella organisation for three schools that offer pathways into the Cambridge system, as well as the exams. The three schools are: *Parnell College*, *Senior College* and *Strathallan*. The Academic College Group schools are independent fee paying co-educational schools.

Senior College: 66 Lorne Street, Auckland 1010; 09 307 4477; http://www.acgedu.com/nz/senior Senior College also offers the IB Diploma Programme. (See below for further details on the International Baccalaureate.)

ACG Strathallan College: RD1 Papakura; 09 295 0830; http://www.acgedu.com/nz/strathallan

Auckland Grammar School: Mountain Road, Epsom, Auckland; 09 623 5400; www.ags.school.nz Auckland Grammar is a traditional boys only state school. Properties within the 'grammar zone' command a premium price tag.

Carey College: Carey College, 21 Domain Road, Panmure, Auckland 1006; 09 570 5873 www.carey-college.com Carey College is a Christian co-educational school.

Hamilton Boys'High School: Peachgrove Road, Hamilton; 07 853 0440; www.hbhs.school.nz A state zoned boys' school.

Hillcrest High School: 141 Masters Avenue, Hillcrest, Hamilton; 07 857 0297; email office@hillcrest-high.school.nz; www.hillcrest-high.school.nz A state co-educational zoned school.

King's College: Golf Road, Otahuhu, Auckland 1133; 09 276 0600; email reception@kingscollege.school.nz; www.kingscollege.school.nz King's is an Anglican independent school, resembling a traditional British public school. Girls are admitted in Years 11,12 and 13.

Lindisfarne College: 600 Pakowhai Road, Frimley, Hastings 4120; 06 873 1136; www.lindisfarne.school.nz An independent boys school.

Macleans College: 2 Macleans Road, Bucklands Beach, Auckland 2014; 09 535 2620; email office@macleans.school.nz; www.macleans.school.nz A co-educational state school with a strong emphasis on academic success.

Palmerston North Boys' High School: 263 Featherston Street, Palmerston North; 06 354 5176; fax 06-354 5175; email admin@pnbhs.school.nz; www.pnbhs.school.nz A boys' state school.

Pinehurst School: 75 Bush Road, Albany, Auckland; 09 414 0960; email: info@pinehurst.school.nz; www. pinehurst.school.nz A co-educational independent school.

St Peter's College: 23 Mountain Road, Epsom, Auckland 1003; 09 24 8108; email admin@st-peters. school.nz; www.st-peters.school.nz A Catholic integrated boys' school.

Samuel Marsden Collegiate School: Marsden Avenue, Karori, Wellington 6012; 04 476 8707; email: enrol@marsden.school.nz; www.marsden.school.nz An independent girls' school.

Western Heights High School: Old Quarry Road, Rotorua; 07 349 5940; www.whhs.school.nz; email info@whhs.school.nz A co-educational state school.

Westlake Boys' High School: 30 Forrest Hill Road, Forrest Hill, Auckland; 09 410 8667; email office@ westlake.school.nz; www.westlakebhs.school.nz An all-boys state school on the North Shore.

Whangarei Boys' High School: Kent Road, Regent, Whangarei; 09 430 4172; email enquiries@wbhs. school.nz; www.wbhs.school.nz An all-boys state school.

Schools that Offer International Baccalaureate (IB)

Auckland International College: 37 Heaphy Street, Blockhouse Bay, Auckland 0600 ; 09 309 4480; email info@aic.ac.nz; www.aic.ac.nz A co-educational private school.

John McGlashan College: 2 Pilkington Street, Maori Hill, Dunedin; 03 467 6620; admin@mcglashan. school.nz; www. mcglashan.school.nz An integrated boys' school.

Kristin School: 360 Albany Highway, Albany, Auckland; 09 415 9566; email kristin@kristin.school. nz; www.kristin.school.nz A co-educational private school.

Queen Margaret College: 53 Hobson Street, Wellington 6011; 04-473 7160; email administration@qmc. school.nz; www.qmc.school.nz An independent Presbyterian girls' school.

Rangitoto College: 564 East Coast Road, Mairangi Bay, Auckland 0630; 09 477 0150; info@rangitoto. school.nz; www.rangitoto.school.nz A co-educational state school.

St Margaret's College: 12 Winchester Street, Merivale, Christchurch 8014; 03 379 2000;email admin@ stmargarets.school.nz; www.stmargarets.school.nz A private girls' school.

Takapuna Grammar School: 210 Lake Road, Takapuna, Auckland 0622; 09 489 4167; email office@ takapuna.school.nz www.takapuna.school.nz A co-educational state school.

State versus Private. Some of the top schools in the country are in fact state schools. High-achieving alumni who had a state school education include New Zealand's former Prime Minister, Helen Clark, who went to Epsom Girls Grammar. The problem for parents is that many of the top state schools operate a strict zoning policy. If the family home is out of zone, they may want to choose a fee paying independent school, if their local zoned secondary school doesn't meet their expectations.

Private education comes at a price. Fees can be as much as $19,300 per child but that's just the start. Add on the cost of the uniform and a laptop computer, as well as the money for school trips and it is clear why parents have to plan ahead, in order to fund their children's education.

Catholic schools, which have now been incorporated into the state system and are known as integrated schools, charge modest fees of a few hundred dollars a year per child over and above the cost of uniforms and school trips. Catholic schools select their pupils and generally ask for references from a priest.

Universities

Whether or not students have attended an expensive independent school, or a state school, makes little difference once they become undergraduates. Apart from courses such as medicine and law, provided a student has attained the necessary entrance standard, entry is open to anyone.

Although one or two of the universities market themselves as better than the rest, with fewer than ten universities, the country is too small to have a two-tier university system. The elite may choose to do their undergraduate degree in New Zealand, or try their luck against fierce international competition for places at Oxbridge, or the Ivy League institutions in the USA.

Each university has strengths in individual subjects and biggest doesn't necessarily always mean best. A bachelor's degree can be completed in three years, while an honours degree takes four. Specialised courses such as teacher training, medicine, law or veterinary science will take longer.

Fees. The University of Otago's tuition fees guide for 2016, which is a useful benchmark, offers a cost comparison between various subjects. Using an example of the cost of a year's study for one full time undergraduate course, selecting from papers in Computer Science, Design, Geography, Information Science, Music and Science, the fees are $6,654. Many students can only afford to study by taking out a student loan, or working part-time. The average student loan debt for a student on a three-year degree course is over $30,000. In 2016 the total amount owed by students in the loan scheme was $15 billion.

Course fees for international students, most of whom come from China and India, start at around $25,000 per year. International students regard New Zealand as safe and a cheap place to study, compared with other OECD countries. Textbooks are expensive, so many of the universities ensure that multiple copies of the required texts are available on short-term loan from the university library.

* * *

HEALTH

The standard of healthcare in New Zealand is good, but there is no comprehensive free health system like the National Health Service in the UK, although there are some free core health services. These are available to residents and temporary residents. Although you have to pay to visit a GP, patients are seen promptly. But for people living in rural areas away from the main centres, serious illness may require that they travel long distances to receive regular treatment. Specialist medical services, which are costly to provide, are concentrated in areas of greatest need, near a larger population centre.

Publicly Funded Health Services

The core services provided free to residents and citizens. Free treatment at a public hospital, free treatment at a public hospital accident and emergency clinic (visitors are also treated for free in A & E).

Subsidies on some prescription items.

Subsidised fees for GP referrals to physiotherapists and osteopath.

Free or subsidised health care for those suffering from acute or chronic medical conditions.

No charge for laboratory tests and x-rays unless carried out at a privately operated clinic.

No charge for health care for pregnant women.

Free prescriptions for patients at public hospitals.

Subsidised GP visits and prescriptions for children under six.

Free basic dental care for all school children.

Breast screening for women aged between 50-64.

Costs

GP Visits. The average cost of visiting a GP varies from $45 to $55 a visit. For weekend and evening appointments, add on a further $15 to $20. Most GPs don't charge for children under thirteen. Check with your GP to see if they are participating in the zero fees scheme.

Prescription charges. For subsidised prescriptions, expect to pay up to $5 per prescription item for up to 20 medicines a year. Over 20, the patient is entitled to a

Prescription Subsidy Card, meaning no further payments need to be made until 1 February of the following year. For children under thirteen prescriptions are free. Pharmac, the government agency responsible for drug purchases will only fund certain drugs, based on cost, even if there are newer and better treatments available. The costs of medicines, which receive partial or no subsidy from the government, are passed on to the consumer.

Visiting a Dentist. The only pain you'll feel after visiting a dentist in New Zealand is in the wallet. While for primary school children a basic free service is available through the School Dental Service, 13 to 18 year olds may be charged. Although the treatment for secondary school age children is meant to be subsidised, dentists aren't obliged to sign up to the scheme and many choose to opt out. For everyone else, expect to pay anything from $100 to $150 for a routine check-up. Dentists are more than happy to add a sparkle to those pearly whites with a range of expensive cosmetic dental treatments, but for those who just want to repair crumbling fillings, the cost of a crown can be between $500 and $1500, depending on the material used.

No Fault Accident Insurance

If you are injured in an accident, you can't sue anyone for damages as the government runs a no-faults claims system administered through the Accident Compensation Corporation (ACC). ACC provides free treatment for both residents and non-residents involved in accidents, whether a motor vehicle accident or an accident in the home. Designed to avoid expensive and drawn out litigation, the Accident Compensation system guarantees those on low incomes access to the justice and compensation often denied them in other countries, where such claims have to be pursued through the courts.

The amount of money awarded through ACC might seem modest, but as claims are processed relatively quickly, claimants can at least then get on with the business of recuperation and recovery, instead of being forced to put their life on hold for what can be many years, with no guarantee that they'll win their case.

The case of a British couple, hit by a drunk driver in 2002, causing permanent injury, highlights the need for visitors to take out comprehensive travel insurance. According to a report in the New Zealand Herald, Tony and Jenny Legge, who live in Wales, were offered just £4200 when Mr Legge estimated that the crash had cost him £400,000 in lost earnings.

Private Health Insurance

Although the ACC system covers individuals after an accident and treatment is swift, routine surgery in the public health system is subject to a waiting list. For some operations, it can take up to two years to get to the top of the queue. Private health insurance allows those with non-urgent conditions to be treated immediately and gives them access to private hospitals that provide a range of procedures. Given that medical insurance premiums have risen as much as 10% or more a year recently, policies with voluntary excesses or those that offer no-claims discounts may be the best value.

Private Medical Insurers

Accuro: Level 1, 79 Boulcott Street, Wellington 6143; 04 473 6185 freephone: 0800 222 876; email: info@accuro.co.nz; www.accuro.co.nz

NIB New Zealand: 48 Shortland Street, Auckland

1010; 0800 123 642; email: contacts@nib.co.nz; www.nib.co.nz

Partners Life: 1/33-45 Hurstmere Road, Takapuna, Auckland 0622 freephone 0800 14 54 33; www. partnerslife.co.nz

Sovereign: Private Bag Sovereign, Victoria Street West, Auckland 1142; 09 487 9963 freephone 0800-500 108 email enquire@sovereign.co.nz; www. sovereign.co.nz

Southern Cross: Private Bag 99934, Newmarket, Auckland ; 09 356 0900 freephone:0800 800 181; email-info@ sxhealth.co.nz; www.southerncross. co.nz

SHOPPING

Car culture and the demise of the public transport system saw shoppers flee the city centres for out of town malls with parking, forcing the closure of many smart department stores. Wellington, which does have reliable public trans-port, is the honourable exception. Wellingtonians mourn the loss of their beloved Kirkcaldies and Stains, or 'Kirks,' as it was known, situated in the heart of the downtown area of New Zealand's capital. The store has been taken over by the Australian company, David Jones, which is the closest you'll get to a Selfridges or a Macys. Where once Queen Street had the stylish Milne & Choyce, now Auckland's department stores, (apart from Smith+Caughey's) seem more like provincial Britain's were 30 years ago – dull and unsophisticated with unimaginative window displays.

Ballantynes in Christchurch is trying to appeal to the younger, trendier crowd with its Contemporary Lounge. But if you really can't do without a regular department store fix, then save up for a trip across the Tasman to Sydney or Melbourne, where you can make up for lost time in David Jones and Myer. The nearest branches of Marks & Spencer are in Singapore and Bangkok.

Teenagers or the young at heart are better catered for with surf wear ranges like Billabong and Quicksilver, Max and Glassons for casual ware. Their older and better off peers search for designers such as Karen Walker, Storm, Zambesi, Trelise Cooper and World. Australian labels like Country Road and Witchery try to bridge the gap between casual and formal wear for both men and women. Pumpkin Patch sell children's clothing.

Expats used to comment that there was no middle ground between the cheaper chain stores and the expensive New Zealand designers. But the arrival of global brands H & M, Top Shop and Zara should help. There's a limited local selection of stylish, well-made shoes for women. Briarwood is one exception, otherwise, shop for imports at sale time. The biggest shopping mall in the country is at Sylvia Park, in south-east Auckland.

Prices. As the median income is only around NZ$51,000 per annum, retailers can't charge too much for everyday items as nobody would buy them. Urban New Zealanders have a passion for shopping and have enthusiastically embraced the consumer lifestyle.

Books are expensive and the price of a weekly supermarket shop is no bargain either, but that's because food is subject to the local equivalent of VAT, Goods and Services Tax (GST) at 15%. But there are ways to reduce the weekly grocery bill, if you shop around, and only buy fruit and vegetables in season.

Electrical goods and cars manufactured in Asia are reasonably priced in New Zealand but expect to pay more for European imports. Briscoes and the Warehouse stock cheap homewares. Freedom Furniture is the closest you'll get to Ikea, but with a reduced range of furniture, home furnishings and accessories. And they don't sell the big ticket items such as flatpack kitchens.

DIY is no longer the national pastime that it once was, as an increasing number of millennials rent, rather than own their home. Bunnings and Mitre 10 are the two chain stores that cater for home renovators and the building trade.

Discount Shopping Centres. There are discount centres selling cut-price homewares, clothes, shoes and sports gear – DressSmart in Auckland and Christchurch and The Fox Outlet Centre in Northcote, Auckland.

Shopping Hours

In the main centres, shops are open seven days a week. From Mondays to Fridays opening hours are from 9.00am until 5.00pm and until 4.00pm on weekends. Expect reduced hours in smaller towns. Late night shopping until 8.00pm or 9.00pm on a Friday or Thursday night gives teenagers the excuse they need to hang out with their mates. Supermarkets in the bigger cities that open seven days a week, 24 hours a day charge a premium for this convenience. Dairies selling basic provisions like milk, bread, papers and grocery items tend to open early and close later in city centres compared with rural areas.

Useful Websites

Farmers: www.farmers.co.nz A middle of the road department store. The online catalogue gives prices and the range and styles on offer.

Countdown: www.countdown.co.nz Countdown is a grocery chain and this site gives the latest prices on grocery items.

Pumpkin Patch: www.pumpkinpatch.co.nz For kids clothes.

Noel Leeming: www.noelleeming.co.nz   Electrical goods for home and office.

Autotrader: www.autotrader.co.nz   Gives current prices for used cars and links to new car sites, otherwise search under the brand name.

Trade Me: www.trademe.co.nz Online site for new and pre-loved anything, including property.

* * *

MEDIA

Newspapers

There's no national daily broadsheet newspaper, although *The New Zealand Herald* tries to lay claim to that title. It has a circulation of 404,000. The news and business sections run national and international stories but the weekend property section covers only the Auckland region. *The Dominion Post* is Wellington's daily, with a circulation of 98,000 and Christchurch's *Press* is 64,000. On Sundays, *The Sunday Star-Times* is the only national Sunday paper with a circulation of 115,730.

Although many buyers prefer to conduct their initial property search online, it's easier to keep track of a short-list with a photograph of each one. All the broadsheet newspapers have extensive property sections with colour photographs (paid for by the vendor), advertising houses and land for sale. Newspapers list the weekly 'open homes', where houses are open for inspection to all-comers without an appointment.

Property Press, published by ACP Media is a free weekly colour print and online publication delivered to homes, or is available from real estate agents. For the online version go to www.propertypress.co.nz. Print versions are available for Auckland, Bay of Plenty, Manawatu, Wellington, Otago and the Southern Lakes District. The online version lists all the other regions including the South Island.

Where to Find International Newspapers. Digital subscriptions are now the only real alternative, since the closure of bookshops such as Whitcoulls in central Auckland, which sold international newspapers.

Radio

The public broadcaster is Radio New Zealand, which operates two radio stations that are advertiser free. National Radio has much in common with the BBC's Radio 4. *Morning Report* from 7-9am, is the definitive morning news and current affairs programme. Concert FM is the classical station. For frequencies for Radio NZ go to www. radionz.co.nz.

The commercial radio station Newstalk ZB attracts those listeners looking for an alternative to National Radio. The Rock FM caters for rock music fans and The Edge plays top 20 hits. The downside to commercial stations is their repetitive advertising.

Sports fans have Radio Sports while students get to hear about what's going on through the student stations, the bNet. The Auckland station 95bFM is reputed to be the best. And the nationwide coverage of iwi (tribal) stations includes the influential Mai FM in Auckland which attracts younger listeners. A Chinese radio station, Chinese Radio FM, Pacific Island station Niu FM and a dance station George FM reflect the diversity of New Zealand's population.

Internet Radio. You can listen live to any station you want over the internet, or via radio on-demand, where programmes can be downloaded and then recorded onto portable devices such as an iPod and an MP3 player for playback at a later time. For further information go to www.bbc.co.uk.

Television

Three types of broadcast digital television operate in New Zealand. Satellite services are run by Sky and Freeview, which also provides a terrestrial service to the main centres. Cable TV is available in Wellington and Christchurch. There are currently eleven national free-to-air channels, two of which are run by the state broadcaster. Television New Zealand operates TV ONE, a mainstream channel and TV2, which is aimed at a younger audience. Television New Zealand, TVNZ is state-controlled and governed by a charter but has to provide a substantial proportion, (currently 90%) of its revenue from advertising and merchandising.

Their biggest competitor is TV3, run by MediaWorks New Zealand, which also runs a number of radio stations as well as the youth-oriented music channel C4. Prime Television broadcasts a mix of prestige imported dramas and documentaries and other more commercial shows. Maori Television was set up to offer programmes in the Maori language, *te reo* as well as English, to enable Maori speakers easy access to their language and culture.

There is no longer a licence fee but viewers have to put up with a constant stream of advertisements on all the terrestrial channels, with one more advertising slot per hour at peak times than in the UK. A film that has a running time of one and a half hours will take two hours to watch. When TV ONE does secure live sports coverage, much of the dramatic impact of the event can be lost as at crucial moments the coverage cuts out and goes to a commercial break. TV ONE offers a selection of imported reality series as well as series drama from the US and the UK.

Locally produced television includes current affairs, news, soap opera. High production costs mean that extensively researched locally produced documentaries are rarely screened.

The New Zealand Natural History Unit, now NHNZ was once the flagship of the state broadcaster but was sold off in the 1980s during the period of intense deregulation.

Satellite Television. Satellite television guarantees access to live sports coverage – at a price. Dedicated night owls can cheer on their favourite English Premier football league team or keep up with the play at Wimbledon. Channels include BBC World, CBS News.

Sky offers a range of different options, which are bundled together to suit the company rather than the subscriber. The Sky News package includes Sky News Australia and Sky News UK. To have both the sport and the movie channels together is the most expensive of all the combinations. Sky also offers radio channels with FM frequencies, which may be the only way that these are available in some of the remoter parts of the country.

At the time of going to press, Sky and Vodafone NZ were in the process of negotiating a proposed merger, to try to entice customers to buy bundled services such as fixed line broadband, pay TV and mobile phones. Competitors TVNZ, Tuanz and Spark oppose it.

* * *

CRIME

New Zealand is a very safe country as the crime statistics below underscore. Bike gangs control the manufacture and supply of certain drugs. When a territorial dispute turns nasty, this can lead to revenge killings, but generally, the public isn't involved. These gangs operate mainly in the larger population centres. It's safe to walk around city centres at night, although it would be unwise to do so in bad neighbourhoods on the urban fringe. Carjackings and violent crimes are rare.

New Zealand is officially one of the world's least corrupt countries. And in local and central government there's a level of transparency that's matched only by Scandinavia. Bribes, kickbacks and corruption in officialdom are infrequent.

Robbery from parked cars and camper vans is on the increase, but as the police point out, this is largely preventable. Isolated scenic spots where tourists leave their cars to go and take photos are an easy target for opportunist thieves. If you plan to hire a campervan on your look-see visit be vigilant about keeping your passport and other valuables with you at all times. Bags left on neighbouring tables when dining out, particularly at night may be the target for petty criminals.

Numbers and Types of Recorded Crimes. The crime statistics for 2014 (the last year crimes were recorded annually) saw a total of 350,389 recorded offences. Over half of these at 182,295 were for dishonesty, which includes burglary and theft as well as fraud and receiving. Drug and anti-social offences came in at 16,543 offences. There were 66 murders throughout the country out of a total of 57,332 crimes against the person, which includes homicide, assault, robbery, harassment and threatening behaviour. There were 4056 sexual offences including sex attacks and indecent behaviour.

Unimaginative politicians with no real policies like to exploit the perception that people aren't safe in their homes anymore. They will go on about 'law and order' being a problem which only their party can solve. Methamphetamine has been implicated in some senseless violent crimes but that doesn't mean that there is now an out- of-control 'P' epidemic.

In the South Island in remote communities, you can still find people who don't lock their doors at night. In the mountainous regions of the South Island, watch out for the winged criminals that roam the skies. The mountain parrots or *keas* like to steal and chew through anything that's left lying around. They're partial to shoes left outside and the rubber seals on windscreen wipers.

* * *

MAORI PLACE NAMES

As you travel around New Zealand, particularly the North Island, once you have a few basic words of Maori, you'll be able to make sense of a great many of the place names. If you get to see the jagged peak of Aoraki Mt Cook, you will know why its translation, 'Cloud Piercer' is so accurate. Or, for those visiting the little town of Te Aroha in the North Island, knowing that the words translate as 'the place of love', may make you want to delve into the origins of the name.

A brief Maori vocabulary

ao cloud

ara path

awa river or valley

hau wind

heke descend

hine daughter, girl

kai food

iti small

iwi tribe

kainga home, village

kaumatua respected elder

mana prestige

marae meeting house

mata headland

maunga mountain

moana sea, lake

moko tattoo

morepork owl

ngati tribe

pa fortified village

pakeha white New Zealander

pounamu greenstone

powhiri welcome at a marae

taonga treasure

utu revenge

waka canoe

whanau extended family

whare house

* * *

PUBLIC HOLIDAYS

In August 2016 it was announced that a new national public holiday is to be created to remember the New Zealand Land Wars. At the time of writing, the date hadn't been decided.

1 January New Year's Day

2 January Public Holiday

6 February Waitangi Day

Good Friday

Easter Sunday

Easter Monday

ANZAC Day 25 April

Queen's Birthday first Monday in June

Labour Day fourth Monday in October

Christmas Day 25 December

Boxing Day 26 December

In addition, each region celebrates an Anniversary Day. In Auckland and Wellington it is held on different days in late January. Taranaki and Otago have a day off in March, while in Hawke's Bay and Marlborough it is held in November. Canterbury and Westland take theirs in December.

* * *

STARGAZING

Astronomy is one of the oldest sciences and was studied by the founders of Ur of the Chaldees and the Ancient Greeks, in India and Egypt and has played an important part in many cultures around the world, including those of Polynesia. The early Polynesians were so proficient at celestial navigation that long before other navigators thought it was possible, they set out fearlessly, across the Pacific to reach the land we call New Zealand. And hundreds of years later, it was because Captain Cook was on a scientific mission to observe the Transit of Venus that his voyage brought him to New Zealand.

Astronomy is one of the few remaining sciences left that allows amateurs to make discoveries, proving that you don't need the resources of NASA to contribute to scientific research. The ideal place to see stars is out in the countryside. On a clear night, you can see satellites and the International Space Station (ISS) as they orbit the earth. But if you don't manage to spot the stars from a remote area, you can still get a superb view of the night sky from a suburban garden. All you will need in the way of equipment is a pair of binoculars.

What's in The Southern Sky? In summer (December to February) you can get a good view of the Southern Cross just before 10.00pm. If you haven't seen the Southern Cross before, beware the 'false cross', which is high in the sky early in the evening. The Southern Cross can be identified by the two brightest stars known as the Pointers. The nearest and brightest of the two Pointers is *Alpha Centauri* and is one of our nearest neighbours in the galaxy. There are five stars that make up the Southern Cross constellation – the false cross only has four. Once you've located the Southern Cross, finding True South is easy. Extend an imaginary line through the long axis of the Southern Cross and then look for the Pointers. Imagine a line between the two Pointers and another line crossing it at 90 degrees. If you were to look downwards where the two lines meet, this is the direction of True South.

Although you may be familiar with the three bright stars of Orion's Belt, you may not realise that it looks rather different in the southern sky. Instead of Orion's sword hanging down, it appears to be raised in the air. The Pleiades or *Matariki*, also known as the Seven Sisters plays a significant role in Maori culture as the Maori new year is marked by the sighting of the new moon and the rise of Matariki. It was thought that the brighter the stars, the better the harvest that year. Matariki falls in and around the shortest day in June when some New Zealanders use it as a convenient time to celebrate an informal midwinter Christmas.

You'll get a great view of a number of the planets, including Venus, Mercury, Mars, Jupiter and Saturn. Venus can be observed at twilight as well as dawn, as it is both the evening and the morning star. Mars, the red planet is easily identified by its distinct colour. If you are lucky you may be able to see Saturn – but to see the Rings of Saturn as well as the most distant planets of Neptune, Uranus and Pluto you'll certainly need a telescope or better still, a trip to an observatory.

While you may be familiar with the Northern Lights – the *Aurora Borealis*, the Southern Hemisphere version, the *Aurora Australis* puts on an equally magical light show. South Islanders will have the best chance of spotting the Aurora Australis. But the best view of all is down on the ice at Scott Base, Antarctica, between March and September. The extraordinary colour displays of green, pink, yellow and violet are caused by electrons and protons from the sun colliding with gases in the outer reaches of the atmosphere.

RESIDENCE AND ENTRY

CHAPTER SUMMARY

Four main ways to obtain New Zealand residency.
Enter the country as a skilled migrant, start or invest
in a business, come for family reasons, or on humanitarian grounds.

British connections. In recent times, over 30% of
the migrants accepted for residency have been British. It is the third most popular destination for UK
migrants after Australia and Canada.

Good health is a must. Potential migrants must
prove that they are in good health, are of good character and have a high standard of written and spoken
English.

Skills Shortage. The Immediate Skill Shortage
List (ISSL) lists shortages in professions as varied
as winemaking, ski and snowboarding instruction to
the racing industry.

The Long Term Skills Shortage List (LTSSL)
advertises vacancies in medicine and health.

Restrictions for older migrants. There are restrictions placed on applications for residency for those
over the age of 55.

Expression of Interest. The Expression of Interest document is the first step in the application process for skilled migrants. Information provided by you on this form becomes the basis for possible selection for residency.

Competition for migrants from other countries. New Zealand has to compete with countries such as Australia and Canada for its migrants.

Non-residents can buy property. The visitor Visa Waiver Scheme and Visitor's Visa means that you can still purchase property and live in your New Zealand home for a few months every year.

Temporary Work Permit. Before you commit to such a big decision as emigrating, work in New Zealand for a couple of years first.

Experience life as a student. Many of those people that want to emigrate have already lived in the country as a student.

Working Holiday. Those aged between 18-30 can come to New Zealand and live like a local on a working holiday.

* * *

OVERVIEW

New Zealand is a relatively young nation and is still building up its key industries, as well as innovating and developing new areas of excellence. To sustain a robust economy, New Zealand needs to actively recruit skilled and well-educated workers from overseas.

On talk-back radio and in the letters pages of news-papers there is angst about the 'brain drain'. Young New Zealanders leave when they complete their degrees to gain the necessary skills and experience they might not be able to get back home. But what the talk-back hosts and letter writers forget, is that many of them return to start a family. And although many educated New Zealanders do leave permanently, there are a great many even better educated, qualified and skilled migrants willing to take their place. Rather than a drain, it would be more accurate to say that New Zealand has experienced a 'brain-exchange'.

Trying to gain residency in any OECD country these days is tough as rules are tightened and reviewed. New Zealand is no exception in applying even more rigorous criteria. Prospective migrants with job offers who don't pass the other requirements are turned away. The world of work has changed drastically in the past 30 to 40 years and many jobs have disappeared. In their place have come those that involve new technology. Workers who have kept up with the changes and have upskilled are the most in demand.

Under the old General Skills Category, many highly skilled migrants (mainly from developing countries who didn't have English as a first language) were unable to get work in their profession and ended up driving taxis. In 2003 the Skilled Migrant category replaced General Skills. The emphasis has shifted to employability instead of just skills, experience and qualifications. Although some appli-cants can be reunited with family members, the majority of migrants from the OECD countries are granted residency through skilled migration.

The changes implemented have largely met with public approval, by being seen to target people who can directly contribute to the workforce. The system appears to favour native English speakers. Applicants with English as a second language must pass a language test and be a 'competent user' of English. Unfortunately, no selective system will ever be perfect.

In recent years New Zealand has shaken off some of its collective low self-esteem and has started to see itself the way that others do – as a desirable destination to live and work. As the volume of enquiries from prospective migrants has risen, the country can afford to be more selective.

Before you take the plunge and apply to move there permanently you should consider going on a temporary basis first – either as a student, on a working or working holiday visa, or as a visitor. Your chances of a successful relocation will be greatly enhanced. When you stay a little longer and experience the workplace and the business culture, sit in rush hour traffic, rent a house or apartment and enjoy Christmas Day at the beach, you really will have sampled the highs (as well as the lows) of living in New Zealand. When the novelty of the new country has worn off and you know what it feels like to be away from friends, that will be the time to apply for residence.

Immigration is a sensitive issue. The government is criticised for being too lax on who it lets in. When the country is already overstretched in providing health and social welfare services for its own people, immigrants are seen as an easy target. Although the New Zealand government wants to ensure that the migration experience is successful, the media are quick to publicise any bad behaviour by foreign nationals.

One inspiring story about the positive contribution made by migrants was the gifting of a substantial tract of land in the Kaipara Harbour for a new national park by Pierre and Jacqueline Chatelanat. The 834 hectare farm was valued at $10 million and become a regional park. Their generosity is one of the country's most significant acts of philanthropy in its history.

Minimum Entry Requirements

Potential migrants have to provide medical certificates and police checks to prove that they are: a) in good health b) are of good character and c) have a high standard of written and spoken English.

APPLYING FOR NEW ZEALAND RESIDENCE AS AN EMPLOYEE

Only New Zealand and Australia currently have any official form of labour exchange that allows citizens of both countries to move between the two to live and work. Citizens of EU countries and North America can come to New Zealand and obtain either permanent or temporary residence.

Skilled Migrant

The main criteria to qualify under the Skilled Migrant category are that you are 55 years or under, have a job offer in New Zealand, have at least two years work experience, along with a tertiary or trade qualification. The Skilled Migrant category is the best way to enter New Zealand permanently, as there are no restrictions placed on your visa and you can't have your residency revoked if you change jobs.

The Immigration New Zealand website provides a check-list called The Skilled Migrant Points Indicator that will calculate eligibility points to help you determine whether or not it's worth putting in a formal application. The Skilled Migrants Points Indicator isn't part of the formal application process and no personal details are retained. You can take the test as often as you like, using different combinations to maximise your points, providing you fulfill the necessary criteria. In October 2016 the number of points required was 160.

Applying under the Skilled Migrant Category. After passing the Skilled Migrants Points Indicator test, the next step is to register an Expression of Interest. Take your time filling in the Expression of Interest, as unlike the Skilled Points Indicator, the information is retained. The Expression of Interest form asks you to provide evidence if you've been offered work in a future growth area, where there is an absolute skills shortage, or outside Auckland. You are also required to provide evidence about your work experience and qualifications, any close family ties to New Zealand and whether your partner speaks English to a required standard.

It is then scored, put into a ranking system and pooled along with all the other applications. Only the highest-ranking applicants are invited to apply for residency. Skilled migrants are much more likely to be successful if they have a New Zealand job offer first. Medical personnel and any other occupations that require New Zealand registration must ensure that they complete their registration before applying for residency.

Anecdotal evidence suggests that world events have a big impact on the numbers of potential migrants registering their interest in moving to New Zealand. In the days immediately after the 2016 Brexit referendum, there was a surge of applications from the UK.

Expression of Interest Statistics. Immigration New Zealand issues a useful fortnightly set of statistics, which makes interesting reading for potential migrants. For the 11 May 2016 selection group a total of 669 applicants had 140 points, compared with 140 applicants who had a points total of 100 or over but under 140. These applicants were then invited to apply for residency. As there is one application per family these figures can represent several people.

Since October 2016 the points required for selection as a skilled migrant was raised to 160.

One of the dilemmas potential migrants face, is whether to apply for residency first and then look for a job, or to find a job first and risk not getting their residency. Anecdotal evidence suggests that applicants with job offers are more likely to be accepted. And if you do have a firm job offer with a specified start date, the authorities are quite helpful in trying to assist you to meet your obligations.

Wanted – Skilled Professionals

New Zealand has some of the lowest unemployment figures in the OECD and as a result is facing an acute shortage of skilled, suitably qualified migrants to fill the growing number of job vacancies.

Medical Professionals – New Zealand Needs You. In April 2016 the Long Term Skills Short List included: anaesthetist, GP, laboratory scientist, midwife, nurse, radiation technologist, registrar (obstetrics/gynaecology), occupational therapist, pathologist, pharmacist, physiotherapist, psychiatrist, psychologist, radiologist, renal physician, palliative physician, surgeon, vet. Whether you work in agriculture, construction and engineering, film animation, ICT and electronics, trades or transport, go to www.immigration.govt.nz for more information on the Long Term Skills Shortage List.

Immediate Skill Shortage List

New Zealand is not just looking for elite, highly skilled and educated professionals with degrees to fill job vacancies. Many vacancies exist in the trades – from plumber to cabinet maker, or in industries such as horse racing. If your occupation is on this list you may be granted an Essential

Skills work visa, which will permit you to work in New Zealand temporarily. You may not necessarily be able to apply for residence.

The Immediate Skills Shortage List (ISSL) – also available from Immigration NZ's website, lists the qualifications it expects those applying to work in New Zealand should have.

Canterbury Skill Shortage List

The Canterbury Skill Shortage List (CSSL) details occupations in critical shortage in the region, needed to help with the rebuild, following the 2010 and 2011 earthquake. If your skill is on the CSSL and you have a job offer in Canterbury, you may be granted an Essential Skills work visa. Whether your occupation is on the CSSL, ISSL, or LTSSL, the end result is the same – if you have the right work experience and qualifications then the likelihood of your obtaining a job offer will be greatly enhanced.

Employees of a Business Relocating to New Zealand

Along with the Entrepreneur category, (see below), this is one of the few categories that doesn't place an age restriction on gaining New Zealand residency. It's only available to key talent in an organisation relocating to New Zealand. As the employee will be working in a New Zealand business environment, the applicant must meet English language requirements.

Work to Residence

If you work in a specialised or in-demand occupation, or are deemed to be an outstanding talent in sports or the arts, then you can apply for a work permit under the Work to

Residence category. The applicant must either have an offer of full time employment from a New Zealand accredited employer with a base salary of at least $45,000 per annum, or an offer of full time employment in an occupation on the Long Term Skill Shortage list. Applicants cannot be over the age of 55 and must hold current registration if their occupation requires that. If applying as an outstanding sports or talent in the arts then this requires sponsorship from the appropriate New Zealand sporting or cultural organisation.

* * *

APPLYING FOR NEW ZEALAND RESIDENCE AS A BUSINESS INVESTOR

Investor and Investor Plus

New Zealand has toughened its rules for business investors. There are two main investor categories, the Investor and Investor Plus. The age limit as an Investor is now 65. Applicants have to have NZ$1.5 million to be invested for a minimum of four years. They are required to have a further $1million as settlement funds to live on. Coming in to the country this way requires the applicant to have three years business experience, as well as meeting character, health and English language requirements. Applicants are required to spend 146 days in NZ for each of the last three years of their investment.

Investor Plus requires a substantial investment of NZ $10 million. These investors need not only a substantial amount of money to invest, but these funds will be held by the New Zealand government for three years, during which time access to the money is very limited. Just having the requisite amount of money to bring in and invest in the country isn't necessarily going to be enough to grant you residency, as you will still have to meet character and health requirements. Gaining permanent residence under this category is not without other restrictions and conditions, which include spending 44 days in NZ for each of the last two years of the investment.

The application procedure for the Investor Category (Investor 2) involves filling out an Expression of Interest in the same way that a skilled migrant would apply. The application will then be assessed from the information that you provide. Once the Expression of Interest has been checked, suitable applicants are invited to apply for residence. At this point applicants will need to provide their documents and once approved, you will need to transfer your money to New Zealand. Applications for Investor Plus (Investor 1) will be allocated a Business Migration Client Manager, by emailing investors@mbie.govt.nz

Entrepreneur Resident Visa

One of the few categories that doesn't carry an age restriction or require the applicant to have formal qualifications, although English language standards must be met. The applicant must have scored a minimum number of points for the Entrepreneur Work Visa, have set up a business working to an agreed business plan, and invested at least $100,000. Some entrepreneurs may be granted an exemption – if their business is in ICT, science, or has export potential.

Once you have an Entrepreneur Work Visa you can apply for residence if you have been self-employed and successfully run your business for at least six months. However, if you are applying after less than two years self-employment, you will be expected to invest $500,000 in your business and have created three new jobs in New Zealand.

APPLYING FOR NEW ZEALAND RESIDENCE ON FAMILY OR HUMANITARIAN GROUNDS

The family category is open to those with immediate family or a de-facto partner who are either New Zealand residents or citizens. Generally, only a spouse/partner, child, sibling or parent is eligible for sponsorship. Although there isn't an English language requirement under this category, entry isn't guaranteed. New Zealand, like all other humanitarian countries accepts refugees under strict conditions.

* * *

TEMPORARY RESIDENCE

Temporary Residence through Work

Job offer. You can apply for a temporary work permit if you have a job offer from a New Zealand employer and are skilled in an occupation that is in demand.

Working on an event. A temporary work permit may also be issued to those who need to work in New Zealand for a specific purpose or event – such as a film or television production, a tournament or other sports tour, or for certain professional reasons.

Joining a partner. You are also eligible for a temporary work permit if you are joining your partner in New Zealand.

Working holiday. Students or trainees wanting to gain work experience are also eligible for a temporary work permit. Those aged between 18 and 30 (18-35 in a few select countries) can visit New Zealand for a working holiday. The Immigration New Zealand website has the full list of countries that have a New Zealand Working Holiday Scheme. These include: Britain and a number of EU countries, the USA and Canada, countries in Latin America, including Argentina and Chile, countries in Asia including Singapore, Japan and Thailand. Australian citizens do not need temporary residence as they are freely allowed to work in New Zealand.

Temporary Residence through Study

International students can study in New Zealand, providing they have an offer of a place from a school, polytechnic or university and their proposed course of study meets specific course requirements. International student fees are high and applicants have to prove that not only have they paid their course fees but that they have enough money to support themselves during their temporary stay. For courses over three months, students need to apply for a student visa. In addition to the academic requirements students have to prove that they are of good health and good character. For stays longer than six months this may include a TB clearance as well as a medical and police certificate.

ENTERING NEW ZEALAND AS A VISITOR

New Zealand operates a Visa Waiver scheme that allows visitors from the UK to travel and stay for up to six months. Nationals from certain other countries, including the USA may be restricted to a three month stay. A visitor's visa is perfect for homeowners over the age 55 who do not qualify for residency by working or owning a business, but who want to spend the northern winter 'Down Under' in their holiday house. If you want to stay longer than your visa-free conditions permit you need to apply for a visitor's visa.

The usual maximum stay for a visitor is nine months in an eighteen month period. Holiday homeowners visiting New Zealand on a regular basis need to keep track of the date they arrived, in order not to exceed the time they are allowed to stay in the country. When travelling in and out, ensure that your flight bookings are organised well in advance as any breach of your visa conditions – even if they were unintentional and beyond your control are taken very seriously by the immigration authorities.

Students who are studying in the country for less than three months can come in as a visitor although they should check with immigration first to clarify whether or not that their country of origin has an agreement with the NZIS that will allow them in on the Visa Waiver Scheme, or whether they need to apply for a visitor's visa.

Health and Medical Requirements. Further information can be obtained about health requirements in the Immigration New Zealand leaflet 1121. New Zealand is particularly concerned about the health of migrants and visitors who have been in countries with TB.

Applying for Residency for the Over 55s

Since 2010 there has been an increase in the number of categories where applicants over the age of 55 can apply for residency, but these require considerable investment. There is both a self-employed entrepreneur and investment category.

There is now a retirement category visa for those aged 65 and over, with family in New Zealand or a temporary retirement visa for applicants with no prior relationship to the country. Even temporary retirees will need deep pockets: NZD$750,000 in investments, $500,000 for maintenance and an annual income from investments and pensions of $60,000.

The parent visa allows those with an equal number or more of their family in New Zealand than anywhere else permanent residence, providing they meet strict financial criteria, including an investment of NZD $1 million. Maintenance and annual income is the same level as the temporary retirement visa. In October 2016 Immigration New Zealand announced that it was reviewing the Parent Category and had temporarily closed applications until further notice.

IMMIGRATION CONSULTANTS

The big advantage of moving with a large company is that all the paperwork involved with obtaining visas and residency is carried out by a professional, freeing up your time to get on with all the other aspects involved in moving. Companies competing with other countries for talented individuals realise they need to offer their relocating staff immigration assistance.

Immigration consultants take the hassle out of filling out all the forms but you still have to pass a medical, collect references from previous employers, pass the police checks and have all the other documentation available for them. And although a good immigration consultant can speed up the process of gaining residency, they can only do this for those who meet the basic criteria. And a privately hired immigration consultant can't influence decisions about residency.

But for those of you who are 'going it alone', without the support of an employer, the question as to whether or not it is worth your while consulting (and paying the fees) of an immigration consultant, without a New Zealand job offer first, is a tricky one. An immigration consultant could help avoid the mistakes that many applicants make which occur at the Expression of Interest stage. Many potential migrants don't realise that their data is being recorded and that this will have a lasting effect on whether or not they get selected for residency. A cheaper alternative is to consult the INZ website and follow the link to: Tips for Lodging Expressions of Interest.

It could be worth your while engaging a consultant if you don't yet have a job offer and your skills, qualifications and experience are in one of the long-term skills shortage occupations, and you have been able to secure New Zealand registration. Immigration officers working for Immigration New Zealand do have discretionary powers if the quota hasn't been filled and a person from a country with a comparable labour market such as the UK and the USA or Western Europe has a set of skills that are in demand by New Zealand employers.

The best way to select a competent immigration consultant is to have a personal recommendation. Be aware that there is no registration required for immigration consultants and anyone can set up in business and claim to be an expert. The test of a good consultant is their willingness to provide a referral from one of their clients. Failing that, check the number of online reviews the company has, or if there are any mentions of them in internet forums. A good consultant should be working not just with individuals but also with corporates. If the company tries to fob you off by citing privacy or client confidentiality, then find one that can provide you with the necessary references. It's a competitive industry, with many players in the market and you should shop around. Expect to pay at least £3000 with VAT plus the cost of visas on top of that.

Immigration Consultants UK:
The Emigration Group: 01244 321 414;
www.emigrationgroup.com

Visa-Go Emigration: 0131 557 1731; www.visa-go.com

Immigration Consultants NZ:
Meridian Immigration Consultants: 09 625 4000;
www.meridian.net.nz

Useful Addresses

Immigration New Zealand Offices – North Island

Auckland Central: Level 4, 280 Queen Street, Auckland 1010.www.immigration.govt.nz Manukau: Level 3, 20 Amersham Way, Wiri, Manukau 2014

Wellington: Kordia House, 109-125 Willis Street, Te Aro, Wellington 6011

There are also immigration offices in the regional centres of Hamilton and Palmerston North. For further details go to: www.immigration.govt.nz/contact/your-nearest-new-zealand-offices **South Island** Christchurch: 110 Wrights Road, Addington, Christchurch 8024

Immigration New Zealand Offices UK:

Immigration New Zealand has offices in a number of countries including The Netherlands, the UK, the USA, Australia as well as South East Asia. The UK and US offices are listed below.

Immigration NZ London: Burwood House, 14-16 Caxton Street, London SW1H 0QY

Immigration New Zealand Offices USA:

Immigration NZ Washington: 1120 19th Street, Suite No. 415, Washington DC 20036

Australian Consular Office in New Zealand:

Australian Consulate-General: Level 7, Pricewater-houseCoopers Tower, 188 Quay Street, Auckland 1010. 09 921 8800

British High Commission in New Zealand:

British Consulate-General: British High Commission, 44 Hill Street, Thorndon, Wellington 6011. 04 924 2888; www.gov.uk/government/world/organisations/british-high-commission-wellington. There is also a consular office in Auckland. Call 09 303 2973.

United States Embassy and Consular Office in New Zealand:

Embassy of the United States of America: 29 Fitzherbert Terrace, Thorndon, Wellington; 04 462 6000; www.nz.usembassy.gov

United States Consulate-General: Third Floor, Citigroup Centre, 23 Customs Street East, Auckland 1010; (09-303 2724; aucklandacs@state.gov

PART II

LOCATION, LOCATION

WHERE TO FIND YOUR IDEAL HOME
NORTH ISLAND
SOUTH ISLAND

WHERE TO FIND YOUR IDEAL HOME

CHAPTER SUMMARY

Sun, sea and seclusion. Northland offers sun, sea and seclusion in the far north. The Warkworth area, one hour north of Auckland combines the best of the outdoor lifestyle yet within commuting distance of the country's biggest city.

Auckland prices. Prices in Auckland are likely to remain buoyant because of the job opportunities.

Get Away from it all in the South Island. The South Island (known as the mainland), has far fewer people and cheaper property than the North Island. Queenstown is the exception, as it has the second highest property prices after Auckland. An apartment may be a better choice as a base for skiing holidays, or else buy in the surrounding district.

Fishing lodges. For a fishing lodge try either the Rotorua Lakes or Taupo.

Help re-build Christchurch. Relocating families moving to Christchurch to help in the reconstruction, will find better value than in Auckland or Wellington.

* * *

OVERVIEW

Whether it's the clarity of the light, the brilliant blues of the sky and oceans, the lifestyle, or the friendly locals, it's a country that creates a lasting impression for many visitors. One UK visitor who first went there on holiday in 1999, reports that like many British people, his perception of the country had been formed long ago, as a small child tucking into New Zealand roast lamb at Sunday lunch, or spreading New Zealand butter on toast. Seeing the Southern Cross and the Milky Way stretching overhead above a midnight beach at Golden Bay took his breath away. A year later, he was moving to Hamilton for a job.

The desire to make the move could have come about from being on holiday and having the time to look at the world a little differently, as the experience of that British holidaymaker illustrates. But whatever brings you to New Zealand, the choice about where to live can be tantalising. Every region contains stunning scenery or the promise of an entirely different lifestyle. So how do you choose?

For some of you, the decision about where to live may have already been made for you – through a job offer, or to be near family. Before you commit to moving, do check out the area first, as otherwise you could find yourself stuck in the middle of nowhere. So before you commit to living 30km south of Auckland at Drury, or at the tip of the Whangaparaoa Peninsula to the north, check out the following section to find your ideal place to live.

You do need to have an appreciation for the natural environment, if you're going to thrive in New Zealand, no matter where you choose to live. Wellington does have theatres and galleries and a lively restaurant scene but it's low key. In Auckland the emphasis is on suburban life, with proximity to the beach, nature and green space. Bars and restaurants are places to be seen.

The smaller cities in the Sunshine Belt, the Bay of Plenty or Hawke's Bay, offer an enviable lifestyle as well as cultural events. These include the attractive little town of Napier, which is noted for its Art Deco heritage, as well as its wine and food tourism. If the beach appeals, try Tauranga. Or, how about that most congenial of little cities, Nelson, a place that's passionate about artistic pursuits, values its heritage, yet has great beaches, a laid back lifestyle and excellent local wine.

Maybe you're looking for a second home – a holiday retreat in the mountains for skiing holidays, or a lakeside retreat. You'll be able to afford more frequent visits to the snow if you avoid Queenstown and Wanaka and buy in Alexandra or Arrowtown. But be quick – these areas are fast catching up with the flashier Queenstown. Or if your ideal way of unwinding is fishing for trout, a weekend retreat on the shores near the Rotorua lakes or Taupo might be an option. For anyone passionate about sailing, Auckland, the 'City of Sails' or the Bay of Islands would be two great options.

Parents raising a young family may choose an area because of the schooling as much as for the lifestyle. If your job is in Auckland then South East Auckland is a good compromise as it has good schooling, it's near the water, yet the houses are around 15% to 20% cheaper than their equivalent in the expensive Eastern Bays or Grammar Zone. Auckland property prices though are on a par with those in South East England. Another child-friendly location is the city of Hamilton, a thriving little place, and an hour and a half south of Auckland, but with more affordable housing.

Or, there's the South Island's biggest centre, Christchurch. It has a dry, sunny climate, great schools, superb skiing nearby and even a beach or two, with better value property. For holidays you can head south to Queenstown and Central Otago, or if you're seeking sun and sand, it's a few hours drive to the delightful areas of Nelson and Golden Bay.

If you're prepared for a more bracing sea experience, you can still find unrenovated properties, a block back from the beach for under $300,000 with views of rugged coastline, near the river city of Wanganui, on the west coast of the North Island. At the southern tip of the South Island in the beautiful empty spaces of Central Otago, a two bedroom unrenovated house on 4.47 hectares (11 acres) with rural and mountain views close to a school, can be had for around $300,000. If you'd like to build your dream house in the remote West Coast area of the South Island, a block of land on 1.26 hectares (3.11 acres) with mountain and native bush views could be yours for just over $250,000.

Christchurch is perhaps the only place in New Zealand where regional identity mattered, because of its supposedly more genteel and ordered settlement in the 1850s. And as you'll see in the section on the area, echoes of this gentility still prevail. In the rest of the country regional identity only starts to matter during a sporting match of rugby or netball. The further down the country you travel, provincial attitudes to city life become apparent. Tell a person from Invercargill that you're from Auckland and they'll shake their head and offer their commiserations.

Here is a brief guide to architectural and real estate terms as used in the New Zealand context. Some of them may be familiar to you, others, especially, are an example of Kiwi vernacular.

Art Deco This decorative style was named after an exhibition held in Paris in 1925. It was widely used in architecture of the 1930s, exemplified by houses with angular or zigzag surface forms. Art Deco houses have flat roofs and are solidly built of stucco or other similar materials. The city of Napier, which was rebuilt in the new style after the 1931 earthquake, has one of the best collections of Art Deco architecture in the Southern Hemisphere.

Bach The Oxford English Dictionary says that the word originated as a shortened version of a bachelor pad, a place where a man lived on his own and did his own cooking and housekeeping. But a bach today can mean anything from a scruffy old holiday cottage to a grand beach house.

Californian bungalow A spacious bungalow, very suitable as a family home, made of wood dating from 1910 onwards with distinct features of the period, including a verandah post on the exterior, window hoods, wide eaves and exposed rafters on gables. The interiors contain extensive wood panelling and sometimes a plate rail, which emphasises the horizontal aspect of the house, creating a feeling of space, which was reinforced by the open plan design. One important and practical design feature of some original Californian bungalows was sliding wood-panelled doors, which closed off the sitting room from the dining room.

Cottage A small, single-storey building, generally with four rooms and without a hallway.

Crib The South Island term for the word bach, more commonly heard in Canterbury and further south. The family crib might be near a lake, a river or the beach.

Indoor-outdoor flow This describes the connection

between the outdoor living space and the house and is a feature of open plan houses.

Kauri *Agathis australis* This timber, which is tall and straight, was felled extensively by the early settlers for house building. Fijian kauri, grown in sustainable forests, is one remaining source of the species. The most famous example of a living kauri in New Zealand is *Tane Mahuta,* in the Waipoua Forest, Northland.

Lifestyle block A ten acre or four hectare hobby farm or smallholding. Usually bought by city folk who have had enough of the rat race, and who don't have to live off the income from their land.

Matai *Prumnopitys taxifolia* a native timber with grey-brown bark once used for flooring and interior joinery.

Monolithic cladding This form of exterior cladding became popular in the 1990s as a cheap way of making a house look like it was built of solid construction. Monolithic cladded houses are shunned by many buyers, as incorrectly applied cladding was implicated in the Leaky Building Crisis – see **Chapter 6 What Type of Property to Buy**, where this is discussed in detail.

O.s.p. An abbreviation for off-street parking, commonly found in real estate advertising.

Relocated house To British readers, living in solid brick houses, the idea that a house could be relocated from one place to another might seem incredible. But it's been going on in New Zealand for years, as old wooden villas have been removed from their original sites and moved elsewhere. It's only thanks to relocation that so many fine examples of villa housing still exist today. A relocated villa is easy to spot from the exterior, as there will be no brick chimney, unless the owners have had it rebuilt. A relocated house may be cheaper than one on its original site, but don't forget to factor in the costs of rewiring and, re-piling. A building will need to have been sprayed for borer or termites before it can be moved, so check with the seller to see if this has been done and ask to see a certificate, as proof.

Rimu *Dacrydium cypressinum* A red pine native timber previously used in interior joinery.

Section The land that the house sits on and the size will be described in sq m or hectares.

Sleepout This describes an extra room for guests, usually away from the main house, which could be a summerhouse or even a converted garage.

Spanish Mission Made of stucco, with a roughcast exterior, Spanish Mission style generally has arched doors and windows, balconies, an orange tiled roof, and long thin windows. The town of Hastings in the Hawke's Bay, which like Napier, was flattened in the earthquake, has a few surviving Spanish Mission buildings still standing, including the Municipal Theatre built in 1914. Elsewhere, the style is found in small low-level blocks of flats, in theatres and in school buildings. Auckland Grammar is one noted example of Spanish Mission style.

Stripped classical A design feature, used mainly in public buildings where elements of classical design have been pared back and ornate features replaced

with simpler ones. The style was said to have originated in Melbourne and contained many features
of the Chicago School. The Harbour City Centre
(formerly the DIC building) in Wellington, the
Wellington Railway Station, Broadcasting House
in Napier and the NZ Guardian Trust building in
Auckland are all of this design.

Tandem garaging Two cars are parked one behind
the other.

Townhouse A house dating from around the 1980s.
Developers will try to cram in three or even four
of these high-density houses onto a site previously
occupied by one house. The house occupies most of
the site, with just enough room to fit a small courtyard garden.

Transitional style Between 1908-1918 approximately, the fashion for the ornately decorative villa
began to fade. During the transitional phase, house
design started to incorporate elements of bungalow
style. Verandah decoration was simplified, roof angles
were flattened and casement windows replaced dou-
ble-hung sash windows.

Villa The first houses to be mass-produced in New
Zealand were wooden houses built in the Victorian
and Edwardian period. Villas are characterised by
a central corridor with rooms leading off on both
sides and high ceilings. Villas are often decorated
with elaborate balustraded verandahs, which extends
right around the house. The best examples are made
of kauri heartwood, which is remarkably resilient to
insect damage. The traditional roofing material for
villas is cast iron. Windows are of the sash variety.

Villas come in three styles. The **single bay villa** generally has an arched pediment with finial fretwork bracketing. The **double bay villa** is characterised by two bay windows at the front of the house. The **square villa** is the smallest and simplest of villa design giving the villa a box-like shape, although some decorative features of the ornate veranda still remains.

Weatherboard This is the wood cladding used on the outside of houses, known as clapboard in the USA.

* * *

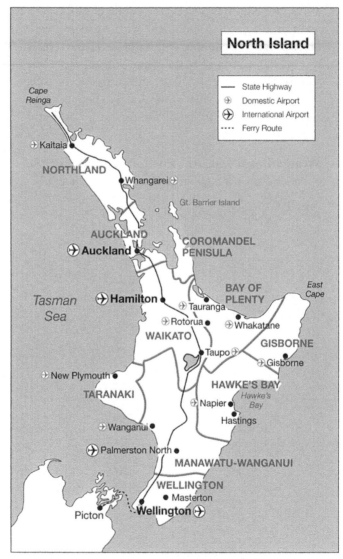

Figure 1 Map of North Island, New Zealand

NORTH ISLAND

UPPER NORTH ISLAND

NORTHLAND

Largest city: Whangarei *Area sq km:*12,600. *Population of region:*151,692 Whangarei: 51,500. *Climate:*Average summer temperature 23.5C. Average winter temperature 15C. Sunshine hours: 2016 per annum. Annual rainfall: 1500mm. *Airports:* Kaitaia, Kerikeri, Whangarei. *Attractions and National Parks:* Bay of Islands, Cape Reinga, Hokianga, Ninety Mile Beach, Poor Knights Islands (one of the world's best diving sites), Waitangi Treaty Grounds, Waipoua Forest, Goat Island Marine Reserve.

Geography and Climate

Northland runs from Cape Reinga at the very tip of the North Island in a long thin curve all the way down to the border of Greater Auckland. It has two natural harbours on the west coast, the Kaipara and the Hokianga. Cape Reinga is where the Tasman Sea meets the Pacific Ocean in a swirling angry mass. For Maori, it is a place of great spiritual significance, where the departed souls leave on their final journey, north to the ancestral homeland, Hawaiki.

On the east coast are white beaches and sheltered bays, including the boaties paradise, the Bay of Islands. It's a beautiful and diverse region with the largest remaining stands of kauri forest left in New Zealand.

In a clockwise direction from Auckland, the geographic regions of Northland are the Kaipara and the Kauri Coast along the Pacific western coastline, the Far North, starting at Kaitaia and includes Ninety Mile Beach and Cape Reinga, some 350km north of Auckland. South of Ninety

Mile Beach are the beaches and settlements of Doubtless Bay and the Karikari Peninsula.

Just south of there is the Bay of Islands, 800km of coast-line with 150 islands. The Whangarei region is south of the Bay of Islands and includes the settlements of Matapouri and the Tutukaka coastline. Then there is the Kowhai Coast, on the east coast, closest to Auckland, which includes the marine reserve Goat Island and the settlements of Wark-worth and the Matakana Valley, a boutique wine region.

Northland is known as the 'winterless north' but in real-ity that's only true north of Kaitaia. Northland has high humidity in summer and frequent rain in winter and spring, especially on the west coast. But instead of annoying drizzle for days on end, the rain falls in bursts, ferocious but short-lived. Parts of Northland can be reached within an hour from Auckland, so it's not surprising that it's a favourite summer playground for those from New Zealand's largest city.

Cheerleaders for Northland point out that it's easier to get to than that other favourite holiday spot, the Coroman-del Peninsula, with two points of access rather than one bottleneck. As well as good access, Northland is steeped in bi-cultural history and retains many of its old buildings. And the beauty of Northland is that even in high summer there are still empty beaches and bays, provided you avoid Paihia in the Bay of Islands. And as you can see from the population statistics, for a region this size, Northland is sparsely populated.

History

Northland, *Te Tai Tokerau* in Maori, and known as the 'Birthplace of a Nation', was the earliest part of the country to be settled by both Maori and Pakeha. In Maori legend, Kupe the great explorer was said to have sailed through the entrance to the Hokianga on the west coast and found it much to his liking, in contrast to a European group in the 19th century, intent on settling in Rawene. With no let up from three solid weeks of rain, they had an abrupt change of plan and packed up and headed off to Sydney.

It seems hard to imagine today that genteel Russell was known as 'the hell hole of the Pacific', in the early days of European settlement. Missionaries tried and failed to convert the debauched sealers and whalers to follow the teachings of the Lord. But they did have more luck with Maori than they did with the sailors. So successful was the French Catholic Mission in Russell that Bishop Pompallier set up a religious printing press, which produced bibles in the Maori language.

It was the lawlessness amongst the visitors that prompted the local Maori chiefs to approach the British Crown in the first instance about imposing authority. This led to the historic signing at Waitangi in the Bay of Islands of the 1840 Treaty of Waitangi. Regarded as New Zealand's founding document, it was signed by Maori chiefs and representatives of the British Crown.

For more information on the Treaty, see the History section in Chapter 1. Almost as soon as the ink was dry, Hone Heke, the Ngapui chief found that the treaty was being breached and showed his contempt for British rule by chopping down the flagstaff at Russell a total of four times.

For the Maori that live in and around Waitangi this is an important centre of Maori culture. The Waitangi Day celebrations on February 6th at the treaty grounds are, on occasion, disrupted by protestors who air their grievances in front of television crews, there to record any verbal upsets between demonstrators and politicians.

The story of Northland is a tale of two coastlines, and the divisions are not merely geographic. The wildly beautiful and empty west coast was once teeming with fortune hunters and opportunists. On this coast once stood ancient native kauri forests, which were cut down to, make ships' spars, houses and furniture.

After the loggers came the gum diggers. Kauris produce a sticky resin, not unlike maple syrup, which was a valuable raw material, used in linoleum and furniture varnishes. When the price for the gum rose, this brought more prospectors. At one stage more than 2000 gum diggers were competing to extract the gum. At first, it was harvested from the kauri stumps left by the loggers but when the supply dwindled, the hunt to find more gum became increasingly destructive until eventually even the ancient kauri swamps were dredged. Once the supply ran out all that was left was a barren and unproductive landscape. Once the shipbuilding boom was over, kauri was an important source of wood for the building and furniture trade. Kauri was fashioned into furniture as well as entire houses.

Although most of the native kauri trees had been felled by the early 20th century, logging for kauri was only banned in the area in the early 1950s when the remaining forest was saved and renamed as the Waipoua Sanctuary. Given the three-pronged attack on the kauri forests, it is remarkable that any kauri survived at all. While there's no real substitute for getting up close and personal with a kauri tree, to whet your appetite you can view the largest and grandest kauri tree of them all by going to http://www. waipouaforest.hokianga.co.nz. Here you will find *Tane Mahuta* – (God of the Forest). This tree stands at 47 m high with a girth of 13m. The oldest known living kauri is *Te Matua Ngahere* (Father of the Forest), more than 3000 years old.

When the gum diggers and the loggers moved on, parts of Northland never really recovered from the environmental damage. The shift to agriculture and farming has had limited success, as much of Northland is unsuitable for grazing and farming.

Because Northland's economy is still overly reliant on natural resources and agriculture, both slow growth industries, the region has never grown sufficiently to lift itself out of the economic doldrums. Northland, particularly in the Far North, has the highest regional unemployment rate in the country at over 8%. Agricultural work is both poorly paid and seasonal, so that young people have left Northland for the cities, seeking a better life. But the tourists on board the luxury cruise ships that regularly call into the Bay of Islands over the summer would have no inkling that this was anything but an idyllic paradise.

Arts and Culture

The Austrian artist and architect Friedensreich Hundertwasser lived and worked in Northland for the last thirty years of his life. He was famous throughout the world for his work with colourful mosaics, and was known for his ability to convert industrial buildings into aesthetic artworks. A new art centre dedicated to his work is currently in the first stages of development. At the time of writing, nearly $13 million had been raised of the total $16.25 required for the Hundertwasser Art Centre, a gallery that will feature over 50 pieces of art in cooperation with the Kunsthaus in Vienna. In addition a second gallery, The Wairau Maori Art Gallery will open alongside the Hundertwasser Art Centre. The Wairau Maori Art Gallery aims to promote mutual understanding between Maori and Pakeha through the medium of contemporary art. The proposed new galleries will become an important addition to the art scene in Northland. In the meantime, the Whangarei Art Museum currently showcases diverse touring and local art.

Typical Properties for Sale

The **Kowhai Coast** around the village-like **Warkworth** offers the best of both worlds. Auckland is only an hour away, the schools are good and property is more affordable than in the city. **Matakana Valley,** nearby, is a boutique wine area where you can dine out among the vines. Whangarei, two hours drive from Auckland, has an attractive harbour and would be suitable for family living or a holiday house, especially in the countryside or out towards the dramatic coastline on the way to Whangarei Heads.

The Bay of Islands, the group of 150 small islands is highly sought after and property on or around the water will be expensive. Russell and Paihia though have barely more than a couple of thousand permanent residents. Kerikeri is a lively little town of fine historic buildings, set in an attractive waterside location.

North of Kerikeri, it's beautiful but remote and suitable for holiday homes or a rural lifestyle, far away from the cares of city life. The fishing village of Mangonui is an attractive little place. The west coast has attracted artists and writers. Available property is scarce and house buyers in this region should note that it is very rural and remote and that the nearest supermarket or medical centre may be up to 20km away.

Properties range from bare land to older style weatherboard houses, modern beach houses, a small number of holiday apartments, as well as houses with orchards, hobby farms and horsey retreats.

Prices in New Zealand dollars, except where indicated. Exchange rate data used throughout this book was calculated October 2016.

Cable Bay: A 790 sq metre section of bare land with sea views over Doubtless Bay. Close to Coopers

Beach shopping centre. **Price:** $128,000 $US 93,240 £UK71,784 $A121,811

Karikari Peninsula: Modern 3 bedroom, 2 bathroom house on 838 sq metres. Views of Tokerau Beach and Doubtless Bay. Close to a golf course, restaurant and winery. **Price:** $519,000.

Kerikeri: 4 bedroom, 2 bathroom house on 1430sq metres of land. Close to a school and the historic centre. **Price:** $629,000.

Mangonui: A house and land package on a .66ha plot with water views. Architect designed house to be built for you within a 110ha gated estate. **Price:** $639,000.

Paihia: A 2 bedroom, 2 bathroom waterfront penthouse apartment in a complex. **Price:** $650,000.

Russell: An opportunity to build your dream home on this 837sq metres plot which comes with a modest 2 bedroom holiday cottage in need of renovation. **Price:** $395,000.

Waiwera: A 2 bedroom holiday apartment with estuary views. **Price:** $390,000.

Warkworth: Between Warkworth and Puhoi, a 6 bedroom, 1 bathroom wooden villa on 4.8 ha. with paddocks, two barns and a stream. **Price:** $1,295,000.

Wellsford: A 4 bedroom, 1 bathroom family home with one bedroom self-contained guest room. **Price:** $445,000.

Whangaroa: A 3 bed, 2 bathroom heritage villa on 2.6 ha. Close to beach, a bus route, bush walks and a school. **Price:** $460,000.

Whangerei: Modern house with 4 bedrooms, 2 bathrooms on 6105 sq metres with coastal and rural views. **Price:** $605,000.

If you plan to spend the New Zealand summer house hunting in the Bay of Islands, you could be sharing it with 30,000 other visitors in January. But if you can delay it until February (surely the most miserable month in the Northern Hemisphere), the kids will be back at school and the prices will be better.

Agents for this area: www.raywhite.com, www.harcourts. co.nz, www.realestatenorthland.co.nz

* * *

AUCKLAND

Largest city: Auckland.*Area sq km:* 5,600. *Population of region:*1.57 million. *Climate:* Average summer temperature 20C. Average winter temperature 13C. Sunshine hours: 245 days per annum. Annual rainfall: 1200mm. *Airports:* Auckland International. Separate domestic terminal nearby. *Attractions and National Parks:* Islands of the Hauraki Gulf including Tiritiri Matangi, a protected bird sanctuary. Waitakere and Hunua Ranges.

Geography and Climate

Auckland sits on a narrow isthmus between two harbours, the Manukau to the west and the Waitemata to the east. From Waiwera in the north to Drury, in the south, Greater Auckland stretches some sixty kilometres. To the west, the city reaches as far as Henderson and the west coast beaches at Muriwai and Piha. Out east, the spread of that urban sprawl is contained by the Hauraki Gulf. Out in the Gulf, Waiheke Island is the eastern most point of Greater Auckland. Auckland's sprawl mirrors that of that other Pacific city, Los Angeles. Twice the size of greater London but with only 1.57 million people, it is one of the least densely populated cities in the world.

With safe swimming beaches in the eastern suburbs and the North Shore and good surfing on the west coast and 20 conservation parks within a 45-minute drive, it's not surprising that Auckland continues to attract new residents. They come for the jobs and of course, the lifestyle.

The Waitakere Ranges has walking and mountain biking tracks, one of which includes the Pohutukawa Glade Walk, leading to Karekare, where scenes from Jane Campion's award-winning feature film, *The Piano* were shot. Out in the Waitakeres are tree ferns, kauri, rata and *pohutukawa* (known as the New Zealand Christmas tree). The forest is the place for bird life such as the iridescent green *tui* and the friendly fantails.

Dotted around in the suburbs are important natural sites including extinct volcanoes (there are at least 50), as well as a mangrove swamp along the foreshore in Remuera. Two of the largest volcanic cones are One Tree Hill (Maungakiekie) and Mt Eden (Maungawhau). Both were once the sites of Maori pa (fortified settlements) and the remains of house sites and food storage pits can still be seen. But it's mainly the views that draw the visitors. But there is one natural landmark that is uniquely Auckland, and that is the third and most dramatic volcano of all, Rangitoto, the sleeping giant, sitting out in the Hauraki Gulf. It was formed a mere 600 years ago after a volcanic eruption. Rangitoto's distinctive conical shape is visible right along the coast from the North Shore down to the Eastern Beaches.

Often referred to as a mini Sydney, Auckland may have

a harbour bridge, beaches and an attractive harbour, but that's about all it has in common with its neighbour across the Tasman. Where Sydney has efficient public transport, Aucklanders are car dependent. And it's a scandal that a city of Auckland's size that the international airport has neither train nor subway connection. Passengers have to take a taxi, rely on friends or family, or wait for an airport bus just to get to the city centre.

The downtown area can disappoint those expecting a big city experience. Auckland doesn't have an opera house or sophisticated shopping, or any of the other facilities that international visitors might expect. The Viaduct area, which has yachts moored nearby, is pleasant enough to while away an evening in a restaurant or bar.

Auckland City Art Gallery and the University of Auckland are set within attractive grounds. A lovely park with a duck pond, a palm house and a winter garden surrounds the Auckland Museum. The best places to eat out are scattered around and not necessarily in the centre of town.

At night the downtown area empties out and can resemble a ghost town as most people have gone home to the suburbs. This can be disconcerting for international visitors. For a livelier experience, just head up to Ponsonby, where the locals go, whereas the waterfront Viaduct area is a place to see and be seen.

Aucklanders are regarded with suspicion by the rest of the country and accused of being brash, showy, shallow and materialistic. But as many Aucklanders know, much of that disdain masks downright envy. After all, Aucklanders seem to have it all. Diners can eat out at a different restaurant every night of the year, and then there's the lifestyle. City types can throw off the suit jacket, jump into sailing gear and be off and away out into the Gulf within 30 minutes of leaving the office.

But this rather myopic view of Auckland belies the

reality. It ignores the fact that Auckland is the world's largest Polynesian city where 11% of the population have Pacific ancestry, that 13% claim Maori ancestry and that 10% of its residents were originally from Asia. As a result, Auckland is the only truly multicultural city in New Zealand, and that diversity is celebrated by all the different cultural attractions on offer.

Aucklanders have a reputation for not being as cultured as Wellingtonians, but that depends on how you define culture. Instead of just an orchestra concert or a play to choose from, Aucklanders could be attending events as diverse as a Pacific Island fashion show or a display of Indian dance.

History

Maori have lived in Auckland for over 800 years, but ever since Ngati Whatua made it their home, they faced considerable challenges from other tribes, eager to capitalise on its riches.

After the Treaty of Waitangi was signed in 1840, William Hobson, the new governor, wasted no time in relocating the capital from Opua in the Bay of Islands further south to Auckland. A Scottish doctor, who lived in Auckland just as it was elevated to its new status was one John Logan Campbell. Known as 'the father of Auckland', Logan Campbell was Auckland's first property speculator, who as well as owning a large tract of land, was able to wield political power by becoming its mayor.

Logan Campbell is fondly regarded, as instead of leaving all his land to his family, he gifted a large area of his estate to the city. The city's dog owners and joggers have been grateful to him ever since. Cornwall Park includes One Tree Hill and is a formally laid out park with exotic tree species from the Northern Hemisphere. Incorporating a home farm, grazing cattle and even a ha ha, all that's missing is the grand stately pile straight out of Jane Austen.

Auckland is the 61st most expensive city in the world to live in and is still cheaper than Sydney (31) and Melbourne (47). Depending on which survey you believe, Auckland is either the third best city to live in for quality of life (Mercer 2016) or ninth (Economist 2015).

Typical Properties for Sale

Auckland now has the highest median house prices in the country, at $821,000 and central Auckland has some of the most desirable real estate in New Zealand. Factors that influence the price of property vary, but being in the right school zone can add as much as 10%. Families will move into a zone just to ensure that they can get their children into either Auckland Grammar (boys) or Epsom Girls Grammar.

Grammar zone includes the 'old money' suburbs of Parnell and Remuera. The other highly sought after areas to live, for those who can afford them are Herne Bay, as well as the Eastern suburbs beside the beach up to and including St Heliers. The most desirable parts of these areas are any that face north and the words 'northern slopes' and 'Rangi views' are shorthand for a view of Rangitoto and that the house faces the right direction for the sun. You'll see little change out of $2,000,000 for 4 bedroom family homes in these areas.

Property development is an Auckland disease: grand old landmark houses have been moved from their original sites and relocated elsewhere. And in their place go grim, boxy townhouses, entirely out of keeping with their surroundings. You'll find many examples of crimes against architecture in Auckland, where colours and materials have been chosen without any regard for the natural environment, or the surrounding buildings. Unlike many other of the world's cities, there was no urban design panel in place in Auckland until recently, so developers could put up pretty much any old monster they liked, with no aesthetic design considerations.

While it is hard to find a piece of bare land to build on anymore, especially near the centre, Auckland offers the potential house buyer one of the most diverse ranges of life-style of any city in the world. Take your pick from a modern apartment at the Viaduct harbour, a clifftop mansion on the North Shore, an inner city kauri villa, or a lifestyle block out west. In South East Auckland it's around 15 to 20% cheaper for houses that often have fine views.

The age and style of housing depends very much on when the area was first settled. Because the North Shore was only linked to the city in 1959, most of the housing stock was built from the 1960s onwards. You'll find older houses in areas, which have had long-term ferry services into the city, including Devonport, Northcote Point and Birkenhead Point. The most desirable areas along the North Shore are those that hug the coastline or have views over the inner harbour.

Ponsonby and Grey Lynn have long been gentrified. Owner-occupiers and renters who can't afford the hefty prices of the inner city are being pushed further and further out to the fringes and beyond.

'South Auckland' is shorthand for parts of Manukau City where there are pockets of urban deprivation. It has a reputation for being unsafe. The majority of residents of Manukau City (down near the airport) are law abiding and industrious. The great many positive initiatives tend to get ignored by the news media for the sake of a good story about gangs and violent crime.

Central Auckland, City Centre: 2 bedroom, 2 bathroom apartment without parking on the fifth floor. **Price:** $550,000 US$400,022 £307,979 A$522,882.

Eastern Suburbs, Glendowie: On a plot of 383 sq

metres this modern townhouse has open plan living and a dining room opening out onto a deck and garden. Double carport. **Price:** $1,040,000.

South East, Half Moon Bay: A 3 bedroom, 2 bathroom house on a 720 sq m plot close to top schools and the Half Moon Bay ferry for commuting into Auckland. **Price:** $1,390,000.

North Shore, Devonport: There is nowhere else on the North Shore that matches Devonport for its seaside village atmosphere, period houses and ferry service to central Auckland. Expats are attracted to the area by the good schooling, as well as the glorious beach on the Cheltenham side. You'll need deep pockets to buy in the area. This renovated 3 bedroom, 2 bathroom villa is on a plot of 377 sq m. Polished floors, an entertaining deck and off street parking for 2 cars. **Price:** $1,695,000.

West, Titirangi: Auckland's answer to Sydney's Blue Mountains. A 3 bedroom, 1 bathroom house on a private bush clad site of 1290 sq m on the fringes of the Waitekere Ranges. **Price:** $760,000.

Piha: A surfer's paradise, this 2 bedroom, 2 bathroom renovated beach house, or quintessential Kiwi bach, with sea views, is on Auckland's wild west coast. **Price:** $1,150,000.

Henderson Valley: If you want space and better value for money, go west. A 3 bedroom, 1 bathroom home on a good sized plot a short drive to a train station and shopping centre. **Price:** $840,000.

Islands of the Hauraki Gulf, Waiheke Island: Handy for the ferry to Auckland, this 2 bedroom, 1 bathroom bach on a site of 883 sq metres has sea views. Enjoy it as it is or build your dream home on the site. **Price:** $749,000.

South, Karaka: A bare block of land of .40 ha in a country setting close to good schools, 45mins to 1hr in rush hour to Auckland. **Price:** $795,000.

Agents for this area. www.barfoot.co.nz, www.prestige-realty.co.nz, www.harcourts.co.nz, www.bayleys.co.nz.

* * *

CENTRAL NORTH ISLAND

WAIKATO

Largest centre: Hamilton. *Area sq km:* 7,363. *Population of region:* 403,638. Hamilton: 156,000. *Climate:* Average summer temperature: Hamilton 23C, Taupo 22C. Average winter temperature: Hamilton 14 C, Taupo 12C. Sunshine hours: Hamilton 2000 per annum, Taupo 1965 per annum. Annual rainfall: Hamilton 1190mm, Taupo 1100mm. *Airport:* Hamilton with regional connections, as well as international to Australia and Pacific holiday destinations. *Attractions and National Parks:* Hobbiton, Waitomo Caves, Pirongia Forest Park, Lake Taupo.

Geography and Climate

The Waikato has a mild climate with high humidity in the summer and the occasional frost in winter. You'll get your first glimpse of the Waikato's pastoral landscape from the top of the Bombay Hills, as you drive south from Auckland. To the east is the ridge of the Kaimai Ranges, dividing the Bay of Plenty from the Waikato and to the south-west the mountains of Pirongia Forest Park. The mighty Waikato River has its source to the south in the volcanic Lake Taupo and wends its way through to reach Cambridge, Hamilton and Huntly finally reaching the sea at Port Waikato, just south of Auckland.

The Waikato is home to all things dairy, and Fonterra, New Zealand's largest dairy company has a base here. Just to the north of Hamilton is Woodlands, a kauri homestead, where the Anchor butter brand was founded in 1886. Even the local football team, Mooloo, is named in honour of the black and white Friesian cattle that made the fortune of many a Waikato farmer.

Although money doesn't grow on trees in the Waikato (sadly they were chopped down to make way for farms), it certainly grows in those fields, or paddocks as they call them in New Zealand. Cambridge and Matamata are the home of the bloodstock industry. Thoroughbred champions of the future take their first wobbly steps in a landscape known as a mini-Kentucky.

Engineering service companies set up to service the dairy industry continue to be a strong earner for the region. It's not hard to see why Hamilton and the Waikato are thriving: there's a reliable infrastructure, good schools, a university and three cities including Auckland all within a 90-minute drive.

History

The European settlers didn't take long to recognise the potential in the Waikato's productive soil. The only problem was that the land belonged to Tainui. The British Crown may have signed a treaty with Maori in 1840, but by 1860 the government was made up of self-interested individuals, who weren't interested in negotiation in the same way as the Crown was.

Maori wouldn't willingly part with their land, even though the government tried to persuade them otherwise. The 1860s saw the start of the Waikato Land Wars where Tainui land was seized by force. In an attempt at elevating the status of Maori to the level of the British sovereign, a breakaway element called Kingitangi, or the King Movement was formed, to try to find a way of controlling the European settlers insatiable demand for land. The base of the breakaway movement was in Te Kuiti, an area that became known as the King Country. It became a no-go area for Europeans. It wasn't until the 1890s that they were permitted to go there. The Maori king, Te Arikinui Kiingi Tuheitia is a descendant of the first Maori king and lives at the Turangawaewae Marae at Ngaruawahia, just north of Hamilton. It was in Ngaruawahia that the historic Raupatu Land Settlement was signed, where Government agreed to pay compensation to Tainui for land confiscated in the 1860s.

Typical Properties for Sale

The Waikato is a prosperous region with substantial houses in the country areas, as well as to the south of Hamilton in Tamahere and near the airport. Cambridge, within a 30-minute drive south of Hamilton, is an attractive country town with good schools and provides a pleasant alternative to living in Hamilton, for those looking to buy a house with some land attached.

Hamilton attracts relocating Auckland families priced out of the Auckland Grammar or Epsom Girls zones, looking to find a more affordable lifestyle. South Auckland is just over an hour's drive, making commuting possible. Hamiltonians can take advantage of all that Auckland has to offer, without necessarily living there.

One of the most beautiful and unspoilt coastal areas within 45-minutes commute to Hamilton is Raglan, with its rugged black iron sand beaches. Rather like Big Sur must have been 50 years ago, this beachside community attracts retirees, families with holiday homes, alternative lifestylers and the surfing community. Raglan plays hosts to international surfing championships and Manu Bay and Whale Bay, 8 kilometres away, are reputed to have the world's greatest left hand surf break. As a contrast to the surfing lifestyle, is a genteel Edwardian spa town. Te Aroha, (the place of love), is at the foot of Mount Te

Aroha, near the Kaimai Ranges. Within a 45-minute drive of Hamilton, Te Aroha is a good alternative to Cambridge for those attracted to a country lifestyle. Property is cheaper than in Hamilton, and there are some beautifully restored villas. Te Aroha's central location provides easy access to the Coromandel and the Bay of Plenty for weekend trips.

The median house price of $458,000 is now above the national average as prices in Hamilton have rocketed up in the past few years. A trickle-down effect from the Auckland boom and a vibrant economy has brought professionals south, looking for better value for money. In the best parts, along the river and around the lake, prices have crept up to rival Auckland's. The best suburb for schooling is in Hillcrest, near the university. New and featureless subdivisions of identical brick houses in the surrounding areas are a blight on the rural landscape.

Most of Hamilton was developed in the 1960s and 1970s, so it's hard to find a house with any character. If you do want a wooden villa or a Californian bungalow, you'll find them in the central city suburb of Claudelands and Hamilton East, along the river. Hamilton Gardens is a delight, where there are river walks as well as themed gardens.

Hamilton was the birthplace of Richard O'Brien, the creator of the Rocky Horror Show. Te Awamutu, a little country town south west of Hamilton was home to the musical Finn brothers of Split Enz and Crowded House fame.

Further south at Taupo, modest fishing lodges are on the market for under $600,000. Lake Taupo is almost as large as an inland sea and lakefront property represents good value, compared with beachfront homes. And Taupo has that stunning mountain scenery as well.

Matamata, or Hobbiton, as it's known to the rest of the world, is now New Zealand's most visited tourist attraction with over 350,000 visitors a year. The house and hobbit village look so authentic that many visitors are disappointed when told that the houses are a film set and not for sale.

Matamata: A modern 6 bedroom house suitable for an extended family on 918 sq m. **Price:** NZ $501,000 US$364,965 UK£ 281,349 A$476,578.

Te Awamutu: A 3 bedroom, 2 bathroom 1950s renovated building in the town centre on 552 sq m with development potential. **Price:** $425,000.

Cambridge: A 3 bedroom, 1 bathroom modern family house with 2 living areas on 3207sq m of land. Near Lake Karapiro so an approximate 45-minute commute to Hamilton. **Price:** $725,000.

Hamilton East: 4 bedroom, 2 bathroom renovated Californian bungalow on 1317 sq m site in a popular school zone, close to the University of Waikato. **Price:** $549,000.

Hamilton countryside: A lifestyle block on 6.95 ha with a 4 bedroom, 2 bathroom house. Fencing and outbuildings. Suitable for equestrian or horticulture. **Price:** $1,400,000.

Hamilton: On the river in a top school zone, this 3 bedroom, 1 bathroom renovated Art Deco home with 2 parking spaces. **Price:** $720,000.

Raglan: North facing beach bach with distant harbour views. 3 bedrooms, 2 bathrooms plus two car spaces.553 sq m. **Price:** $565,000.

Raglan: Build your dream surfing retreat on this raised 0.12 ha block of land 750 metres from the beach. **Price:** $320,000.

Taupo: With views of the Waikato river, a modern double glazed 4 bedroom, 2 bathroom detached house on 1266 sq m. **Price:** $639,000.

Taupo: 3 bedroom, 2 bathroom house on 662 sq m with spectacular views of lake and mountains. **Price:** $875,000.

Agents for this area: www.rwhamilton.co.nz. www.harcourts.co.nz, www.lodge.co.nz.

THE GULLY SYSTEM

Hamilton's gully system is a series of streams that snake their way through the suburbs. Conservationists are encouraging homeowners to restore these nature reserves with native plants to bring back *tui*, the white throated and raucous New Zealand native bird species, which was all but wiped out in Hamilton because the surrounding area has been so extensively farmed.

* * *

EAST COAST

COROMANDEL PENINSULA

Largest town: Thames. *Area sq km:* 23,530 *Population of region:* 28,000 Thames:7,000 *Climate:* Average summer temperature 22C. Average winter temperature 13C. Sunshine hours: 2200 per annum. Annual rainfall: 1400mm. *Airport:Whitianga* – limited service flying scheduled scenic flights between Auckland and Great Barrier Island. *Attractions and National Parks:* Cathedral Cove, Hot Water Beach, Karangahake Gorge, Coromandel Coastal Walkway.

Geography and Climate

The Coromandel Peninsula is technically part of the Waikato but because of its coastal position, distinct identity and popularity, it warrants a separate section. The Coromandel is the finger of land that juts out into the Hauraki Gulf, to the east of Waiheke Island. On the western side is the Firth of Thames and on its eastern side, the Pacific Ocean. Dawn breaking over the Coromandel mountains is a truly breathtaking sight. Wags say that if you can see the Coromandel clearly then it's going to rain, but if clouds obscure it, then it's already raining. And rain it does, near the mountains, which explains why the area is so green.

The Thames Coast, which is on the western edge, is the most direct route up to Coromandel Town. The narrow, treacherous but scenic road twists and turns its way along for 35 kilometres. Fringed by *pohutukawa* (Metrosideros excelsa), known as the New Zealand Christmas tree, their stunning red flowers are in full bloom in December.

The infrastructure in the Coromandel, particularly the narrow roads, helps keep the area free from tour coaches, but getting around can take time, even though the distances may be short. Fans of the Coromandel willingly put up with the poor access via the one route in and out, by ensuring that they avoid Easter and Labour Weekend. One way to avoid the tailbacks in the summer is to take the passenger ferry service from Auckland. It's an hour each way by boat, and you may even spot dolphins. Tourism, mining and forestry are the main industries here as well as mussel and oyster farming off the coast of Coromandel Town.

History

Long before the European settlers arrived a significant population of Maori lived on the peninsula, mainly in the sheltered areas along the east coast. They hunted the moa, the largest flightless bird ever to roam these lands. In 1852 the aptly named Charles Ring found gold at Driving Creek, just north of Coromandel Town. As gold fever took hold, the town became the temporary home to more than 10,000 settlers. That first gold rush was followed by further discoveries at Thames, Coromandel and Karangahake. But it's not just gold in those hills, but semi-precious stones including amethyst and agate.

As well as gold, it was kauri that attracted prospectors to the area. Kauri logging was big business for 60 years until all the kauri ran out. Tree ferns have grown where once the mighty kauri stood. Now and again you can spot a young kauri, which will have self-seeded. Even these stragglers give visitors a tantalising glimpse of how different the landscape must have once looked when it was thick with virgin forest. And as in Northland, the gum diggers descended on the area after the loggers.

Gold mining, unlike most of the other extractive industries, didn't cease in the 19th century but has been the major source of income, on and off over the years in the little town of Waihi.

At Hot Water Beach you can dig your own spa pool as water from a hot spring bubbles up under the sand. The Karangahake Gorge has some easy, flat walks where visitors can find out about the area's historical links to gold mining. The Coromandel Forest Park has long distance walks with basic accommodation for overnight visitors.

Typical Properties for Sale

Coromandel Town attracts writers, artists, conservationists as well as those escapees from the rat race. But it's not yet fashionable in the way of Byron Bay or Dartmouth in Devon. There's still a pioneering spirit up there and you're more likely to see a local driving a tractor than doing tai chi on the beach.

On the east coast, you'll find a different crowd. The low-key resort of Whitianga is a mecca for holidaying Auckland and Waikato families. Pauanui is glitzy, while Whangamata suits families. There's good surfing here along a beautiful beach.

The Coromandel suits telecommuters and creatives. It's not ideal for relocating families, as there's not much in the way of schooling or many facilities. And in winter it's very quiet. A town further inland such as Paeroa gives families more commuting options. The prices on the western side of the Coromandel, looking out on to the Firth of Thames, are cheaper than the east coast but there's only a few scattered settlements and therefore not much available for sale. Here, the beauty is not in the built environment but the surroundings. Buyers gravitate to the east coast for the beaches and the ocean views. Waihi Beach mostly consists of 1960s and 1970s solidly built houses that are functional but mostly without charm.

People who have bought recently buy these properties both for capital gain and as a development for the future. Others are content to leave as is, kitting the house out with basic furniture, creating a relaxed atmosphere, far away from the stresses of city life. Properties in the Coromandel range from modern beach houses, bare land to build on, a few holiday apartments and country homes on larger blocks of land.

Paeroa: This well-preserved little town, known for its antique and craft outlets is at the junction of two rivers. There's a golf course and good fishing available nearby. A 3 bedroom, 1 bathroom wooden bungalow with period features. **Price:** $395,000 US$287,692 £221,779 A$375,363.

Pauanui: It's all about location in this popular holiday resort, around two and a half hours drive from Auckland. 4 bedroom, 3 bathroom waterfront luxury home in a modern development. **Price:** $1, 500,000.

Port Charles: You might need a four-wheel drive vehicle to get to this remote area near the top of the Coromandel Peninsula as the access road is gravel for part of the way. A 2 bedroom, 1 bathroom house on a 400 sq m plot. **Price:** $415,000.

Tairua: With a river estuary and an ocean beach, this is a popular base. The Shoe and Slipper Islands and the Alderman Islands offer some of the country's best diving. 599 sq m plot cleared for building. Elevated site with views across the harbour and the ocean. **Price:** NZ $449,000.

Thames: A 3 bedroom 1 bathroom solid brick house in need of modernisation on a 645 sq m plot in walking distance of the town. **Price:** $439,000.

Waihi Beach: 1.85 ha elevated building plot, 260 m above sea level, with panoramic ocean views to Mayor island. **Price:** $1,900.000.

Whangamata: At the coastal holiday resort of Whangamata, a 4 bedroom, 2 bathroom townhouse. 400 metres from the beach. **Price:** $690,000.

Agents for this area: www.coromandel.harcourts. co.nz, www.bayleys.co.nz

HOLES IN THE GROUND

In December 2001 several houses collapsed into a disused mine shaft in the little town of Waihi, home to the Martha

Mine. Drainage from the mineshafts below caused some support structures to rot. Waihi Beach, which is some kilometres away from the mining area was not affected. If a house is built near disused mine shafts then this information should be recorded on the LIM (Land Information Memorandum) reports held by the local council.

* * *

BAY OF PLENTY

Largest city: Tauranga *Area sq km:* 12,247 *Population of region:* 267,741 Tauranga: 117,600 *Climate:* Average summer temperature. 23C Average winter temperature. 14.7C *Sunshine hours:* 2260 per annum. Annual rainfall: 1198mm. *Airports:* Tauranga, Whakatane and Rotorua. *Attractions and National Parks:* White Island (Whakaari), Mt Maunganui (Mauao) as well as outstanding beaches.

Geography and Climate

The Bay of Plenty was so named by Captain Cook in 1769, and the region has lived up to its bountiful reputation ever since. Today, it's an important area for fruit cultivation including kiwifruit, citrus and avocados. The coastal area of the Bay of Plenty has a microclimate, making it one of the sunniest areas of the country. The rest of the region has a warm, moist climate with few extremes of temperature, creating ideal growing conditions. Rotorua's lakeside location makes it slightly cooler than the coast.

Situated mid-way down the North Island on the east coast, the Bay of Plenty reaches south as far as the fascinating geothermal region of Rotorua. Joining the Coromandel at Athentree at the western end, the Bay of Plenty hugs the ocean past Whakatane and Opotiki towards the east.

The Raukumara Range provides a rugged backdrop to these two coastal settlements.

With over 100km of sandy ocean beach and more sunshine hours than Biarritz, the area is a mecca for sun worshippers and lotus-eaters. Whether you want to swim, surf, fish, dive, or merely gaze at it, the azure blue waters of the Bay of Plenty are truly mesmerising. Pavement cafes and restaurants make the best of the local produce. Mills Reef in Tauranga and Morton Estate at Katikati combine dining with wine tasting. Music fans will enjoy Tauranga's annual Easter jazz festival.

But it's not all hedonistic play. As well as a bustling centre for trade, Tauranga is the biggest commercial centre in the region. Timber, dairy products and the region's fruit are all shipped through the Port of Tauranga, the nation's busiest export hub. Domestic tourism is an important industry, which is fuelling the growth in the service sector.

History

The region has always held special significance for Maori. The monument at Maketu commemorates the landing place of the *Arawa* canoe, which according to Maori legend was one of the first to sail from the ancestral homeland in Hawaiki.

In 1864 one of the most significant battles in the New Zealand Wars took place in the little settlement of Gate Pa. Government troops set up a blockade in the area, as they believed local Maori were aiding the Maori king in the Waikato. Although Maori were heavily outnumbered, they nevertheless survived the bombardment. The Mission cemetery in Tauranga honours the dead of both sides who fell in battle.

The Bay of Plenty has two distinct economic and commercial regions, west and east. Tauranga and its ocean-side neighbour, Mt Maunganui, known affectionately as 'The Mount' are the hub of the Western Bay of Plenty while Whakatane with a population of just 18,000 is the main settlement of the Eastern Bay. While Tauranga is the commercial centre, as you head east it becomes much more rural, the towns are much smaller and thinly populated. Tauranga's location at the entrance to a large natural harbour has been a key factor in the city's growth. In the 1950s when Tauranga and Whakatane were both sleepy beachside backwaters, the two were very much on a par. But when Tauranga was chosen over Whakatane as the new export port for the Bay of Plenty region, this fuelled an immediate growth in both jobs and population.

Tauranga is one of the fastest growing cities in New Zealand and if that trend continues, it will soon overtake Dunedin as the fifth largest in the country. But Tauranga is no metropolis and not likely to become one, although, over the Christmas and New Year summer break when the place fills up with holidaymakers, it can seem that half of Auckland has decamped to the seaside.

Once regarded as a place to retire to, Tauranga and Mount Maunganui are attracting a younger crowd, pushing the average age down to 38. The climate, lifestyle and work opportunities continue to attract incomers to the area, many of whom have ditched urban living for a more balanced approach to work and life. And as well as attracting relocating New Zealanders, the region has long been popular with those looking to move from other parts of the globe. The Western Bay of Plenty's growth has put pressure on local infrastructure. Mount Maunganui and Tauranga are connected by a bridge that becomes a traffic bottleneck at rush hour.

POST EARLY FOR CHRISTMAS

The hardware store that doubles as a post shop in Bethlehem, Tauranga, enjoys a brisk trade at Christmas not just from residents but from all over the world, so that post can carry that coveted Bethlehem postmark.

Whakatane is unlikely to see anything like the same level of development as Tauranga. Although increasingly popular as an area for second homes, 300km is too far from Auckland for families to drive to at weekends. State Highway 2 which is an A road with passing places, is not only the main route to Tauranga but the Coromandel as well. There are regular bottlenecks at the northern end at Easter and at other holiday weekends.

Whakatane's isolation means that in winter it can be very quiet. Although it's a pretty little place, there's not much to do when it's raining, apart from family or community activities.

Apart from the suburbs, the alternatives in Rotorua are close to the lakes, especially for keen anglers.

Typical Properties for Sale

Many New Zealanders lump Tauranga, Mt Maunganui and Queenstown together as examples of the level of development they don't want to see in the rest of the country. There may be high-density apartment blocks but developers aren't permitted to build higher than eight storeys. And unlike Australia's Gold Coast, public access legislation precludes beaches from ever passing into the hands of property developers.

Even though condominiums and apartments at Mount Maunganui have replaced the scruffy kiwi beach baches, the built environment has yet to spoil the first sight of that magnificent mountain and that stunning ocean.

Location and views are the key factors in determining what price you'll pay for property here. A two bedroom apartment or townhouse with harbour views is now around $730,000. A two bedroom house with an ocean view with one bathroom and one parking space will cost over $850,000. A three bedroom house with a garage and two additional parking spaces, one bathroom, but with no views starts at $525,000.

Apartment living at Mount Maunganui offers that perfect lock up and leave lifestyle, for those who plan to divide their time between New Zealand and homes elsewhere. In blocks with on-site management, absentee landlords can opt for full management so that their apartment becomes part of a rental pool. Although the best prices and highest occupancy rates are during the summer, it's still a popular area for weekend breaks in the off-season.

A four bedroom family home in Tauranga, close to good schooling, will cost from $800,000 upwards on a smaller site. Three bedrooms in a similar area are around $650,000. Prices are cheaper the further east you go towards Whakatane for family homes, but not for second homes near water. Paying $850,000 for a plain and unlovely two bedroom holiday cottage with basic facilities might make you think again.

The hidden gem of the area though has to be Tauranga's magnificent inner harbour, which curls around in hidden inlets and waterways from Tauranga right up as far as Athentree. Prices drop the further out from Tauranga, but the lifestyle is tranquil and very liveable. On the river near the little town of Katikati, $990,000 buys a four bedroom three bathroom house on one acre with a boat mooring.

A million dollars may still buy you not just a home, but also income from the land, depending on location. Kiwifruit, compared with avocados is a more reliable crop, although it's becoming increasingly difficult to make a decent living as prices drop. Avocados are a high value industry and production barely seems to keep up with demand. But avocados are difficult to grow, according to industry insiders and crop yield can vary significantly year to year. Anyone looking at buying a horticultural business should do their sums very carefully and take the best advice they can. No matter how scientific horticulture has become, it's still a precarious way to make a living, unless you grow your crop in a polytunnel, or under glass. A freak storm can wipe out an entire outdoor crop.

Katikati: A Cape Cod style holiday retreat with 3 bedrooms and 2 bathrooms with water views. Comes with self-contained flat and a garden with fruit trees. **Price:** $865,000 US$630,131 £485,762 A$822,834.

Kauri Point: In a great fishing spot, between Katikati and Waihi Beach, a 1012 sq m building plot with harbour and farmland views. **Price:** $285,000.

Mount Maunganui: 1960s 3 bedroom, 1 bathroom renovated wooden bungalow on 625 sq m flat land with garage for one car and parking spaces for two other cars. **Price:** $549,000.

Omanawa: Horse heaven. 3.92 ha of flat pasture with 8 paddocks. A 4 bedroom house, study and 2 bathrooms. Within 30 minutes drive of Tauranga. **Price:** $699,000.

Pukehina: 2 bedroom, 1 bathroom traditional wooden bach on 905 sq m, beside a tidal estuary with views. **Price:** $625,000.

Tauranga Modern and characterless 3 bedroom brick house with 2 bathrooms and double internal access garage on 540 sq m. **Price:** $625,000.

Te Puna: Large family home in the country on 3345 sq m with landscaped garden. **Price:** $750,000.

Whakatane: On a 698 sq m block of land a 3 bedroom 1 bathroom wooden 2 storey house with distant views of the sea. **Price:** $439,000.

Agents for this area: www.actionrealestate.co.nz, www.claridgesrealestate.co.nz, www.eves.co.nz

FLOODING AND SUBSIDENCE

Buyers in coastal areas in the Bay of Plenty should pay particular attention to the information in local searches and ask for an engineers report if necessary, for matters relating to flooding and subsidence. In May 2005 a storm, which particularly affected the little settlement of Matata, saw some houses topple off cliffs. Many of the remaining properties were declared unsafe and were subsequently demolished. The parts of Tauranga that suffered similar problems will now have this information recorded on the LIM (Land Information Memorandum) reports held by the local council.

* * *

GISBORNE

Largest town: Gisborne. *Area sq km:* 15,487. *Population of region:* 43,653 Gisborne: 30,000. *Climate:* Average summer temperature 24C. Average winter temperature 14.5C. Sunshine hours: 2180 per annum. Annual rainfall: 1050 mm.*Airport:* Gisborne *Attractions and National Parks:* East Cape, Mount Hikurangi, Te Urewera National Park, Lake Waikaremoana.

Geography and Climate

The Gisborne region is blessed with mild winters and hot, dry summers. It has a drier climate than Auckland and Northland, and in February temperatures can reach the 30s. It has a thriving horticultural industry, supplying produce for both local and international consumption. Gisborne has been one of the major wine regions in New Zealand and is particularly noted for its chardonnay.

Gisborne became the first city in the world to host the Millennium celebrations. The sacred mountain, Mt Hikurangi, 1754 metres, the highest non-volcanic peak in the North Island, is the first place to see the sun.

Gisborne is one of the least populated regions in the North Island and because of its isolation, one of the least visited. Going to the region is like stepping back in time. The Pacific Coast Highway, the 1170km (728 miles) coastal route that starts in Auckland and ends in Napier, passes through Gisborne and on to Waikaremoana. It is one of the roads least travelled, yet is one of the most spectacular drives in the country and is the ultimate 'get away from it all destination'. It's an unspoilt wilderness with beautiful bays and beaches, golden sands and surf beaches. Like Northland, Gisborne and the East Cape are areas that reflect a strong Maori influence and that culture is evident throughout the region. The local tribe is Ngati Porou.

Visitors should be aware that because they don't get many tourists, that some locals may be shy and want to keep to themselves. The region is home to the tiny settlement that featured in the film *Whale Rider*. On your travels you will pass many ornately carved *marae* (meeting house) and painted Maori churches. It's best to check with the local tourist office regarding marae visits, as there are protocols to observe.

Out along the beaches, you will see local children riding

horses bareback. Surfers are attracted especially to Wainui Beach, one of the best surfing beaches in the whole country.

Further south is the magical Lake Waikaremoana and the Te Urewera National Park. This is one of the last remaining wilderness areas, with the largest stand of untouched native forest in the North Island. Outdoor activities in the park include horse trekking and white water rafting. You can go fishing for trout or water ski on the local rivers. The Lake Waikaremoana Track is one of New Zealand's Great Walks.

Homebuyers looking for the great escape from city life will be attracted to the area for its climate and scenery. While Gisborne does have a cinema, there isn't much else in the way of entertainment apart from eating out. For a town of its size, Gisborne does have a café and restaurant culture and many of the local eateries are near the beach or the harbour. It has a number of parks and outdoor spaces as well as an arboretum, with extensive woodland plantings and easy walking tracks, just out of town.

History

Although Northland may lay claim to being the first area to be settled by both Maori and Pakeha, Gisborne and the East Cape were the first places where both set foot on dry land. Just as Maori had arrived in their *waka* (canoe) many years before, it was in 1769 that the surgeon's boy Nicholas Young first spotted land from the mast of the *Endeavour*. The peninsula was named Young Nick's Head in his honour but it was at Kaiti Beach near Gisborne where Captain James Cook first stood on New Zealand soil.

Typical Properties for Sale

The downside to Gisborne, especially for those looking to buy a second home is its isolation. It's a 509km drive from

Auckland and 534km from Wellington on a road network without a motorway. For couples and small families, the faster and more convenient option would be to fly and then hire a car.

Like most regions, there's a fair selection of different styles of property to choose from and the prices are still some of the best in the country. The apartment market is limited to the city centre. Bare land for building is for sale near beaches. Gisborne has a good selection of original villas with character.

> **Gisborne:** A classic 6 bedroom, 2 bathroom 1912 2 storey wooden villa. Ideal for a home plus income, such as a bed and breakfast business on 1214 sq m. **Price:** $580,000 US$422,513 £325,713 A$551,727.

> **Gisborne:** 3 bedroom, 1 bathroom renovated wooden villa with period features and polished floors on 860 sq m. **Price:** $285,000.

> **Gisborne countryside:** A 1930s 3 bedroom house with separate sitting plus dining room on 17 ha. of fully fenced grounds 35 minutes drive from Gisborne. Your own stand of native bush with trout fishing nearby. **Price:** $349,000.

> **Tiniroto:** Lifestyle property on 5.27 ha with a 3 bedroom, 1 bathroom Californian renovated wooden bungalow with period features and polished floors. A country primary school and pub within walking distance. Tinoroto is in a remote, rural region 61 kilometres from Gisborne. **Price:** $299,000.

> **Tokomaru Bay:** A hilly 3 ha block of land to build your own dream home. Not far from the jetty. The area has a grocery store, a pub and two primary schools. **Price:** $125,000.

Wainui Beach, Gisborne: A 2035 sq m building plot, walking distance from the beach. **Price:** $275,000.

Wainui Beach, Gisborne: 4 bedrooms, 2 bathroom open plan modern lock up and leave house with a small garden and courtyard on 893 sq m, near one of New Zealand's best surfing beaches. **Price:** $670,000.

Agents for this area: https://gisborne.ljhooker.com, www.raywhite.com, www.harcourts.co.nz.

* * *

HAWKE'S BAY

Largest town: Hastings *Population of region:* 151,179 Hastings: 61,696. *Area sq km:* 14,111 sq km Sunshine hours: 2,190 per annum. Annual rainfall: 800mm *Airport:* Hawke's Bay. *Attractions and National Parks:* Te Mata Peak, Cape Kidnappers, home to the largest and most accessible gannet colony in the world, Art Deco Napier, Lake Tutira Wildlife Refuge, Kaweka Conservation Park.

Geography and Climate

On the east coast, half way down the North Island is the fertile region of Hawke's Bay. The Mediterranean style climate makes it one of New Zealand's warmest and driest places in the country. The Ruahine and Kaweka Ranges are high, forested mountains that flatten out to the Heretaunga Plains where the cities of Napier and Hastings are located. The clifftops of Cape Kidnappers cut a dramatic swathe across the coastal landscape.

Te Mata Peak is 400 metres above sea level, and the Maori legend associated with it is that *Te Mata* was a sleeping giant and leader of the Waimarama tribes. A rival tribe from the Heretaunga Plains sent a fair maid to capture his heart. Te Mata proved his devotion by devouring the hills between coast and plain but died in the process. His unfinished work can be seen at a place known as The Gap. His body in repose forms Te Mata Peak.

The climate combined with the unique soil has made the Hawke's Bay area one of the most productive agricultural regions in the country. It has a thriving Farmers' Market, as well as roadside stalls selling fruit, honey, cheese and chocolate, so that travellers can put together impromptu picnics. In addition to orchards and wineries, there are lavender gardens and olive groves. Hawke's Bay is New Zealand's premier region for wine and food tourism. There are over 40 wineries to visit, many of which showcase the local produce in their restaurants, including Craggy Range and Sileni Estates.

There's plenty to do in the area for locals and visitors alike. Hawkes Bay hosts the Art Deco Weekend in Napier, the Horse of the Year, Harvest Hawkes Bay, and the International Mission Estate Concert. The best surf beaches in the region are along the coast from Cape Kidnappers at Ocean Beach and Waimarama Beach.

Matariki – the Maori New Year. *Matariki* is the Maori name for the seven stars or 'seven sisters', the Pleiades. Matariki appears in the eastern sky around the shortest day, towards the middle of June. It marks the start of the Maori New Year. Hastings is the place to be for Matariki, where the week's celebrations are rounded off with a night of fireworks.

Tourism, agriculture and wine are the major industries in the region. Napier is a go-ahead little city, which ran the very successful 'Win a Life' promotion that received over 2700 entries from all over the world. The winning family from Britain started a trend with a further 50 families emigrating as a result of the campaign. In 2005 the 'Win a Dream Job' campaign was launched with the prize as six month's work at a winery.

History

Cape Kidnappers was named in honour of Captain Cook's Tahitian cabin boy on Cook's first voyage in 1769. Local Maori thought he was being held prisoner and tried to kidnap him, but he managed to escape and swim back to the ship, as Cook's crew fired upon the canoes.

In 1931 Hawke's Bay was the site of New Zealand's worst earthquake disaster, measuring 7.9 on the Richter scale. The city of Napier and parts of Hastings were flattened. Land rose up from out of the sea, some 40 square kilometres of it, such was the strength of the quake. Out of this disaster, in which over 250 people were killed, a new city was rebuilt in the classic architecture of the time – Spanish Mission, Stripped Classical and Art Deco.

Napier and Havelock North attract city dwellers looking to move somewhere smaller, where the pace of life isn't so frenetic, and where there's a real sense of community. The schools are good so that it's a great area for relocating families. Although the beach at Napier is stony rather than sandy, surfing beaches are within a 30-minute drive. Hastings is the main service area for all the surrounding farms, orchards and vineyards.

Typical Properties for Sale

Nearly all the wooden buildings pre 1930, were flattened during the earthquake. In Napier, you'll find the antique and curio shops selling the Art Deco accessories needed to complete the look.

Central Hawke's Bay: A 45-minute drive out of Hastings is a 3 bedroom, 1 bathroom house on 0.82 ha. Views to the coast. **Price:** NZ $395,000 US$287,757 £221,889 A$375,760.

Hastings: 5 bedroom, 1 bathroom relocated Californian bungalow on a flat 885 sq m site. **Price:** NZ $369,000.

Havelock North: The country village of Havelock North is a prosperous and thriving little place with large family homes and an arts community. The area is known for good schools. In an established, leafy area, a 4 bedroom 2 bathroom house on a 842 sq m site.**Price:** $600,000.

Napier: A 3 bedroom, 1 bathroom partially renovated villa on 442 sq m in a street full of other houses of the period. **Price:** $445,000.

Napier Hill: Up on the hill overlooking the bay, a 3 bedroom, 2 bathroom 1980s style townhouse on a small 305 sq m plot. **Price.** $678,000.

Mahia Peninsula: Across the road from the beach a 3 bedroom, 1 bathroom old style Kiwi bach on 931 sq m. **Price.** $600,000.

Waipukurau: In this country town, a 4 bedroom 1 bathroom single storey family home built in the 1960s, on a spacious 814 sq m site with single garage and parking for two other cars. Within walking distance of a country primary school. **Price.** $260,000.

Waipukurau: Equestrian lifestyle property on 16.82 ha with basic 2 bedroom house. **Price:** $849,000.

Agents for this area: www.tremains.co.nz, www.raywhite.com, www.propertybrokers.co.nz

THE LONGEST PLACE NAME IN THE WORD

Sorry, Wales, but there's a much photographed signpost in Mangaorapa, central Hawke's Bay, longer even than the famous Welsh place name: *Llanfairpwllgyngyllgogerychwyrndrobwilliantysiliogogogoch.*

It describes where, in Maori legend, *Tamatea Pokaiwhenua*, a chief known as the Land Eater, gobbled up the land as he walked. At Mangaorapa he stopped to play music to his beloved. *Taumatawhakatangihangakoauauotamatateaturipukakapikimaungahoronuk-upokaiwhenuakitanatahu.*

* * *

TASMAN COAST (WEST)

TARANAKI

Largest centre: New Plymouth *Area sq km:* 7,273. *Population of region:* 102,900. New Plymouth: 49,100 *Climate:* Average summer temperature: 21.5C. Average winter temperature: 13.5 C. Sunshine hours: 2,174 per annum. Annual rainfall: 1,436mm *Airport:* New Plymouth with regional connections to Auckland and Wellington.

Attractions and National Parks: Egmont National Park, Mt Taranaki, Whitecliffs Walkway.

Geography and Climate

Taranaki is on the west coast, approximately halfway down the North Island. For a small region, it packs in a great deal – mountain scenery, a rich pastoral landscape interior along with brilliant surfing beaches.

Mountains create their own microclimate, and Mount Taranaki is no exception. In the foothills expect 7000 mm of rain per annum compared to around 1500 mm in coastal New Plymouth. Taranaki has the third highest rainfall and third highest number of wet days in the country. The west coast location does mean that it can blow a gale, but that's mitigated by over 2000 hours of sunshine per year. Rain combined with the rich volcanic soil creates lush green pasture and Taranaki, like the Waikato, has grown rich on the dairying industry.

The perfectly symmetrical cone atop of Mt Taranaki (2518 metres) has ensured that the iconic mountain is one of the world's most photogenic. And it's not hard to see why it doubled for Mount Fuji in the Tom Cruise film, *The Last Samurai*. And as the surfing Hollywood star found out, Taranaki is indeed one of the few places in the world where you can ski and surf on the same day.

In 1959 natural gas and oil reserves were discovered off the Taranaki coast. The largest natural gas field, Maui, which has contributed significantly to the area's economy, has larger reserves than once thought. Maui has ensured that the regional economy stays buoyant. Taranaki isn't solely reliant on oil and natural gas, as the production of synthetic fuel, dairying, as well as manufacturing, are all important industries.

Taranaki has one of the lowest crime rates in New Zealand with violent crime infrequent. The strong community spirit and co-operation meant that in 2005, after the tragic murder of a German backpacker, police were able to apprehend the suspect within a matter of weeks. Community support has helped the many parks and gardens in the region to flourish. One garden, in particular, Pukeiti Rhododendron Trust is particularly lovely. At the foot of Mount Taranaki, Pukeiti puts on a dazzling display of azaleas and rhododendrons in spring, a 'must see' for every keen gardener.

Arts and Culture

New Plymouth is the only urban centre in the region and is particularly noted for its outstanding art gallery and museum, Puke Ariki. A city in amongst a farming community, halfway between Wellington and Auckland is not the most likely spot for a contemporary art gallery. Although there is a long history of artistic patronage by wealthy individuals in Europe and America, the Govett-Brewster gallery started with just $100,000 from a bequest by long-time resident Monica Brewster. One of the conditions of the bequest stipulated that not only should New Plymouth have its own world-class gallery, but that it should be run by an individual of national standing in the arts. It holds an important archive of New Plymouth's most famous son, the artist and kinetic sculptor Len Lye. New Plymouth hosts the annual WOMAD (World of Music and Dance) festival, hosting international world music acts from across the globe.

History

Taranaki has more than dairying in common with the Waikato. Taranaki's rich pastoral landscape was as much a prize to European settlers as the Waikato was and when local Maori couldn't be coerced into selling, the problems between settlers and Maori erupted in the first of the Land Wars of 1860. As the Taranaki chiefs had neither signed the Treaty of Waitangi, nor recognised British sovereignty, their actions were treated as rebellion. For ten years Maori engaged in guerrilla warfare.

Typical Properties for Sale

In September 2016 the median house price in Taranaki was $350,000. It is a thriving little province with a stable economy and strong employment. The region attracts gardeners, surfers, windsurfers and those with an interest in the visual arts. The black sand surf beaches offer some of the best surfing and windsurfing in the country, but are unsuitable for swimming, particularly for families with young children.

Those looking to relocate may be employed in dairying, retail, health, education, property, business or hospitality. The lower than average house prices attracts buyers seeking a good standard of living. Holiday houses are cheaper on this windswept coast as it lacks golden sands and safe swimming beaches. But the views are stunning, with glorious sunsets over the Tasman Sea. It's a four hour drive to Auckland and Wellington.

Coastal Taranaki: Near Mokau, a 3283 sq m elevated block of land with fantastic ocean views. **Price:** $320,000 US$233,120 £179,800 A$304,413.

Egmont Village: 2024 sq metre flat plot with 3 bedroom 1 bathroom early 1900s renovated villa with period features. Established trees and a rose garden. **Price:** NZ $580,000.

New Plymouth: Modern and well decorated 4 bedroom 3 bathroom house on 1158 sq m. Open plan living and dining area with glass wrap around balcony. **Price:** $699,000.

Stratford: 4 bedrooms, 2 bathrooms in need of renovation. Suit a potential tourism business opportunity on .21 ha. 200 metres from the 'Forgotten World Highway' in one of New Zealand's fastest growing adventure tourism regions. **Price:** $200,000.

New Plymouth: Sylishly renovated 4 bedrooms, 2 bathrooms early 1900s wooden villa on 962 sq m.

Landscaped with decking and a brick patio. **Price:** $630,000.

New Plymouth: 3 bedroom 1 bathroom house needing renovation with good views to the harbour on 540 sq m. **Price.** $760,000.

Rural New Plymouth: 2.31 ha. of lush gently undulating countryside with rural and mountain views. **Price:** $320,000.

Agents for this area: www.remax.co.nz, www.bayleys.co.nz, www.harcourts.co.nz, www.tsbrealty.co.nz.

* * *

LOWER NORTH ISLAND

MANAWATU AND WHANGANUI

Largest centre: Palmerston North. *Area sq km:* 22,215 *Population of region:* 189,790 Palmerston North: 83,500; Wanganui, 39,400. *Climate:* Average summer temperature: 22.4C. Average winter temperature: 12.4C. Sunshine hours: 1,723 per annum. Annual rainfall: 963mm *Airports:* Wanganui – domestic. Palmerston North – domestic. *Attractions and National Parks:* Whanganui National Park, Manawatu Gorge, Tongariro National Park, a World Heritage Site. As well as active volcanoes Mt. Ruapehu, Mt. Tongariro and Mt Ngauruhoe, the park contains Whakapapa, Turoa and the Tukino ski fields.

Geography and Climate

Manawatu-Whanganui stretches as far as the west coast of the North Island between New Plymouth to the north and

Wellington to the south. Inland to the north it encompasses the area known as the Volcanic Plateau, a mountainous region with a variety of native plant life. Here you'll find the Tongariro Northern Circuit Track (known as the Tongariro Crossing), one of New Zealand's great walks.

The Tongariro National Park, given World Heritage status for both natural and cultural values in the 1990s, with three active volcanoes and ski fields nearby, sits right in the centre of the North Island. National Park is a four drive from Wellington or Auckland.

The hinterland of the Manawatu is steep and hilly and is an area known for sheep and dairy farming. The Whanganui River, New Zealand's longest navigable river, begins its journey high up on Mount Tongariro as a mere trickle. It flows for 290km (180 miles) flattening out as it reaches the flat alluvial plains, widening and disappearing into the Tasman Sea at Wanganui.

The river is the major centre for recreational activity in the region. With more than 200 rapids, it is nevertheless still graded as suitable for all levels of kayakers. Kayak and canoe are still the best way to experience the peace and tranquillity of the river, although thrill-seekers will enjoy the jet boat trips. The alternative and quieter option is a riverboat cruise.

Wanganui (the city) has retained its European spelling, while Whanganui (the river) and the district retains the Maori one. A referendum on whether to change the name of the town to match the river in March 2006 resulted in 80% of voters preferring to retain the status quo. But Wanganui is going to have to do more than unify its spelling to alert New Zealanders that live outside the town of its existence. With no real swimming beaches to entice local summer holidaymakers, the region rarely makes it onto the itinerary of international visitors either.

The Manawatu Gorge is 15 kilometres north-east of

Palmerston North. It's a spectacular setting for a hike and can be walked in a few hours. The Manawatu region is traditional sheep and dairy farming territory, and as local farmers may tell you, it's the backbone of the economy. And here you'll find a breed of people unsentimental about animals and conservative in their politics.

The majority of workers in the Manawatu-Wanganui region aren't employed in the rural sector but in manufacturing, the retail trade and health and community services. In Palmerston North, education is a major employer.

Palmerston North, on the banks of the Manawatu River, is the only city in the Manawatu. It is 145 kilometres north of Wellington and 70 kilometres to the south-east of Wanganui. Palmerston North came about because of its strategic importance as a major crossroads. It is home to Massey University, the second largest university in New Zealand. Palmerston North, like Hamilton, was selected as a site for a new university in the 1960s. When the students are in residence it has a livelier feel than at other times of the year. Palmerston North, though, lack's Hamilton's ethnic diversity, and can seem to outsiders to be rather dull and provincial, with no real character or identity.

Wanganui was settled much earlier than Palmerston North and has well-preserved buildings with a mixture of villas, bungalows and stucco housing. The riverside setting provides an attractive backdrop. Wanganui Collegiate is one of the top private schools in the country. Wanganui is 190 kilometres from Wellington. And like New Plymouth, Wanganui has a highly regarded gallery, the Sarjeant Gallery specialising in photography. The Whanganui Regional Museum is reputed to be New Zealand's finest provincial museum. And just because locals don't appreciate what they have on their own doorstep, this shouldn't deter overseas buyers from relocating to the area. Whanganui-Manawatu is one of the cheapest regions to buy property in the North Island.

Away from the two cities, the hinterland of the Manawatu may appeal to those seeking a rural holiday home or
commuters looking for a country lifestyle. Feilding, named
as New Zealand's most beautiful little town, stands out
amongst the nondescript country settlements in the area.

History

Although the river is now used mainly for recreation, from
1886 to the early 20th century it was a major transport hub
with commercial steamers connecting Wanganui all the
way up Taumaraunui in the central North Island. In the
early 20th century the Whanganui River was billed as the
'Rhine of Maoriland', attracting as many as 12,000 tourists
a year both locally and internationally. Steamboats and
paddle steamers would ply the Whanganui River, a difficult
and sometimes dangerous undertaking. The river was and
still is the site of many Maori settlements.

Both Maori and Pakeha settled Wanganui early on.
When the New Zealand Company in the 1840s ran out of
land in the Wellington region, the remaining settlers went
to Wanganui.

The mountains of National Park have no doubt brought
great joy to those who have conquered them. But with joy
also comes sadness. On Christmas Eve, 1952 the Wellington to Auckland train was derailed by a *lahar* or overflow
from the crater-lake on Mount Ruapehu. The train was
swept off its tracks at Tangiwai, just as it was crossing a
bridge. This was New Zealand's worst rail disaster.

Typical Properties for Sale

In September 2016, the median house price in Manawatu
was $256,600. In Wanganui, the median was still well
under $200,000, making it one of the cheapest places in
the country to buy property.

House buyers don't come to Manawatu and Wanganui for sun and sea. The sea is too rough for swimming, although the beaches are great for walkers. The best outdoor recreation on offer has to be on and around the Whanganui River and in the Tongariro National Park.

Holiday houses are better value along the Manawatu coast, than they are in the Nelson region in the South Island. Because it's under a two-hour drive from Wellington, the Manawatu could provide a second home option for those based in Wellington, or as an affordable place to live for artists or writers. Those looking for a mountain hideout should head for the friendly little mountain town, Ohakune. Mountain lodges aren't just for winter sports – the mountain air is perfect for walking in summer and autumn.

Coastal Manawatu: 3 bedroom 2 bathroom house and land package in an estate. Short stroll to lovely beach. **Price.** $315,000 US$229,477 £176,990 A$299,657.

Dannevirke: In a town named for its Danish settlers (the name means Dane's Work), a 4 bedroom 1 bathroom wooden bungalow on 1014 sq m. **Price:** $279,000.

Levin: In a country town within commuting distance to Palmerston North, is a 1980s 4 bedroom, 1 bathroom house on 1.95 ha. Property comes with 2 paddocks. Needs upgrading. **Price:** $565,000.

Manawatu: A country retreat with an established pet caring business. Or convert for other work from home possibilities. A well-decorated and modern 4 bedrooms, 2 bathroom house on 4048 sq m. **Price:** $550,000.

Palmerston North: 4 bedroom, 3 bathroom villa with period features. Close to schools and shops. Comes with fully self-contained studio and a double garage. 870 sq m site. **Price:** $575,000.

Palmerston North: A renovated 3 bedroom, 1 bathroom rendered bungalow with period features on a 657 sq m plot. Single garage. **Price:** $320,000.

Wanganui: Lake views from this 4 bedroom contemporary town house, with 3 bathrooms, 1 ensuite, double garage on a 757sq m site. **Price:** $540,000.

Wanganui: Seafront with unrestricted sea views from Kapati Island to Taranaki. 5 bedroom, 2 bathrooms in need of renovation on 7662 sq m. **Price:** NZ $600,000.

Wanganui: On a 797 sq m flat plot, a 3 bedroom, 1 bathroom early 1900s villa with period features in need of renovation. **Price:** $259,000.

Wanganui: 3 bedrooms, 1 bathroom villa on 337 sq m for renovation. **Price:** $123,000.

Wanganui surrounds: A 2ha. lifestyle block with 3 bedrooms, 2 bathrooms, fenced paddocks and out buildings. **Price:** $699,000.

Agents for this area: www.ljhooker.co.nz, www. rwpalmerstonnorth.co.nz,www.harcourts.co.nz

* * *

WELLINGTON AND WAIRARAPA

Largest centre: Wellington. *Area sq km:* 8,124 *Population of region:* 496,900 *Climate:* Average summer temperature:

20.3C Average winter temperature: 11.3C Sunshine hours: 2053 per annum. Annual rainfall: 1246mm. *Airports:* Wellington. Main domestic hub between the North and South Island. Wellington's international connections are via Australia and the Pacific because of a short runway. *Attractions and National Parks:* Kapiti Island Nature Reserve, Karori Wildlife Sanctuary, Waiohine Gorge, Castlepoint, Cape Palliser.

Geography and Climate

Wellington sits on the edge of a beautiful harbour, surrounded by verdant green hills at the southern tip of the North Island. Positioned over an earthquake fault line and with its steep streets, wooden houses and large harbour, Wellington has much in common with San Francisco, although without the damp fog. Catch Wellington on a calm day, and it's idyllic. But when the gales sweep into the harbour from Cook Strait and the southerlies blow all the way from Antarctica, it lives up to its reputation as 'Windy Wellington'. Gusts can reach over 93kph for up to 60 days per year.

Formed as a result of the flooding of a large valley and an earthquake, the city sits to one side of the harbour. Houses cling to the steep wooded hillsides. Pressure on space for a growing population meant that greater Wellington spread out into two narrow valleys, the Hutt Valley and Porirua some time ago.

The design of Wellington's inner city high-rise buildings compound the effects of the wind as a sudden gust in a wind tunnel can lift you off your feet. To thrive in Wellington during wind and rain, you'll need to learn the correct way to walk – at a steep angle. And a raincoat with a hood is a must as nobody has yet come up with a Wellington-proof umbrella.

New Zealand has a reputation as the adventure capital of the world, but there's one white-knuckle ride the capital's cheerleaders forget to mention. Landing at Wellington airport is spectacular. Crosswinds, down draughts, Wellington has it all, but to the highly skilled pilots who fly this route, it's all in a day's work.

The dormitory suburbs outside the city area in the Hutt Valley and Porirua are rather soulless. Lower Hutt is a good choice for those looking for houses with decent sized gardens. Lower Hutt's gem is the Dowse Art Gallery. Like the Govett-Brewster in New Plymouth, the Dowse is the venue for contemporary art. On the opposite side of the harbour from the central city are Day's Bay and Eastbourne. Day's Bay was the setting for Katherine Mansfield's finely crafted short story, *At the Bay*. Eastbourne, just around the corner is quiet and dignified and with its pebbly beach has a lot in common with its English namesake.

The Kapiti Coast, north of Wellington on the western side is becoming an increasingly popular area for commuters, although it can take over an hour to drive into the city at peak times. The alternative is to take the train, which runs all the way to Paraparaumu. There are sandy beaches and fine views on this coast. Kapiti Island is run as a bird sanctuary by the Department of Conservation. Visitors to this offshore haven need to book far ahead, especially on weekends in the summer.

Arts and Culture

Cultural attractions include Te Papa, The National Museum of New Zealand. The capital is also the home of the NZSO (New Zealand Symphony Orchestra), and the National Archives, which displays the original Treaty of Waitangi. Wellingtonians are loyal supporters of the arts, especially cinema and theatre. Wellington hosts a bi-annual international arts festival.

Wellington, unlike Auckland has a lively downtown area, which is compact enough to be easily navigable on foot. The suburbs are connected via commuter trains and buses.

Wellington has good shopping for a city of its size. David Jones is the best department store in the country with excellent customer service. And foodie heaven can be found just off Courtenay Place, in the shape of the gourmet food market, Moore Wilson. Wellington boasts more cafes and restaurants per capita than there are in New York and with all things considered, this is a very liveable city.

But when Wellingtonians aren't playing they're getting down to serious work. The largest industries are business and property, then retail, health, community services and then government and defence. As the capital, Wellington is the administrative centre, Auckland is known as the commercial centre. Wellington is the centre of the film industry, home to Peter Jackson's Weta Workshop. Weta works with Hollywood studios and film-makers from across the globe.

The Wairarapa, to the north east of Wellington is cut off by the rugged Rimutaka hills. At the foot of the Tararua Ranges, the word in Maori means 'Glistening Waters'. The area is named after the 800 hectare Lake Wairarapa. Because of its inland location, the Wairarapa has a more benign climate than Wellington.

Wairarapa has pretty country towns and is a popular weekend destination. Martinborough is the centre of wine tourism in the region and hosts the annual Toast Martinborough festival. The Wairarapa's rugged but spectacular coastline is home to a large breeding colony of fur seals at Cape Palliser, the southernmost tip of the North Island. An hour's drive east from Masterton is Castlepoint where there is a beach suitable for bracing walks.

History

The *Ngati Tara* people first inhabited Wellington. Abel Tasman and Captain Cook tried, but failed to enter the harbour, defeated by the treacherous weather. In 1840 the eccentric Edward Gibbon Wakefield, through his New Zealand Company, purchased a tract of land in the area, which was originally named Britannia.

In 1865 Wellington became the capital. The treacherous seas off Wellington have claimed many lives, as ships have foundered and sunk in fierce storms. In 1968, the inter-island ferry, *Wahine* sunk just outside the harbour with the loss of 50 lives. Those who survived were rescued off Eastbourne beach.

Typical Properties for Sale

The market in Wellington, New Zealand's second largest city, is buoyed by its status as a capital and the fact that land in the city is scarce. It is therefore not all that surprising that median house prices are $480,000, although still around half those of Auckland's. Pressure on land to build on has meant that there has long been an apartment market in Wellington. The areas around Parliament (the Beehive) empty out on weekends as MPs and civil servants go home to their families.

Although Wellington has been better than Auckland at preserving its heritage, sadly, the oldest area of all, Thorndon, (birthplace of Katherine Mansfield), was sliced in two to accommodate a motorway, some years ago.

The country lifestyle on offer in the Wairarapa really does represent that perfect escape to the country but with seemingly fewer of the drawbacks. There seems to be a real respect for heritage out there, as many old homesteads have been lovingly restored, often at considerable cost. You'll find these homes featured in magazines read by expatriate New Zealanders living in cramped flats and apartments in London, Sydney or New York, who, no doubt, dream of owning one on their return.

It's not out of the question to commute the hour and a half from the Wairarapa to Wellington, especially if you can work from home for part of the time. On the surface, this is the archetypal New Zealand farming community, with its white sheep dotted around the hillsides, but conservative Carterton elected the first ever transgender mayor in the 1990s. Georgina Beyer then went on to become an MP.

Carterton: A 3 bedroom, 1 bathroom wooden bungalow on 1472 sq m with parking for two cars.

Price: $280,000 US$203,980 £157,325 A$266,361.

Greytown: 4 bedroom 2 bathroom wooden bungalow on 942 sq m. Established garden with vegetable plots. **Price.** $570,000.

Kapiti Coast: Allow an hour to Wellington at peak times from this modern and stylish 3 bedroom, 2 bathroom house on 4973 sq m. Double internal access garage and minutes from the beach. **Price:** $825,000.

Martinborough: A 4 bedroom 2 bathroom weatherboard villa. Well presented and renovated, the house comes with a separate self-contained 2 bedroom cottage, ideal for guests. On 1627 sq m. **Price:** $635,000.

Wellington: 3 bedroom 2 bathroom villa renovated to a very high standard. Additional study and comes with polished concrete floors and underfloor heating. In an established area close to the city centre. Open plan living with doors that open onto a deck. **Price:** $925,000.

Wellington: Superior apartment with 3 bedrooms and 2 bathrooms. Gourmet kitchen and terrace. A short stroll from the beach. Covered parking for 2 cars plus storage. **Price:** $1,100,000.

Wellington: 4 bedroom, 3 bathroom townhouse with large open plan kitchen. Living space opens out onto a patio. Double internal access garage. **Price:** $575,000.

Agents for this area: www.professionals.co.nz, www. leaders.co.nz, www.loweandco.nz.

Figure 2 Map of South Island, New Zealand

SOUTH ISLAND

UPPER SOUTH ISLAND MARLBOROUGH

Largest centre: Blenheim.*Area sq km:*12,494. *Population of region:* 43,416. Blenheim: 30,600. *Climate:* Average summer temperature: 23C. Average winter temperature: 13.3 C. Sunshine hours: 2400 per annum. Annual rainfall: 655mm.*Airport:* Blenheim.*Attractions and National Parks:* Marlborough Sounds including the Queen Charlotte Track and the Molesworth road.

Geography and Climate

Marlborough is the sunniest and driest area of New Zealand and sits at the northeast tip of the South Island. The Marlborough Sounds, Kenepuru, Pelorus and Queen Charlotte are a series of forested inlets and bays that rise steeply from the deep green waters. With over 1500 km (930 miles) of coastline, the Sounds contain over 55 recreational reserves. The Queen Charlotte Track hugs the coastline on an easy flat walk through native forest.

Salmon and mussel farming are important industries in the Sounds. Marlborough is an area that was once dotted with woolly Romney sheep. Today, many of these slopes have been converted to grape production. Inland Marlborough is still sheep country, and home to Molesworth Station, New Zealand's largest farm at 180,000 hectares. Between November and until Easter, visitors to the region can drive the Acheron Road through Molesworth Station (daylight hours only) to experience the New Zealand high country. Marlborough is the largest grape-growing and winemaking region in the country. It's here that you'll find Cloudy Bay, the award-winning Sauvignon Blanc wine.

History

Abel Tasman stopped at D'Urville Island in 1642, the first European to take shelter in the Marlborough Sounds after many months at sea. Over 100 years later, Captain Cook made detailed charts of the area. Some 50 years after Cook, French navigator Dumont D'Urville found the narrow strait now known as French Pass. *Te Awaiti* (now Picton) was originally a whaling station and in 1827 the first European settlers arrived.

The Wairau Plain was the site of a conflict between the new settlers and Maori tribes in 1843. A disputed land deal by the New Zealand Company brought two *Ngati Toa* chiefs to the area, one of whom was the powerful *Te Rauparaha*. An armed party led by Arthur Wakefield, the brother of the governor of New Zealand went to meet them. Ngati Toa met the party in peace, but the settlers chose force over diplomacy, which had disastrous consequences as the settlers shot Te Rangihaeta's wife. Ngati Toa demanded *utu* or revenge and 22 of the *pakeha* (white people), including Wakefield were killed and the event became known as the Wairau Massacre. A monument in memory of those killed is at Taumarina, 20km south of Picton.

Typical Properties for Sale

Marlborough is in what's known as the Sunshine Belt, along with the Bay of Plenty and Nelson. It attracts alternative lifestylers, retirees and migrants. From 1986 to 2001, the population of Marlborough increased by 18.4%. House price data bundles Marlborough and Nelson as one region and prices have been rising steadily in the past ten years. In 2006 the median house price was $262,500. Ten years later it's $450,000. Attracted by the dry warm climate, new residents in Marlborough find the easy going rural lifestyle amenable to gardening, enjoying vineyard lunches, and taking advantage of the outdoor lifestyle on offer. In a major centre for wine production, it's not so surprising that there were a number of employment vacancies in 2016 in wine growing, wine making and related industries.

Anakiwa: At the head of Queen Charlotte Sounds, a 1861 sq m block of land, ideal for a holiday home. **Price:** $240,000 US$174,825 £135,656 A$227,714.

Blenheim: A 2 storey 4 bedroom, 3 bathroom homestead, built in the 1880s on 2356 sq m of flat land. Garage for 4 cars. **Price:** $660,000.

Blenheim: 3 bedroom, 1 bathroom villa with separate self-contained studio. A 786 sq m site. **Price:** $339,000.

Havelock: Well cared for 3 bedroom, 1 bathroom house with views to the Sounds, in need of modernisation. Well-tended garden and double garage. **Price:** $525,000.

Kaikoura: In the coastal town where tourists flock for whale watching, a 3 bedroom, 1 bathroom wooden bungalow, on a flat 4,000 sq m block of land with views to the Kaikoura Ranges. **Price:** $392,000

Marlborough Sounds: Overlooking Pelorous Sound, an 8000 sq m bush clad site. **Price:** $140,000.

Picton: In the picturesque port, known as the gateway to the South Island, Picton is the place to explore the Sounds. A 4 bedroom, 2 bathroom wooden bungalow. House on 1037 sq m. **Price:** $479,000.

Agents for this area: www.harcourts.co.nz, www.bayleys.co.nz, www.marlboroughrealestate.co.nz.

* * *

NELSON AND TASMAN

Largest centre: Nelson *Area sq km:*10,207. *Population of region:* 87,000 Nelson: 46,000. *Climate:*Average summer temperature: 22.3C Average winter temperature:12.2 C Sunshine hours: 2400 per annum. Annual rainfall: 970mm. *Airport:* Nelson. *Attractions and National Parks:* Abel Tasman National Park, Nelson Lakes, Farewell Spit and Heaphy Track (a NZ Great Walk), Kahurangi National Park.

Geography and Climate

Nelson, to the west of Marlborough at the top of the South Island, has a similar climate to the south of France. And unlike neighbouring Marlborough, sunny Nelson doesn't dry out so much in the summer. Nelson is bounded by the Richmond Range to the east with Mt. Richmond (1756 metres) and the Arthur Range to the west. Its tallest peaks are Mt. Arthur (1795 metres) and The Twins (1809 metres).

The Waimea River and the Motueka River are two of the largest rivers in the region, starting high up in the Nelson Lakes area, flowing down lush green river valleys, before widening out on the flat plains and out to sea. Tasman Bay is a wide bay with tidal inlets dotted along the coast from Nelson to Motueka. There are golden sand beaches from Kaiteriteri westwards through the Abel Tasman National Park.

The three national parks in the region offer a variety of scenery and conditions. The Abel Tasman includes the Abel Tasman Coastal Track. The Kahurangi National Park is a wilderness and contains the Heaphy Track, which because of its westerly position can be a wet walk. The

Nelson Lakes includes Lake Rotoiti and Lake Rotoroa and contains mountains high enough for skiing.

History

Maori first came to the region in the 16th century. The first tribe was *Ngati Tumatakokiri*, who attacked Tasman and his crew at what was named Murderer's Bay (now Golden Bay) in 1642. Fierce inter-tribal rivalry wiped out most of the Maori population and those that were left put up no resistance by the time the first European settlers arrived in the 1830s with the New Zealand Company. Problems immediately arose over the right to the land, which had to be resolved before it could be distributed to the settlers. Disaster befell the New Zealand Company in 1843 when 22 of Nelson's citizens were massacred at Wairau. In 1844 it went bankrupt, leaving the settlement with nothing.

The Nelson region has long had a reputation for attracting artists to the area. As well as painters there are potters, ceramicists, sculptors and glass blowers. In the 1970s the Motueka River Valley was home to a hippie commune. The alternative lifestylers lived amongst the conservative orchardists and tobacco growers.

Although the hippy community has dispersed, in their place have come winemakers and those involved in the tourist trade. The Nelson region today is a thriving and lively place with an interesting mix of people. One event that sums up the successful harnessing of creativity and entrepreneurship is the World of Wearable Art Award, started in 1987. Many Nelson locals were sad to see it move to Wellington, although there is still a WOW gallery in the city. Despite the high profile of the artists in the region, it is agriculture, forestry and fishing and horticulture that are the mainstays of the economy.

Typical Properties for Sale

Nelson's mixture of great climate, laid back lifestyle and creativity has attracted many new incomers. The city centre is compact, with good restaurants and cafes, serving the local wine. Nelson has both character and charm, as well as a lively art scene. Nelson has some fine period buildings that have been carefully restored. There are excellent schools, including Nelson Girls and Nelson Boys Colleges to keep those families with school age children happy.

Property statistics are combined with those of Marlborough and for the past five years the market has been characterised by slow growth, followed by huge gains with prices dropping back. The median house price now stands at $450,000. A wide variety of lifestyles are on offer from early 20th century villas, lifestyle blocks in the countryside and modern architecturally designed coastal property. There isn't much of a selection of apartments as most residents live in detached houses.

Mapua: 3 bedroom, 2 bathroom house and land package. **Price:** $575,000 $US418,724 £UK 325,055 $A545,000.

Motueka: A stylish 3 bedroom, 2 bathroom house on .52 ha in a rural location not far from town. Beautifully landscaped gardens. Views to Durville Island and Stephens Island. **Price:** $800,000.

Nelson: 4 bedroom, 3 bathroom 1990s house with views of the harbour and mountains. Dated decor and some upgrading required. On 648 sq m flat site with garden. **Price:** $599,000.

Nelson: On an elevated site overlooking the port and marina at Nelson Bay, a renovated wooden character home renovated throughout. 4 bedrooms,

1 bathroom and parking for 2 cars on 567 sq m site. **Price:** $595,000.

Riwaka: A country life. 4 bedroom, 1 living, 1 bathroom Victorian era house with period features on 2323 sq m. Swimming pool. French doors opening out to landscaped gardens and mature trees. Double garage. **Price:** $575,000.

Takaka: The steep and challenging drive over the tortuous Takaka Hill keeps Golden Bay as an exclusive retreat. 4 bedroom, 2 bathroom beach house. Requires maintenance and modernisation. Sea views. **Price:** $659,000.

Agents for this area: www.rwrichmond.co.nz, www.mikepero.com, www.havenrealty.co.nz.

* * *

CENTRAL SOUTH ISLAND CHRISTCHURCH & CANTERBURY

Largest city: Christchurch *Area sq km:* 45,346. *Population of region:* 539,433. Christchurch: 367,800. Timaru: 43,929. *Climate:* Average summer temperature. 22.5C Average winter temperature. 11.3C. Sunshine hours: 2035 per annum. Annual rainfall: 635mm *Airport:* Christchurch International and domestic terminals. *Attractions and National Parks:* Aoraki Mt Cook National Park, Arthur's Pass National Park, Banks Peninsula, Hanmer Springs, Lake Tekapo, Lake Pukaki, whale watching at Kaikoura, Mt. Hutt ski fields, Lake Coleridge.

Geography and Climate

Canterbury is the largest land area in New Zealand and borders Marlborough to the north and Westland to the west as far as the Southern Alps. The Waitaki River forms the southern boundary with Otago. There are diverse micro-climates, including an alpine one in Arthur's Pass National Park and Aoraki Mt Cook. Away from the coast it will be hotter in the summer and colder in the winter. As Canterbury and the rest of the South Island have distinct seasons, this can come as a shock to Aucklanders not used to seeing bare trees in winter.

North Canterbury includes the coastal district of Kaikoura. The deep waters around Kaikoura are a rich feeding ground for all manner of marine life, including sperm whales. Whale watch tours take visitors to see these magnificent creatures. To the west of Kaikoura is the Hurunui in which lies the alpine and thermal village of Hanmer Springs. To the south-east of Hanmer Springs is the exciting new wine region of Waipara Valley.

Mid Canterbury includes Waimakariri, just north of Christchurch along the coast and includes the country towns of Rangiora and Kaiapoi. It is known for its fishing, beaches, scenic countryside and local produce. To the west of Christchurch, jutting out into the Pacific is Banks Peninsula, a pretty but sparsely populated area that includes Canterbury's oldest village, Akaroa. Banks Peninsula is, in marked contrast to the flatness of the Canterbury Plains, the only hilly area in the region. The waters off Banks Peninsula are the place to spot the rare Hector's dolphin.

A large part of Selwyn, extending from the Christchurch border to Arthur's Pass National Park includes high-country lakes and forest park. The surrounding areas are sparsely populated. Ashburton to the south is farming country and includes the popular ski field, Mt. Hutt and extends along the plains to reach the coast.

South Canterbury includes the region's second largest town, Timaru, in the Waimate district and out west is Mackenzie country, home to the glacier-fed blue lakes of Tekapo and Pukaki. And the Mackenzie country is home to New Zealand's tallest and most majestic of mountains, Aoraki Mt Cook (3755m).

North Islanders regard Christchurch as more English than even parts of England. There are the English names on most street corners and the River Avon, where visitors can go for a leisurely punt. Christchurch Cathedral, built between 1864 and 1904, and once visible for miles in this flat city, lost part of its spire and tower in the 2011 earthquake. In 2012 because of safety risks, the tower had to be demolished. A temporary replacement, known as the Cardboard Cathedral, has become a symbol of hope and the rebuild of the city.

Called the Garden City, Christchurch takes pride in its gardens and public parks. Some locals are questioning whether this branding is stuck in the past, as it fails to reflect the energy and passion brought by those involved in the rebuilding of the city since the earthquake.

As well as living in a city that looks to its English past, Cantabrians, especially those from Christchurch are accused by other New Zealanders of holding on to colonial class-based values. The contrast with Aucklanders couldn't be more marked. In Christchurch, where you went to school matters: in Auckland it's where you live.

Arts and Culture

Canterbury has the second largest population after Auckland, yet Christchurch has a new art gallery, while the visionless Auckland planners refused to spend the money on a new building and compromised by extending their old one. The Christchurch Art Gallery is a metal and glass architectural statement and has considerably enhanced the city's reputation as a place to view the best of New Zealand art.

As well as a showcase for contemporary art, Christchurch is known for its contribution to science, chiefly its scientific links with Antarctica. As the nearest city to the great southern continent, Christchurch was the place where Captain Scott set off on his ill-fated expedition. Today it is home to the administration headquarters of the NZ, US and Italian Antarctic bases, a centre for international scientific co-operation. The International Antarctic Centre is a visitor attraction offering Antarctic education and entertainment, including a simulated 'Antarctic Storm' with a wind chill factor of minus 18.

History

Christchurch's English heritage dates back to 1850 when the Church of England chose it as a place for an ordered settlement. It was a time when farms were run by the gentry, who made a great deal of money from the wool trade. With the failure of the New Zealand Company to gentrify the rest of the country, the Church of England was determined to uphold Christian values in Christchurch. They set about building churches for worship and frowned upon pubs. Fortunately their influence was short-lived.

Banks Peninsula, to the west of Christchurch, has an altogether different colonial past. Akaroa, meaning 'Long Harbour' in Maori was the site of the country's first French settlement. In 1838 Jean Langlois, a French whaling captain bought Bank's Peninsula from local Maori and then returned to France. It took him two years to set up a trading company and by the time 60 French settlers arrived in 1840, Britain had beaten France to it by signing the Treaty of Waitangi. Had it not done so, then the history of the

European settlement of the South Island could have been distinctly Gallic. The settlers were met by a British warship but were allowed to stay in Akaroa. In 1849 they were joined by a large group of British settlers and their land claim was sold to the New Zealand Company. A handful of streets in Akaroa still retain their French names.

Typical Properties for Sale

With a median house price of $434,250 in the Canterbury region and over $450,000 in Christchurch, the housing on offer ranges from farming homesteads to inner city apartments. Christchurch is ideal for relocating families: it has excellent schooling and large family homes. As the pressure on land increases, it is likely that more owners with land will be tempted to subdivide. Let's hope they do a better job of creating more attractive in-fill housing than in Auckland, which has resulted in some very ugly developments in the once leafy suburbs.

As house prices are at least 40% lower than Auckland's, Christchurch could be the ideal place to move to, for those looking to combine the best of city life, yet with access to an unspoilt landscape. Skiers will enjoy the ski field at Mt. Hutt, within a two-hour drive of Christchurch. Mount Hutt has the longest ski season in the Southern Hemisphere. And what's more, Christchurch has beaches and harbours all within easy driving distance.

For those looking for the country life, a base around the little country town of Geraldine could be an option. One of the nearest settlements to the wondrous Mackenzie Country, Geraldine is now attracting artists as well as remaining a rural town with a strong sense of community.

Ashburton district: Lifestyle block of 4163 sq m of gently undulating terrain ready for building.

Mountain views. **Price:** $172,000 US$125,004 £70,747 A$118,512.

Banks Peninsula: Bare land of 16.30 ha to create your own lifestyle block. Elevated views over Charteris Bay and Lyttelton Harbour. **Price:** $300,000.

Christchurch: 4 bedroom, 1 bathroom 2 storey wooden house, requiring upgrading and modernisation. Off street parking and garaging for one car on 612 sq m of flat land in popular school zone. **Price:** $410,000.

Christchurch: 3 bedroom, 2 bathroom brand new townhouse with double glazing, courtyard and parking for one car. **Price:** $599,000.

Christchurch: 4 bedroom, 2 bathroom brick and tile single storey house on 756 sq m flat plot laid to lawn, double internal access garage. Some modernisation of the bathrooms required. **Price:** $650,000.

Geraldine: Wooden single storey 3 bedroom, 2 bathroom Victorian villa with original features on .49 ha of land. Double garaging and landscaped garden. Outbuildings including a home office. **Price:** $699,000.

Timaru: 5 bedroom, 2 bathroom 2 storey character property in central location. In need of some upgrading. Double garage. On 1011 sq m plot. **Price:** $459,000.

Agents for this area: www.rwmetro.co.nz, www.harcourts.co.nz, www.bayleys.co.nz.

* * *

WEST COAST

Largest centre: Greymouth *Area sq km:* 23,336. *Population of region:* 32,148. Greymouth: 12,894. *Climate:* Average summer temperature: 19.5C. Average winter temperature: 12 C. Sunshine hours: 1850 per annum. Annual rainfall: 2575mm. *Airport:* Hokitika. *Attractions and National Parks:* Franz Josef and Fox Glaciers, Paparoa National Park, Mt Aspiring, Coastal Okarito – home to the *kotuku* or white heron.

Geography and Climate

The West Coast (or Wet Coast, as it is sometimes known) is the long slender strip of coastal land bordering the Tasman Sea, bound by the Southern Alps to the east. The wettest area in the entire country, it's a wild and rugged place with rainforests, glaciers and a rocky and windswept coastline. Lonely Planet named the drive along this coastline as one of the world's most spectacular – although you'll need a car with efficient windscreen wipers to appreciate the view. Captain Cook named an area on the West Coast Cape Foulwind, after being stuck offshore there for a week.

Whether it's the icy wonders of the Franz Josef and Fox Glaciers, or the geological formation of Punakaiki's pancake rocks, the West Coast abounds with unique natural features. The pancake rocks are but one feature of the Paparoa National Park, which contains forests, minerals and a variety of ecosystems.

The West Coast's rivers have cultural significance to Maori, as this is where *pounamu* (greenstone or jade) can be found. Greenstone was carved for weapons as well as jewellery.

Okarito, the largest wetlands in New Zealand, is a major feeding area for birds, of which 70 different species have been recorded. The only breeding sanctuary for the *kotuku* or white heron is nearby at Whataroa.

History

The towns along the West Coast owe their existence to the gold mining that went on there in the 1800s. The little settlement of Reefton in the 1860s was the first place in the Southern Hemisphere that had a public electricity supply. After gold mining came coal mining and today dairy farming and the timber industry support the economy of the West Coast. The people of the region, 'Coasters' as they're known, are hardy, rugged but very hospitable. Coasters find that the geographical isolation from the rest of the country lets them get on with life.

Typical Properties for Sale

The West Coast is the only region in the country to experience a decline in population as the boom and bust of the extractive industries, such as coal mining have seen many job losses in the past few years. In 2005, the Coast saw a reversal of fortunes, when a reprieve for coal was meant to create over 200 new jobs. And as a result, the port of Greymouth, which was threatened with closure, was upgraded. The risk that coal miners have to endure to earn a living was brought home in November 2010, when two explosions at the Pike River mine caused the deaths of 29 miners. In such a small community, this was a devastating tragedy.

The Coast isn't the place for city types looking for an easy life, nor is it going to suit families with school age children, either. But anyone looking for splendid isolation at a reasonable price, or for those interested in the environment, this could be the perfect place for a holiday retreat. In 2015, the Move to Westport campaign went nationwide, hoping to lure retirees to the area. Those who moved had money left over after they'd bought their homes outright.

The statistical sample is too small for specific house price data, but it is fair to say that here you will find some of the cheapest property in the country. Don't buy property here if you're counting on a capital gain. Its unique lifestyle doesn't suit everyone but for those that do make a home here, they'll feel like they have the whole place to themselves.

Greymouth: Lifestyle block of 20 ha with rustic 4 bedroom, 3 bathroom home in need of modernisation. 15 ha of pasture, suitable for equestrian or dairy. Plus outbuildings. **Price:** $465,000 US$ 338,128 £262,846 A$440,624.

Hokitika: Potential bed and breakfast business in this 6 bedroom, 4 bathroom home on 850 sq m. Some upgrading required. Parking for up to 10 cars. Close to bush walks and the sea. **Price:** $480,000.

Karamea: You could buy three properties on the Coast for the same price as one property anywhere else. This 3 bedroom 1 bathroom (plus cloakroom) wooden bungalow on 1719 sq m. **Price:**$225,000.

Moana: With views overlooking Lake Brunner, a 3 bedroom, 2 bathroom bach on 506 sq m elevated plot. **Price:** $368,000.

Agents for this area: www.harcourts.co.nz, www. rwburnside.co.nz.

* * *

LOWER SOUTH ISLAND

OTAGO

Largest centre: Dunedin *Area sq km:* 31,990. *Population of region:* 202, 470. Dunedin: 123,000 *Climate:* Average summer temperature: 18.9C. Average winter temperature: 9.9C. Sunshine hours: 1,590 per annum. Annual rainfall: 809mm *Airports:* Dunedin, Queenstown and Wanaka. *Attractions and National Parks:* Lake Wanaka, Lake Hawea, Lake Wakatipu, Mt Aspiring National Park, Ski fields at Treble Cone and Cardrona, Otago Peninsula, Royal Albatross Colony.

Geography and Climate

Weather statistics belie the reality of the huge variations in temperature and climate. Dunedin is wetter and cooler than other areas in the region. In central Otago, summer temperatures can soar as high as the 30s. In winter when the snows fall, they can drop to below freezing in the high country.

Otago includes the lakes area of Queenstown and Wanaka, which along with the majestic trio of mountains known as the Remarkables, continues to draw visitors to the area. The Remarkables offer some of Australasia's best skiing and snowboarding. Unlike much of the landscape, there is a familiarity with the lakes and mountains, reminding visitors of the Swiss Alps or Italian Lakes.

Sandwiched between Canterbury and Southland, Otago stretches along the coast as far as Oamaru, then spreads inland past Wanaka to its western boundary with the West Coast. Central Otago includes the picturesque settlements of St Bathans and Alexandria. The flat golden plains of the area, known as the Maniototo, with their backdrop of the mountains, are a favourite subject matter of New Zealand landscape artist Graham Sidney. This is farming country, with dairying, deer and sheep as the principle agricultural businesses.

History

Out in Central Otago, you'll find the little settlements, all with Scottish names, such as Sowburn and Wedderburn. Links to further Scottish influences are evident, when, weather permitting the game of curling (bowling on ice) takes place. All over the Maniototo and indeed in many other parts of Central Otago, are the remnants of its gold rush past. Some of the old coaching inns and old stone buildings have been restored. But before gold-rush fever hit Otago, sheep farmers who were members of the Free Church of Scotland settled the area.

Otago's main city is Dunedin (the Gaelic name for Edinburgh) and whose settlers were obviously so homesick for Scotland, they even put up a statue of Robert Burns. Home to the University of Otago, Dunedin attracts students (known as 'scarfies' for their trademark neckwear) from all over the country. It has a reputation as a party town during term time.

Typical Properties for Sale

In the Otago area the median house price is $296,000, while in the Central Otago Lakes Area, which includes Queenstown, the median is $694,500. In Dunedin, the median house price is $315,185 making it one of the cheapest cities in the country. Property buyers in Otago are as diverse as the area itself. Dunedin attracts many owner-occupiers, most of whom have been lured to the region from the North Island.

A successful marketing campaign promised jaded

Aucklanders lower house prices, no traffic jams and easy access to the ski slopes. As well as that, there are many investors attracted to Dunedin by the captive student population. Because of the shortage of good property, landlords have done very well out of this market. The relationship between landlord and student tenant hasn't always been an easy one. Tenants accuse landlords of providing expensive sub-standard accommodation, which they are forced to pay for during the summer holidays, while landlords complain that there's no point in providing decent fixtures and fittings as they get trashed. Observers say that this situation was blown out of proportion by the news media and that the bad landlords have been forced to provide better quality digs.

If there's one part of the country that is entirely unsuited to wooden villas, with their draughty single glazed windows, high ceilings and lack of central heating, it's Dunedin, yet the city is full of them. Dunedin does, though, have the largest and best-preserved collection of Victorian and Edwardian public buildings in the country.

Locals prefer the quieter Wanaka area to Queenstown for their holiday homes, although prices have shot up there recently too. Wanaka is like Queenstown was 20 years ago and its residents hope it doesn't get as developed. Not surprisingly, the area attracts wealthy local and international buyers. The actor Sam Neill not only lives in the area but also owns a boutique vineyard, Two Paddocks, which produces some very respectable Pinot Noir. Shania Twain was criticised when she took the lease on an iconic sheep station. Her initial plans to build a house were rejected but were accepted when the project was scaled back. Five years later she split from her husband Robert Lange and he took control of the land. He has since donated 52 hectares to New Zealand's National Trust, allowing public access to over 20 trails on the property.

Another international buyer whose Queenstown property

purchase didn't go unnoticed in his home country of Australia was Bob Carr, who was then State Premier of New South Wales. Many Australians were angry at his hypocrisy. He had imposed punitive taxes on property purchasers (and sellers) and then went and bought a house in a country that still imposes no stamp duty, even for second homes.

Trophy and coastal property is the one area where New Zealanders, particularly indigenous people, are understandably sensitive to the issue of foreign ownership. They see the Overseas Investment Commission, the body that oversees sales of coastal and trophy property over a certain size, as being too soft. But the reality is that much of New Zealand has been in foreign ownership for many years. It's just that the locals don't like to be reminded of it.

> **Dunedin:** 4 bedroom 2 bathroom refurbished brick and tile house on 385 sq m. Parking for 2 cars. Ideal as an investment. **Price:** $419,000 US$305,184 £239,296 A$397,919.

> **Dunedin:** 3 bedroom, 1 bathroom wooden villa in south Dunedin with large garage on 373 sq m. Close to schools and shops. **Price:** $270,000.

> **Queenstown:** A 1 bedroom 1 bathroom apartment of 50 sq m. Garaging for 1 car. **Price:** $415,000.

> **Queenstown:** 4 bedroom, 3 bathroom townhouse in need of upgrading with double garage. Lake and mountain views. 30 minutes walk to centre of town. **Price:** $1,295,000.

> **Wanaka:** 4 bedrooms, 2 bathroom, 1 ensuite executive house solidly built of local stone. Office, feature gas fireplace, open-plan kitchen. Elevated decks and views. Double garage. **Price:** $1.3 million.

Agents for this area: www.bayleys.co.nz, www.
ljhooker. co.nz, www.raywhite.co.nz

* * *

SOUTHLAND

Largest centre: Invercargill.*Area sq km:* 34,000 *Population
of region:* 97,300. Invercargill: 51,696. *Climate:* Average
summer temperature: 18.6 C Average winter temperature:
9.5C. Sunshine hours: 1,600 per annum. Annual rainfall:
1,111mm. *Airport:* Invercargill. *Attractions and National
Parks:* Rakiura National Park (Stewart Island), Catlins
Coast.

Geography and Climate

Tucked away in the southernmost tip of the South Island,
there's nothing between Southland and the great Southern
Ocean. Southland stretches as far south as Stewart Island,
across Foveaux Strait. It borders the Fiordland National
Park to the west and Otago to the east.

The weather certainly isn't Southland's greatest attraction. With the lowest average summer and winter temperatures and the second highest number of rainy days, there
are no real redeeming features about the climate. The bad
news doesn't stop there if you look at the sunshine hours
statistics. And there are the 17 days a year when the wind
speed gusts over 93kph.

But this is one of the least populated regions in the
country. It's lush and green, and here you'll have the
opportunity to encounter wildlife along the beautiful
empty Catlins Coast, or hike in a pristine forest wilderness. And Southland's rivers are a magnet for brown trout
enthusiasts. Curio Bay has a petrified forest of kauri and

other trees dating back to Jurassic times. Stewart Island is a bush-covered paradise teeming with bird and marine life. The island is one of the best places to see the nocturnal kiwi in its natural habitat. At night they come out to feed on the beaches.

Southland includes the main regional city Invercargill. The city once had a reputation for being drab and dull and it is rather flat and featureless. It does, though, have a collection of historical buildings. Invercargill is no longer the butt of jokes and the town has come a long way in the past 40 years. When the Monty Python team was last there, one of the group ordered a three-egg omelette. He got an omelette with three fried eggs on top.

Invercargill's mayor Tim Shadbolt hit on an innovative plan to attract people to the region as it had lost 12.7% of its population in the years from 1986 to 2001.

A tertiary education provider, the Southern Institute of Technology promised its students a free education. This was enough to persuade many to move to the area and finish their education. And in 2005 Invercargill was the proud host of the premiere of Roger Donaldson's feature film about motorcycle legend Burt Munro, *The World's Fastest Indian*.

History

One of the first towns in New Zealand to be settled by Europeans in 1850 is also one of its most isolated. Some 30 kilometres south of Invercargill, the port of Bluff started as a sealing and whaling station, even earlier, in 1824. Stewart Island was named after Willliam Stewart the first officer on a sealing vessel that arrived in 1808. In the 1830s Stewart Island was a thriving logging centre for the island's indigenous *rimu* forest.

Southlanders have a reputation for being reserved,

perhaps because many of them work out in the isolated farming country, but once you get to know them they can be very hospitable. By employee numbers, the largest industry is neither fishing nor farming but manufacturing, followed by the retail trade and the health sector.

Fishing, salmon and mussel farming are important industries. The most famous delicacy of all in Southland is the deepwater Bluff oyster. Superior to rock oysters, these sweet tasting and juicy little bivalves are celebrated at an annual oyster festival.

Typical Properties for Sale

The median house price in Southland is now $200,000 and the median for Invercargill is $210,000, making it one of the cheapest places to buy real estate in the country. Recently there has been a surge of interest in buying investment property in Southland. Students migrating southwards all need somewhere to live and investors have been attracted by the low house prices. Southland is only going to attract a certain type of person, because of its geographical isolation. Big city lights are a long distance away. Christchurch is 575 kilometres from Invercargill, an eight-hour journey by road. The region may suit those looking for a fishing lodge, or those who want to live a rural lifestyle, far removed from the rat race.

Coastal Southland: 2 bedroom, 3 bathroom modern holiday home. Double glazing. Easy access to the beach. **Price:** $409,000 US$297,990 £233,434 A$388,564.

Gore: A 4 bedroom, 2 bathroom 2 storey brick and tile house in need of modernisation on 1.15 ha. Rural views.Comes with 2 large paddocks. **Price:** $540,000.

Invercargill: 5 bedroom, 2 bathroom Californian bungalow with double garage. Landscaped garden on 809 sq of flat ground. **Price:** $335,000.

Rural Southland: Lifestyle block on 5 ha. Temporary accommodation on site while you build your home. 2 ha of fenced (currently sheep) paddocks, house site, orchard, vegetable gardens. **Price:** $320,000.

Stewart Island: Very basic crib (or fishing retreat) which would be better pulled down. In an idyllic part of this very special island, with bush access to swimming beach. Potential for sea views from new house. On 1204 sq m. **Price:** $155,000.

Te Anau: Te Anau is the gateway to Milford Sound and Fiordland and is two hours from Queenstown. 707 sq m land for building with views to the lake. **Price:** $120,000.

Winton: In this country town, a 3 bedroom, 1 bathroom Victorian single storey villa on 850 sq m. Retains some original features. Garaging for 1 car. **Price:** $220,000.

Agents for this area: www.harcourts.co.nz, www. raywhite.co.nz, www.sre.co.nz.

PART III

THE PURCHASING PROCESS

FINANCE

FINDING PROPERTIES
FOR SALE

WHAT TYPE OF
PROPERTY TO BUY

RENTING A HOME
IN NEW ZEALAND

FEES, CONTRACTS &
CONVEYANCING

FINANCE

CHAPTER SUMMARY

Banks. For such a small population, banking in New Zealand is a fiercely competitive business with a number of banks in the market. Some banks target new residents by assisting them in opening accounts before they get there. You can't withdraw any money until you get to New Zealand and have presented yourself with your passport to a local bank officer. Not all types of accounts are available to non-residents.

Credit card applicants who are non-residents need to hold some other investment account with the bank.

Transferring funds. Predicting which way the exchange rate will go is best left to the professionals.

Mortgages. In 2016 the rules for mortgage lending were tightened. Thirty year loans are common, particularly in areas where property prices are high such as Auckland or Queenstown. Many New Zealanders fix their mortgage rate to avoid the high floating rates.

Economy. New Zealand is a nation of homeowners where money is tied up in property rather than in other forms of savings.

Unemployment. New Zealand has one of the lowest rates of unemployment in the developed world.

Taxes. There is no Stamp Duty payable on house purchases. There is no Capital Gains tax. Those who are resident for tax purposes in New Zealand pay tax on all their income as there is no tax-free personal allowance. Only the self-employed pay an ACC levy.

Insurance. Third party car insurance isn't compulsory because of the no-fault Accident Compensation scheme. It's the car and not the driver that is insured in New Zealand.

* * *

BANKING

The image that the New Zealand high street bank likes to convey is that of the friendly local branch, willing to lend a sympathetic ear when a customer comes in looking for a loan. But the reality is, that apart from Kiwibank and the TSB, the rest are owned by offshore business interests.

Banks have closed loss-making rural branches and even if you are lucky enough to have a bank in your neighbourhood, it is but one small cog in a large corporate enterprise. As anonymous bank officials control the purse strings centrally, it scarcely matters anymore, for personal customers at any rate, which branch holds your account. All banks offer telephone and internet banking which will enable you to operate your account, wherever you decide to live in New Zealand.

Opening an Account from Abroad

High street banks have realised that migrants are a potentially lucrative sector of the personal banking market,
particularly if they are bringing capital into New Zealand.
Now there are whole departments set up specifically to
assist the banking needs of new migrants. The ASB, through
the Commonwealth Bank of Australia, has an office in
London, which allows those moving to New Zealand to
open accounts before they leave.

But whether you open an account through an overseas
office, or via a high street bank's website, you can only
put money in. You can't make any withdrawals until you
get to New Zealand, as your passport and other original
documents have to be verified, in person, by a bank official
of the ASB. While most of the high street banks will open
accounts for non-residents, not all of them offer a full range
of accounts. Check the banking websites for more details.

Bank Charges. Like banks everywhere, New Zealand
banks charge you for holding on to your money; whether
that is by imposing fees for processing cheques, using an
ATM belonging to another bank or running your accounts.
You can reduce your transaction charges by maintaining
a minimum balance. Don't overdraw without an authorised overdraft facility, as you will incur hefty fees. If you
write a cheque without having sufficient funds, it won't be
honoured.

Resident and Non-resident Accounts

Banks need to know if you are either resident or non-resident
for New Zealand tax purposes so that they can determine
whether or not they are required to deduct Non-Resident
Withholding Tax (NRWT) from the interest credited. The
rate of withholding tax depends on which country you are

considered as tax resident. Banks require their customers to complete a Non-Resident Declaration to confirm their status. Note that the criteria for residency for tax purposes is unrelated to your immigration status.

Credit Cards

Non-residents can apply for a credit card, but banks generally prefer the applicant to hold an additional investment account with them. Credit card limits, particularly for new customers, are set at a much lower level than in the UK.

Bank Contact Details

ASB: www.asb.co.nz. *ASB London Representative Office:* Commonwealth Bank of Australia, Financial and Migrant Information Service, Senator House, 85 Queen Victoria Street, London EC4V 4HA; 0845 074. email asbbuk@cba.com.au (referencing migrant banking)

ANZ: www.anz.co.nz.

BNZ: www.bnz.co.nz.

National Bank: www.nationalbank.co.nz.

Westpac: www.westpac.co.nz.

TSB Bank: (formerly the Taranaki Savings Bank) www.tsb.co.nz.

Kiwibank: www.kiwibank.co.uk.

Bankdirect: (the direct banking arm of ASB) www.bankdirect.co.nz.

The Economy

At the end of 2005, the current account deficit stood at 8 percent, which was one of the worst rates in the OECD. Now it is 3 percent of GDP, much lower than the UK, which is 6.9%. The macro economy is in relatively good shape and it is expected to grow at 2.8% until 2019. The GDP per capita is $52,000 and the unemployment rate as of September 2016 was 4.9%.

But there is little cause for complacency, as many New Zealanders live from pay day to pay day. When the weekly pay cheque comes in, instead of depositing a proportion of that money into a 'rainy day' account or long-term savings plan, many New Zealanders are struggling to make ends meet, by the time they have paid their hefty mortgages.

Owning a home is still a dream of the majority of New Zealanders, who would rather control their financial destiny by buying property, than pay commission to a fund manager or share broker. There are many who still believe that property has risen higher than shares in recent years. Problems start to occur though when the investment is tied up solely in the main home and there are no spare funds left to repair or maintain it.

It used to be that New Zealand's average salary was well below that of other countries, but the country has since caught up and it is now equivalent to £25,000, compared with the UK, which since the recession has barely shifted and is £27,000.

As house prices have risen, New Zealanders have started to feel richer and there are some who have begun to unlock the capital in their major asset – borrowing off the house to buy cars, go on expensive holidays as well as pay to fix the roof. Of course, this 'spend rather than save' mentality is by no means unique to New Zealand and is in part due to the change in attitudes of baby-boomers who seem determined to spend their kids' inheritance while they're still fit enough to enjoy it. But New Zealand, unlike other OECD countries, has a very tight domestic economy as well as a poor savings record. The worry is that some vulnerable householders, who are already deeply in debt, may no longer be able to service their mortgage.

Interest Rates

The official cash rate (OCR) was lowered to 2% in August 2016, which might be good news for borrowers, but not so good for savers. To check the best interest rates on offer for borrowers and savers, go to www.interest.co.nz. In October 2016 the cheapest advertised floating mortgage rate was 5.19% with Resimac. HSBC was offering the lowest rate on two-year fixed mortgages at 3.79%. The best rate on five-year fixed mortgages was 4.79% with BankDirect (source www.mortgagerates.co.nz).

UK MORTGAGES

Buying a second home in New Zealand could see you taking out a second mortgage on your UK property, as a convenient way of financing the purchase. The amount you will be able to borrow depends on your fulfilling the bank's usual lending criteria and the amount of equity you have available in your house.

NEW ZEALAND MORTGAGES

The Reserve Bank of New Zealand (RBMZ) brought in new Loan to Value (LVR) rules at the end of 2016. Most investors will now require a deposit of 40%, while most owner-occupiers are going to have to find a 20% deposit. It is hoped that these new rules will put the brakes on rocketing house prices. The Retirement Commission has spoken out against the trend for long mortgages, warning borrowers that paying off a loan over the shortest possible term, not the longest will help them save money in the end.

Types of Mortgage

Repayment Mortgage. The most straightforward of all the loans on offer. Initially, the repayment pays off the interest but towards the end of the loan the principal (the original amount of the loan) is paid off. Borrowers see their mortgage debt decrease over time.

A Home Loan, Savings and Transaction Account. This type of loan offers a safety net, which ensures that the loan is paid off within the time that the borrower specifies. The best way to use such an account is to have any salary and other income credited into the account. It also allows borrowers to redraw any additional amounts they have paid in, over and above the repayment schedule.

Revolving Credit. Although the theory behind this type of account is that it gives the borrower greater financial freedom, it is only suitable for the fiscally responsible who are not going to exploit their credit facility.

Fixed Interest Rate. With a fixed rate you know the exact amounts that your repayments will be and it is worth fixing if you believe that there will be upward pressure on interest rates.

Variable Rate. The advantage of a variable rate is that borrowers aren't penalised, should they wish to pay back lump sums. Some borrowers choose to fix the bulk of their loan and put a smaller amount on a variable rate so that if they do have any extra cash, they can make lump sum payments.

Interest Only. This type of loan is only suitable for those who know they are going to be paying off the principal of the loan from time to time.

IMPORTING CURRENCY

The money you are transferring from abroad will need to be converted into New Zealand dollars, as you will have to pay for the property in local currency. You will be exposed to fluctuating exchange rates at the time of purchase and if and when you eventually come to sell the property.

There are a number of different ways to import currency and transfer funds, and these are listed below. Bringing in large amounts of cash isn't one of them. Any more than NZ$10,000 in cash (around £5,000) has to be declared in a Border Cash Report to New Zealand Customs. Anyone with excessive amounts of cash on them will be questioned about money laundering activities and the assumption will be that the money is being used for criminal purposes. Given that security measures have been tightened considerably in all countries around the world since 9/11, it's not worth taking the risk, just to avoid commission charges.

Electronic CHAPS Payment. The CHAPS system is an electronic interbank transfer, which the banks claim, arrives as cleared funds on the same day if it is sent from the UK.

Bankers Automated Clearing System (BACS). Transferring funds via BACS takes 3-4 working days. Internet transfers are usually sent this way so allow at least four days for funds to clear.

Cheque. Remitting funds to New Zealand via cheque is

a slow process as cheques can take weeks to clear.

Remitting Large Sums. This can be done by opening a foreign currency account with a New Zealand bank and keeping the bulk of the funds in there while waiting for the best rate of exchange. Or else you can use a specialist currency trading company.

Fifteen years ago, some lucky migrants were getting as much as $3.30 for the pound. Those days are long gone. Since then the dollar has remained strong against all the major currencies such as the pound and the US dollar. Financially savvy consumers could track the dollar for themselves and have the money in an overseas transaction account and elect to move their money when the rate hits a certain level.

A currency broker can offer better exchange rates than banks, without charging commission. This gives you the possibility of 'forward buying', agreeing on the rate that you will pay at a fixed date in the future, or with a limit order, waiting until the rate you want is reached. If you prefer to know exactly how much money you have available for your property purchase, forward buying is the best solution, since you no longer have to worry about the pound against the New Zealand dollar working against you. Payments can be made in one lump sum or on a regular basis.

Another option is to use the services of a law firm in the UK to transfer the money. They can hold it for you until the exact time that you need it and then send it through a currency dealer. Currency dealers include:

Currencies Direct www.currenciesdirect.com

The Telegraph Financial Services
http://www.telegraph.co.uk/financial-services/
currency-exchange/international-money-transfers/

UK Forex www.ukforex.co.uk

OFFSHORE ACCOUNTS

You can operate your offshore bank account via the internet. Whether or not offshore banking is tax efficient will depend on where you are tax resident. EU expats are likely to be subject to an automatic withholding tax, under the European Savings Directive.

TRUSTS

The most relevant form of trust for home buyers in New Zealand is a family trust. You don't need to have substantial assets to set one up, although there are initial costs as well as administration charges.

The purpose of a trust is simple – a person or an organisation agrees to hold your assets, and because you give away your assets to the trust, it's then treated for tax purposes as though it's not your money. But trusts can't be set up solely as a way of minimising your tax liabilities. There must be other legitimate reasons for doing so, such as protecting your family home in case your business fails, to set up a fund to pay for your children's education, to ensure that a family asset or business remains in the family, or as a way of ensuring that children receive their inheritance.

The latter case is particularly relevant in the light of there being so many more blended families. Assets held in a family trust can't be classified as relationship property and is therefore not subject to division in the unfortunate case of a separation or divorce. The trust must, though, have been set up long before the relationship started to founder, as otherwise, a good matrimonial property lawyer could try to prove that the trust was set up purely to exclude the new partner.

By setting up a family trust, you own fewer assets in your own name. But the advantage is that even though the trust owns the assets, you still have control over them, provided this is written up in the deeds. For example, if your house is sold to the trust, you will most likely still live in it, even though you don't own it.

TAX IN NEW ZEALAND

The received wisdom is that New Zealand has high taxes but international comparisons prove otherwise. There are fewer of the 'stealth' taxes, such as National Insurance, that UK taxpayers have to pay. The Goods and Services Tax (GST) is 15%, which is less than VAT in the UK. However, levying GST on all goods unfairly penalises the poor. The excuse that it would too difficult to manage any exemptions is rather a thin one, especially as the UK can exempt children's clothing and certain foods. And unlike the UK and Australia, wage earners are taxed on all their income. There's no personal allowance, as an incentive to go out to work. As you can see from the tax rates below, you don't have to earn all that much to qualify as a top rate taxpayer.

2016 INCOME TAX RATES

Up to $14,000 10.5 cents in every dollar

$14,001 to $48,000 17.5 cents in every dollar

$48,001 to $70,000 30 cents in every dollar

$70,001 and above 33 cents in every dollar

Social Security Contributions. While you might not get a tax holiday on low earnings, employees pay no additional social security payment either. The self-employed must pay a levy to fund the no faults Accident Compensation scheme (ACC). Income from the management or operation of a business is considered in the calculation of the ACC levy.

For more information on how much you will need to pay, contact ACC: ACC Business Service Centre, PO Box 795, Wellington 6140. Tel: 0800 222 776; email business@acc.co.nz; www.acc.co.nz

Access to a retirement pension is automatic for New Zealand citizens and residents, unlike the British system, which relies on you having a full contribution record. However, those with pensions from abroad need to see the information below:

State Pension Provision for Those with Overseas Pensions. While anyone who has no pension provision and retires in New Zealand will be looked after by the state, this is not necessarily the case if you've worked overseas and have accrued money in either a private pension scheme or a compulsory state one. Retirees from the UK don't get any index-linked increments from their UK state pension, once they move abroad to certain Commonwealth countries, including New Zealand and Australia.

Obtaining an IRD Number. All those eligible to pay tax in New Zealand are allocated an IRD number. You can apply for an IRD number in person at any Inland Revenue Department office or download the form from the internet and print it out. As documented proof of your identity, such as a certified copy of your birth certificate or passport has to be provided with the application form, it can't be emailed but must be sent to your local IRD office.

Calculation of Overseas Income. Anyone who receives income from overseas has to calculate the value of this income in New Zealand dollars. The IRD issues currency conversion tables, which enable you to calculate the exchange rate on the day you received your income.

Allowances Available through the Tax System. The Inland Revenue Department website has a fuller explanation of the various tax breaks available which are designed to ease the tax burden on families with dependent children.

These include: Working for Families Tax Credits, Working for Families Assistance, Child Support and Paid Parental Leave. There is as yet no paid paternity leave in New Zealand.

IRD CONTACT INFORMATION www.ird.govt.uk. See the website for the contact numbers and addresses, as they differ, depending on the nature of your enquiry.

MOVING TO NEW ZEALAND

UK Residents. Employees should ensure that they receive their P45 from their employer. Contact your local office of HM Revenue and Customs and notify them that you are leaving the UK. If you are leaving part way through a tax year, you may be due a refund, so that it's important to fill out a tax return to sort this out.

You become non-resident if you leave the UK permanently or for three years or more to work abroad. There are a number of other criteria, which determines whether or not you will be resident for tax purposes in the UK. Over a period of four years, your visits to the UK should not exceed an average of 91 days or more a tax year, not counting the day of arrival and departure.

US Citizens. US citizens and resident aliens are expected to file an annual tax return. They are liable for US taxes on worldwide income until they become permanent residents of another country. The USA has a double taxation agreement with New Zealand so that you shouldn't end up paying tax twice. The criteria for residency are: either you have been a resident of New Zealand for a full tax year, which in the case of the USA is the same as the calendar year, or you must have been physically present in New Zealand for 330 days during a period of twelve months. The US Internal Revenue Service (IRS) has an extremely comprehensive and clearly written booklet called

Tax Guide for US Citizens and Resident Aliens Abroad, Publication 54. It can be downloaded from the internet at www.irs.gov.

Other Taxes

Currently, there is no stamp duty for property purchases, nor is there any capital gains tax. However, if the property isn't a main residence, any gains made will be taxed as income.

Goods and Services Tax (GST). GST isn't charged on the sale and purchase of residential property, unless the property is used by the vendor as part of a business. A GST exemption applies to the split use of a property, which would apply if you were buying a commercial building with both commercial and residential tenants. While GST would be levied against the commercial part of the building, the residential part would be exempt.

Local Taxes. Each council charges rates on the property for rubbish collection, street maintenance, lighting, transport, parks and the environment. The system used to assess rates relies on a visual inspection of the property from the roadside, as well as the local information held on the property by the council. For rating purposes, a dilapidated three bedroom home with a garage will be assessed at the same rate as a renovated one. The total rates for a three bedroom home with a small garage in Auckland's eastern suburbs for 2015/6 were $3477. 71. Rates have gone up in Auckland in line with the rise in property values. Homebuyers should note that rates are payable on a property whether or not it's occupied. Rates can be paid online.

Pet owners should note that dogs must be registered with the local council and that an annual registration fee is payable. The dog registration fee in Auckland for 2016 was $131. All you get for your money is an identification tag that is used to match animal and owner, in case your dog is found wandering. Fines are steep for anyone caught with an unregistered dog. Pleading ignorance about the law might work the first time that you're caught. The revenue collected is used to pursue dog owners with unregistered dogs and to police areas where dogs are banned, such as beaches during summer. Any unregistered dog is rounded up and carted off to dog jail. Dogs that aren't collected within seven days may be put up for adoption, or end up on death row, if they aren't suitable for re-housing. All vehicles have to be licensed. Payments can be made for six months in advance rather than the full year.

Wills

After purchasing a property in New Zealand, you'll want to ensure that your will is up to date and that you leave your New Zealand property assets to your nominated heirs. It makes sense to make a will with your solicitor at the time of the property purchase. They'll advise you on whether your UK assets should be incorporated into the New Zealand will, or kept separate. For those whose financial affairs are less complicated, a free will writing service is available online via the New Zealand government owned Crown entity, the Public Trust. Providing you make the Public Trust your executor, the service is free and can be updated at any time. Public Trust: www. publictrust.co.nz

INSURANCE

When buying a house through a bank or a mortgage broker, they'll be keen to sell you buildings, contents and car insurance at the same time, as this is where they are going to be earning commission. While it can be convenient to buy insurance at the same time that you buy your house, make sure that you're adequately covered.

Drivers should note that it is the car and not the driver that you insure in New Zealand. Even if you are involved in an accident caused by another party, you could find yourself paying for a hire or lease car while you wait for yours to be repaired, unless you paid extra and took out a policy that provides this. If your car is off the road for several weeks, you could be paying out several thousand dollars in car hire, which may or may not be covered by the other party's insurer.

As one panel beater remarked recently, if he had to have a car for everyone involved in an accident he would need a whole fleet of them. And unless you happen to strike it lucky, courtesy cars are inferior to most late model high-performance cars.

There is no compulsory third-party insurance required in New Zealand because of the no-fault accident compensation system. In Britain, the prohibitive cost of third party insurance keeps the number of teenage drivers on the roads to a minimum but in New Zealand teens can and do obtain their licenses at the age of sixteen.

Despite the high-profile road safety campaigns, including the tragic testimony by a teenage boy who talks about how his mother was killed by a speeding driver, no government wants to be the one to put their hand up and introduce compulsory third party insurance because of the cost implications. The high rate of road accidents (many of which are caused by irresponsible young drivers) costs the country millions of dollars and causes life-long misery for the families and friends of the victims.

FINDING PROPERTIES
FOR SALE

CHAPTER SUMMARY

Estate agents. British buyers may find the hard-sell tactics in the larger cities more overt than they are used to. Revealing your upper price limit will only encourage agents to show you properties in a higher price bracket that may or may not be negotiated downwards.

Prices. Buying at auction is common practice in New Zealand. Even houses advertised for sale by negotiation may not have prices.

Open Homes. Properties are marketed via the 'open home' system. House buyers can spend the weekend walking around houses on the market, without an appointment.

Word of Mouth. In areas where there is a strong sense of local community, potential buyers need to prove to locals that they will participate in community life.

Hard-sell Seminars. Don't be taken in by the marketing hype. Poor quality property is sold at such events.

* * *

CHOOSING WHERE TO LIVE

In **Chapter 3 Where to Find Your Perfect Home**, the snapshot of the types of houses on offer may have given you a better idea of where you might want to live. If you're moving to New Zealand with an employer, then it's likely that this decision will be influenced by the travelling time to work. Given that most people live in the North Island, with the majority of those based in the northern part of the country, this is where you're most likely to end up.

Checklist for Buying in a Particular Location

Affordability: It's only natural to aspire to live in the best possible area when moving to another country. You wouldn't want to travel all that way, just to end up living somewhere ordinary. But if you can't afford the median house price, it will take longer to find something suitable, especially in smaller areas where fewer properties come on to the market. It might just be that there aren't enough available properties to choose from. One couple, who emigrated from Israel, found themselves stuck in the expensive Queenstown Southern Lakes area, unable to afford a house because of rising prices. Despite the fact that they ran a successful business in the area, people like them are finding that living in paradise is becoming increasingly difficult.

Travel times: Part of the pleasure of moving to this beautiful country is that you can share it with family and friends when they come to visit. If you want your friends to come and see you, or if you need to travel frequently for work, factor in the distance from a regional airport.

Schools: For parents of school age children, proximity to a good school is essential.

Shopping: The further away from the shops you are the more reliant you will be on your car. In rural areas, the local petrol station functions as general store, newsagent and source of the best gossip.

Health: In isolated rural areas there is a shortage of general practitioners and dentists, as young graduates head to cities or overseas so that they can pay off their student loans. If you live in the countryside and get ill, you may have to travel long distances to receive specialist treatment.

* * *

ESTATE AGENTS

The majority of real estate agents are decent people, trying to make a living. But when they receive no base salary and are paid purely by commission, it's not surprising that there are a few who will give prospective buyers the hard sell. Agents are self-employed, although they may represent a particular firm. There are no restrictions placed on numbers of agents or agencies operating in any one place. In an overcrowded market, many of them live from one sale to the next.

Beware the sales tactics when buying property in areas where the market is overheated, such as Auckland, Queenstown, Tauranga and Mount Maunganui. If a sales negotiator hears an overseas accent, they will assume that you are a cashed up buyer able to afford a very expensive property or, a recent arrival who doesn't know the system. If you come from the UK, that means London and the South East with their sky-high property prices and every American is, of course, from California. You will receive many a phone call about fabulous (and expensive) properties for sale, unless you divert their call to voice mail. Australian and US buyers will have encountered similar sales techniques back home.

Country agents know that if they sell to an overseas buyer, they'll be seeing them around the place, so there's an incentive to get them the right property. Real estate agents have to be registered and to have passed a basic qualification. Trainees don't need academic qualifications to take the 40 hours course, just fluency in English. Despite the minimum training requirement, agents are permitted to not only negotiate contracts on behalf of the vendor but can agree on clauses in the Sale and Purchase Agreement which would usually be authorised by a qualified solicitor in the UK. For more details on this, see **Chapter 8 Fees, Contracts and Conveyancing**.

Real Estate Advertising. The regulations governing real estate advertising aren't as strict as they are in the UK. As a result, the real estate ads make entertaining reading, especially when an agent makes creative use of the English language. And the companies that deal with expensive properties are some of the worst offenders. 'A prism of ocean views', 'serious sellers demand action', 'investors love a winner', and yes, that old stalwart, 'deceptively spacious.' But the best yet was in the details of an advertised house in Auckland: 'The Yacht Club is situated at the Eastern end and has become a breeding ground for the future sailors.'

Although hyperbole may be allowed, deliberately mis-leading buyers isn't. One test case saw an agent promoting a so-called waterfront property, complete with an enticing photograph of the beach. The photograph was taken from another house, and the house for sale had no view and wasn't near water.

Agents don't provide the comprehensive flyers that are standard in the UK, detailing chattels, building materials, type of construction and most importantly – room dimensions. While you will get an overall size of the property in square metres, if you want to know the size of individual rooms, you'll need to measure these yourself. More expensive properties are marketed by very flattering photographs taken from the best angles.

Price. If there is one aspect of the house buying process that irks buyers from overseas more than anything else, it's the failure in New Zealand by agents to disclose an asking price. Agents act for the vendor and will argue that if a price is disclosed, it can't be negotiated upwards. And because market conditions fluctuate so much in a 'hot' property market, they will tell you that they can't accurately put a price on a property. The cynic might believe that putting a ceiling on the price of property puts an upper limit on the agent's commission. And if agents in the UK can put a price on, where house prices are higher, why can't agents in New Zealand do the same?

The way that agents avoid disclosing a price ranges from the pompous – 'expressions of interest invited' (that is, only those with serious money need apply) to the baffling FSBN – For Sale by Negotiation. Then there is 'buyer enquiry welcome from $500,000'. Where there is no price disclosed you will see the unhelpful, 'Price: By negotiation'. Some agents are more straightforward and at least give the buyer a price to start from: 'In the $900,000 range', 'mid-high $500,000' or 'buyers upwards of $600,000.' Overseas buyers are best to check the median value of a particular area as a way to assess whether they can afford to buy.

Government Recruitment Events

The New Zealand government runs regular recruitment drives to attract skilled migrants to the country. Primarily an employment event, this is nevertheless an opportunity to have your questions about New Zealand answered in person. Events in 2016 took place in Paris in September 2016 (working holidays) and in Birmingham and London in October. For further information go to :

https://www.newzealandnow.govt.nz/events-expos

HARD SELL PROPERTY SEMINARS

Property seminars, promoted in newspapers, are still unregulated. They target the first-time property investor, promising very high returns on rental investments, but often the figures are over-inflated. Investors are ripped off by paying over the odds for the property and secondly by being forced to pay a high commission to the intermediary running the seminar.

These sales pitches are often disguised as 'lectures' by so-called property 'experts' who will have some impressive qualifications from a university that doesn't exist. The expert will have written a book revealing the secrets of his property success, which you'll be able to buy for a 'special price for a limited time only' at the seminar. They make their money by charging the 'mum and dad' investors or buyers from South East Asia a large fee for the privilege of attending the seminar. This was how some of the more dubious shoebox apartments in central Auckland were sold. Enticements to attend can include the promise of a 'free' holiday to somewhere such as Australia's Gold Coast.

Property Viewing

The best way to ensure that one particular agent doesn't target you is to attend what are known as Open Homes. Incredulous as this may sound to the British buyer, houses (apart from trophy property) can be inspected without an appointment. American and Australian buyers may already be familiar with the Open Home system.

Advertised in the property press of the daily newspaper, Open Homes are usually held on weekends, Sunday being the most popular day. They attract a fair number of Open Home tourists, who like to take a look at the neighbours' houses when they're out, or to pick up some decorating tips. Expect to hear opinions on everything, from the décor to the photographs and the wines the vendors' have in their cellar. It's easy to spot an Open Home – just follow the line of cars and the advertising signs. Attendees are expected to sign in and leave a telephone number and the diligent agent will follow this up with a phone call and ask for your feedback.

* * *

THE INTERNET

Savvy agents know that the internet is one of their best marketing tools, particularly for 'trophy' property. With increasing use of new technology, prospective buyers can have a virtual tour of the house and grounds. But be aware that buying online, sight unseen is a huge risk. If a property seems cheap, compared with similar properties in the location, or the location itself seems very reasonably priced, there's always a reason for this.

One buyer from the UK fell in love with a rural property online. The post and rail fencing and the long driveway with the cute little house looked perfect. But when she viewed the house, the reason why the photograph had been taken at an odd angle suddenly became apparent. Barely 50 feet away was an enormous power pylon, which was but one of many unfurling across the landscape. The countryside was flat and featureless; the nearest shop was five kilometres and the house appeared to be built out of nothing more solid than plywood.

Useful Websites

www.realenz.co.nz Run by the Real Estate Institute of New Zealand, this is the definitive site for advertising New Zealand real estate. A multi-agency site with residential, commercial, lifestyle and waterfront listings.

www.tradme.co.nz Trade Me is the country's most popular website. Set up as local alternative to eBay, it's been trading new and used property since 2005. In October 2016 Trade Me launched Property Insights, a new free app of property information which includes previous sales history and an estimate of current value.

www.harcourts.co.nz Harcourts are a national chain.

www.ljhooker.co.nz This Australian-owned firm is well-represented throughout New Zealand.

www.bayleys.co.nz Bayleys list more expensive property, although they claim that they deal in all price ranges.

Property Press: PO Box 90106, Victoria Street West, Auckland 1142; Tel: 0800 477 677; email: custserv@ propertypress.co.nz; www.propertypress.co.nz These weekly glossy tabloid format listings are published throughout New Zealand. Property Press lists the details of the weekly Open Homes on its website.

www.nzherald.co.nz The New Zealand Herald is the daily newspaper for the Auckland region. A weekly property pullout section with photographs is published every Saturday as well as the times and dates for Open Homes.

www.propertystuff.co.nz This site, run by the publishers Fairfax, has handy links to all the other newspapers in New Zealand. There's a map detailing which newspaper covers which region. The newspapers are: *Waikato Times* (Hamilton and the Coromandel), *Manawatu Standard* (Palmerston North), *The Dominion Post* (Wellington and Wairarapa), *The Nelson Mail* (Nelson and Golden Bay), *The Marlborough Express* (Marlborough and the Sounds), *The Press* (Christchurch, Canterbury and the West Coast), *The Timaru Herald* (South Canterbury), *Otago Daily Times* (Queenstown and Southern Lakes), *The Southland Times* (Southland and Stewart Island). Links on the site will tell you how to find a hard copy of the paper. The online version of the property listings includes an email alert, which will automatically send you notification of property that fit your criteria.

UK Property Magazines

Australia & New Zealand: 01179 323586; www.australia-magazine.co.uk. This glossy bi-monthly magazine publishes a digital version and has features not just on property and where to live, but covers all aspects of moving 'Down Under'.

Word of Mouth

In prime coastal areas, the word goes out within the local community that a property in a sought after location is for sale. Properties such as these may be sold privately, without ever reaching the market. If word gets out that an overseas buyer is in an area looking for property, the assumption will be that they are prepared to pay over the odds. While one or two may be tempted to cash up and sell to you, the community-minded may want to see evidence that you will 'fit in'. Locals only get upset when international buyers choose to come to a friendly egalitarian country like New Zealand, and promptly shut themselves away in a fortress and won't integrate.

WHAT TYPE OF PROPERTY
TO BUY

CHAPTER SUMMARY

Buying land. In rural areas where there's limited housing stock, you can buy a piece of land and either build on it or move a house on to the site.

Relocating a house. A great house in the wrong part of town can be given a new lease of life by relocating it. It's probably one of the cheaper ways to invest in a holiday home. Check that there are no building covenants on your land that prevents you from doing so.

Restored wooden villas. In the smarter city neigh-bourhoods, many of the restored old wooden houses retain the façade but have been completely rebuilt inside.

Test moisture levels. A building inspector should test a house for moisture levels if it was built between 1990 and 2005 with monolithic cladding.

Carbon neutral. You can commission an architect to build a carbon-neutral house.

How New Zealanders Live Now

New Zealanders who grew up in old and draughty wooden houses aspire to more modern homes. Unrenovated Edwardian era houses are considered to be outdated and uncomfortable. But any house, whatever its age, is going to deteriorate if badly maintained. And it's true that wooden houses require regular painting, as well as more maintenance than those made out of brick or other solid materials.

The poor design of some houses means that they are cold in winter and too hot in summer. It doesn't help that Aucklanders, in particular, are in denial that there is a winter. One recent new arrival in Auckland compared the attitude towards central heating in New Zealand to that of Spain, where there seems to be a similar apathy and refusal to acknowledge that wintry conditions in houses are unpleasant.

The first thing that many buyers from overseas do when looking around New Zealand houses is look for the radiators and are surprised when they don't find them. While individual rooms may have some form of heating and central heating via a heat pump is now more common, there are still thousands of homes with poorly fitting single glazed windows that lose all their heat in winter. As most people tend to buy a new house in spring or summer, it's easy to forget about heating, especially when the vendor and agent tell you that it doesn't get cold.

Most new houses built by developers are designed for show, rather than comfort, with the emphasis on making the most of the summer months. North Islanders in particular aspire to new, open-plan houses with good 'indoor-outdoor' flow. The ideal position for the living, dining and kitchen area is at the back of the house, which should preferably be north facing. The transition between the living area and garden should be seamless, so that when the back doors are open, it's difficult to define where the house ends and the outdoor entertaining area begins.

In winter, a poorly designed house is austere and uninviting. The much-trumpeted 'indoor-outdoor' flow is just another way of saying that it gets draughty. While a new house is going to be better insulated than an older one, smart granite worktops, tiled bathrooms and no carpets will be unwelcoming in winter, unless you have good heating.

Up until a few years ago, a request for double glazing would meet with a blank stare, although now some newly built properties, (mainly in the South Island) have it installed. Now, even developers, (of luxury apartment blocks) in the bigger cities have woken up to the soundproofing benefits of double glazing. Other New Zealanders are only now starting to realise how much money they could save on heating bills if they had a more energy-efficient house. One drawback of the modern New Zealand open-plan house is that it doesn't cater for families with teenagers. If there's no way of closing off a television or music room – the rest of the family have to endure the loud music.

A considerable amount of effort and money goes into landscaping the outdoor entertaining area, as so much time is spent out there in the summer. A professional landscape designer can help ensure that it integrates with the house, but be careful not to blow the budget. A heated pool, outdoor lighting, gas patio heaters and a brick oven will look fabulous but might mean you've overcapitalised on the property and may not get the money back when you come to sell.

In the past fifteen years in urban areas, back gardens have shrunk to such an extent that to find a house with a garden big enough to put in a pool is becoming increasingly difficult. The classic 'quarter acre section' that many New Zealand children grew up on have become a quarter of that size.

* * *

TYPES OF HOUSES

Figure 3 Villa, Te Aroha

Villas

Built in Edwardian times, villas made out of weatherboard were the first style of house to be mass-produced in New Zealand. The different style of villa includes the classic *flat-fronted villa* and the *bay villa* (so called because of its bay window). Villas are characterised by their high ceilings, sash windows and craftsmanship. The best examples were made of native timbers, especially *kauri* heart wood. The traditional roofing material was iron.

The typical villa has a wide arching central hallway with rooms off to the side. The design flaw of the villa becomes apparent in winter. Although the high ceilings look magnificent, this makes them very hard to heat. There is no porch with an inner door to provide protection from the elements as the front door opens onto the street. In the main cities it is becoming increasingly hard to find villas that haven't been extensively remodelled inside and 'improved.'

State Houses

The boom years in the early 1950s heralded a new era of prosperity. As the country thrived, new houses were needed for the workers who were helping to build a strong economy. Those who were dependent on welfare weren't forgotten about either as New Zealand embarked on a building programme of public housing.

Known as state houses, these detached wooden bungalows were situated within generous grounds. Built by skilled workers, state houses have a reputation for sound construction, with gardens big enough for a lawn and a vegetable patch. These properties are now highly sought after, either as starter homes or as investment properties. When a house is advertised as ex-state it will always attract buyer interest. For public housing tenants, conditions aren't as good as they once were. Councils in some areas are moving the original state house to the front of the grounds and building a second one behind it, much to the dismay of long-term residents.

Townhouses

The word *townhouse* refers to a detached house in an urban area, built within the past 20 years or so on a small site, usually with a courtyard garden to the rear. Overseas buyers coming to New Zealand for the wide open spaces are often dismayed to find that as many as three detached houses can be built one behind the other on one original site. These houses lack privacy and are overlooked by the neighbours.

There will be a shared driveway and only the front town house will have a street frontage.

Auckland's North Shore coastline now has million dollar houses squeezed onto small sites, which might have distant sea views – once you look past all the other houses. If a house is at the top of a ridge the occupants may be able to see inside their neighbours' houses. Amazingly though, many New Zealanders value the view over the lack of privacy and are fans of new townhouses. They like the fact that they won't need to spend any money in the first few years and that the garden is low maintenance.

Figure 4 Art Deco House Napier

Art Deco

These houses aren't just popular with Art Deco fans but with buyers who want a solidly built house that requires less maintenance than a wooden villa. Dating from the late 1920s and early 1930s, there are fine examples of Art Deco style throughout New Zealand, but the best are in Napier. When the town was destroyed by the 1931 earthquake, the city chose to rebuild in this style. Built of solid stucco, the only drawback is that the flat roofs can leak if the house isn't well maintained.

Figure 5 1930s bungalow Auckland

Californian Bungalows

Californian bungalows built in the 1920s and 1930s range from grand family homes in the older established suburbs to smaller, more manageable three or four bedroom homes. For those looking for a house with character, the Californian bungalow is a better option than the villa, as the ceilings are lower and it'll be easier to heat. Like any house made of wood, these houses are high maintenance. But if you're prepared to put in the work, these are very attractive houses to look at as well as live in. They contain many period features such as hardwood flooring, leadlight windows and finely crafted doors.

Second Homes

It's the location rather than the house itself that attracts locals to flock to the beach *bach* for their annual summer holiday. International buyers don't understand why so many New Zealanders are willing to give up the comforts of home over the summer, in exchange for a modest and architecturally uninspiring family bolthole. They don't see the attraction of the rather plain beachside settlements that have sprung up around the country, that have little in the way of facilities, apart from a dairy and a petrol station.

But for bach fans, some of the appeal is that it is a 'back to basics' experience. The point of the bach is to use it as a base to return to in the evenings, after a day out fishing or at the beach. And there's a great sense of community amongst second-homers who return year after year. The family beach bach bought for mum, dad and the kids in the 1950s will now be used by the extended family.

Buy for low maintenance rather than looks when searching for a second home. A wooden bach might look cute but if you have to close it up for the winter you'll be spending all summer re-painting it. A 1970s brick and tile house is a much better option and the factory brick can be disguised with a coat of paint.

Other options for second homes include lakeside or mountain retreats. If you enjoy challenging restoration projects, how about renovating a big country house in an area like the Wairarapa, where you could create an ideal country lifestyle. Or better still, get the benefit of the previous owner's hard work and buy one already restored.

Figure 6 Apartments Auckland

APARTMENT LIVING

Owning a detached house with room for children to play was once the dream of many a New Zealander. While those who can afford the most expensive suburbs close to the city centre are still living the good life, many young people are starting to look for alternatives. As apartment living on a large scale is a recent concept, the building regulations and the infrastructure have been slow to catch up. Noise problems from neighbours are the most common complaint by apartment dwellers, yet councils are only now realising that some inner city buildings have inadequate soundproofing.

If you're going to give up a house and a garden in the suburbs, there needs to be plenty going on in town to compensate. Many new residents in Auckland complain that more needs to be done to liven up the city centre. Council planners could learn a lot from their European counterparts, where cities are lively places for residents and visitors alike.

Modern Apartments

Apartments built for wealthy owner-occupiers downsizing from the suburban family home will be spacious, have balconies and good views. In Auckland, you could be paying $900,000 for a leasehold apartment with two bedrooms, a view, one car park and a storage locker. Onsite facilities such as a gym and pool will involve hefty annual maintenance charges.

At the opposite end of the scale are the investor apartments, which were supposedly built to house all the foreign university students coming to New Zealand to study. After a change of governance in 2005, Auckland Council was forced to stipulate minimum apartment sizes, as the tiny units being built for the foreign student market were so small that many of them could barely fit a bed. In 2014, no doubt after pressure from developers, minimum sizes seem to have shrunk by 5 metres and the law states that two people can inhabit an apartment of 30 sq m.

It's Aucklanders who will have to live with the consequences, long after the developers have made their tidy profit. Councillors have vowed not to repeat the same mistakes as their predecessors in allowing such horrors as multi-occupancy buildings with so-called 'internal bedrooms' (without a window). Whether or not they keep their promises remains to be seen. It's a great shame that so many fine historical buildings were ripped down, in the name of this 'progress'. The people of Auckland deserve better.

Older Apartments

The blocks that were built before 1990 in the cities are generally spacious and well built. The best have the greatest number of owner-occupiers and are highly sought after. The conversion of older buildings into apartment developments has been a feature in the main centres. These older style conversions may lack such features as balconies, but the fact that many are made of stone or brick does mean that the exterior of the building is of solid construction.

Apartments with On-site Facilities

The more expensive blocks offer resort-style facilities with on-site security, a pool and tennis courts. An apartment in such a complex will be as expensive as a suburban house in a top area. If a building has a doorman, a marble entrance and lifts, buyers have to factor in the hefty annual maintenance charges, or the body corporate fee as it is called. One recently advertised property selling for around $700,000 had annual body corporate fees of $12,500. That's a sizeable amount to find every year and money that could be spent paying off a mortgage.

BUYING LAND

In rural areas where there is limited housing stock, sometimes the best alternative to get the house you want is to buy the land and either build on it or move a relocated house on to the site. Buying a plot of land (called a section) and then overseeing the construction of the building is one way to be certain of the quality. But as Mike Cole says in **Chapter 13 Case Histories**, it's important to choose the right section and the best place to build on the site.

Before you buy, commission a geotechnical survey that assesses drainage and soil stability. The LIM (Land Information Memorandum) will detail the services provided while the district plan will tell you about zoning and other requirements. Be aware too that banks aren't willing to lend as much on a section as they would on a completed house.

HOUSE AND LAND PACKAGES

Steps to Take When Buying a House and Land Package

Ask to see what other developments the developer has built.

Talk to an owner of one of their properties.

Check that the builder belongs to a registered trade organisation.

Ask if any of the developer's other properties have been subject to claims regarding weather tightness (see Leaky Building Syndrome below).

Ask what materials the house is to be built from. Only buy from that developer if the house is to be of solid construction.

Ask for a higher level of insulation than is standard for the area and be prepared to pay more if necessary. It will save you money in the end on heating bills.

Ask if a ventilation system can be put in to counteract the high levels of humidity and minimise the risk of damp.

Check that the house comes with a guarantee.

* * *

LEAKY BUILDING SYNDROME

New Zealand's leaky homes crisis surfaced in 1998. Residents in a trendy Auckland neighbourhood noticed that their houses, which were barely 18 months old, were beginning to rot. Built of weatherboard and stucco, the complex, a townhouse/terraced housing development of double-storied houses had upstairs balconies. There was a mixture of owner-occupiers and rental investors, all of whom got together and spent considerable time and energy on trying to get redress for their shoddy development. From the outside the houses showed none of the obvious signs that all might not be well underneath. And weatherboard, or clapboard as it is known in the USA, is a building material that has been used for over 100 years on houses that have never suffered more than the occasional dripping roof.

But the weatherboards in this development hadn't been put up by builders with anything like the same standards as the craftsmen that built the Victorian and Edwardian villas. A combination of a lack of ground clearance and cladding buried in concrete was just one of the contributory causes that led to leaking. More serious was the failure to ensure adequate control joints in the stucco plaster, which cracked, allowing water to seep in. Behind the plaster, instead of a waterproof membrane, was unsealed and untreated fibreboard. This board acted like a sponge that soaked all the water up. In an area prone to high humidity, it didn't take long for the houses to start to rot from the inside. A potentially hazardous toxic mould developed in some of the properties, producing respiratory problems for the unlucky homeowners.

Other reasons for the rotting given in this first test case for the Weathertight Homes Resolution Service was a failure of the waterproofing in the decks, flat roofing and inadequate flashings. Many of the other larger developments in Auckland (built by the same developer, Taradale Properties) with the same problems, might have looked from the outside that they were built of solid materials. But for these types of buildings, a simple test can be carried out, which gives the prospective purchaser an indication as to whether or not a house is solid. Simply by knocking on an outside wall will confirm whether what looks like solid concrete, is, in fact, hollow monolithic cladding.

Monolithic cladding has been a popular product in the building trade for residential construction in recent years. For a developer with an eye on maximising profits, it was seen as a cheap product and one that was quick and easy to apply. A cladding of sheet material with an applied coating gives the building the appearance of one built in concrete, plaster or masonry. Referred to colloquially as 'chilly-bin' or 'plastic' houses, these types of dwellings have been most affected by leaky building syndrome.

In a landmark ruling in March 2005, the owners of Ponsonby Gardens were awarded $700,000 each to fix their rotting homes. The developer, Taradale Properties, a company liquidated in 2003, escaped blame. The site manager, the project manager, the architect, the waterproofing company and Auckland Council, which signed off on the building code compliance certificate were found liable. The local council, (funded by taxpayers) was the only party that paid up. All the others avoided their moral and fiscal responsibility by dissolving their limited liability companies. And in another twist, as the parties were found 'jointly and severally' liable, Auckland Council has had to bear the full cost. Ultimately it'll be ratepayers who'll fund any future repairs.

Many New Zealanders are seduced by house style, rather than substance. It wasn't difficult for developers to find a market for their Mediterranean inspired housing as plaster-style houses in various hues of terracotta were built. And as soon as the houses were built, they were snapped up by enthusiastic buyers, unwitting victims of the leaky building crisis. With summer temperatures regularly matching those of the Mediterranean, those who bought into the lifestyle of these new 'low-maintenance' houses might easily have felt the house would look after itself. But one soaking in a sub-tropical Auckland downpour puts paid to any notion that the top half of the North Island has a climate like southern Italy. The rain, when it falls does so in bursts, sometimes leading to localised flooding.

And while houses in Spain and Italy are generally built out of natural materials such as local stone, sometimes with walls a foot thick, earthquake regulations in New Zealand require that buildings have to be built out of materials that have some 'give', so that they can withstand the occasional jolt. But second-rate structures clad in plasticised fibrous plaster or stucco weren't the answer, as thousands of home-owners found out.

The Role Of Untreated Timber

In early 1990 the timber industry campaigned to promote the use of untreated kiln-dried pine. They reminded regula-tors that houses in New Zealand were built with untreated timber before 1950. But what they failed to mention was that the timber back then was of much higher quality than fast-grown commercial sapwood. And all those older houses had eaves. Their proven durability is such that the Victorian and Edwardian villas and the 1930s Californian bungalows are still sought after, restored or not. And it is likely that many of them will still be standing, long after many poorly built 21st century houses have passed their use-by-date.

The forestry industry saw that cost savings could be made if the product they exported to Australia and Asia, untreated timber, could be used in New Zealand. And another advantage was that untreated timber was dry and wouldn't shrink and could be used immediately by builders, compared with chemically treated timber, which was wet.

Where Did the Problem Start?

The leaky homes crisis became public knowledge in 2002, but New Zealand wasn't the first country to be affected. The USA and Canada, in particular, had warned of the problems of monolithic cladding and untreated timber. A report on Vancouver's leaky condos was in New Zealand as early as

1998. These problems were attributed to poor construction and the recommendations in the report were ignored.

The Building Industry Authority, councils, developers, architects and builders all sought to absolve themselves of the responsibility of paying to fix the problem. The initial estimate of 20,000 homes affected by the crisis was wildly inaccurate. In the end, 80,000 homes were said to be sub-standard.

Stigma Affects Property Values. Anecdotal evidence from a study conducted from a small sample group in Auckland suggested that property values had been affected by the stigma attached to leaky building syndrome. Buyers avoided houses built between 1990 and 2002 with Mediterranean-style monolithic cladding (fibrous plaster or stucco), a flat roof, no eaves, internal balconies, untreated kiln-dried timber, situated in an area with high winds. Such properties took longer to sell and many were marked down in price down by at least 10%.

Help for Prospective Homebuyers. Although the rule '*caveat emptor*,' or buyer beware applies in New Zealand as much as it does in Britain, the sellers of Mediterranean style monolithic clad homes will need to prove to future buyers that if their homes have leaked that adequate repairs were carried out. The onus is on prospective buyers to study the LIM report, which will reveal this. As it is 15 years since the problem was identified, most, if not all of the houses affected should have been identified and rebuilt to a better standard.

Moisture Detection

Before you buy a property, ensure that you get the building inspected by a company that can measure the moisture content of timber, so that a thorough check for leaks can be done. A system of probes aims to act as an early warning device to detect leaks before damage occurs. This should be done on any house you buy in New Zealand, not just those with monolithic cladding. So many of the untreated timbers were used in the frame of the building, which anyone carrying out just a visual inspection would easily miss. For further information on monolithic cladding see: https://www.consumer.org.nz/articles/monolithic-cladding

* * *

RELOCATED HOUSES

At night, the sight of a convoy of large vehicles lumbering towards you down the highway, balancing what appears to be a house sliced in two, can give many a car driver a fright. But don't worry, it will merely be one enterprising homeowner's solution to the 'right house wrong neighbourhood' dilemma. The buyer purchases an empty section, ensuring that there are no covenants on the title, and then hunts around for a suitable house to move onto the site.

Buying a piece of land and moving a house onto it was one way many New Zealanders found as a way of owning a little slice of paradise, which didn't cost the earth. And it wasn't just the humble little bach that started life somewhere else, either. Many lovingly restored country landmarks may once have been one of the earliest houses built in Parnell or Remuera, but whose relocation has been so successful that they look part of the landscape. Relocated houses are cut in half, moved on to the site and then re-piled, which involves new wooden supports placed at regular intervals under the floor, which should be mounted on new concrete footings. One way to tell if a house has been relocated is to check the exterior for original brick chimneys.

Who Buys Them?

While many younger New Zealanders may find an inner-city apartment more in keeping with their urban lifestyle, relocated houses are still popular with canny investors or those looking for a holiday home. Fans of older houses love the craftsmanship and detail that modern houses just don't have. And even though a badly maintained villa is going to cost a lot of money and effort to restore, the chance to own an old building with exquisite original features makes the hard work seem worth it.

What Type of House is Suitable for Relocation? While a house removal company will tell you that almost any building is removable, a two-storey house with a concrete floor is going to be more costly to move than an older wooden villa, even one complete with wrap around veranda. Some of these older houses are worth far less than the land they sit on so that developers remove them to make way for multi-unit developments. But rather than demolish them, these houses are recycled.

Where to Find Houses for Removal. Some house removal companies have houses on site so that potential buyers can view them, in the same way that you would go shopping for a new sofa, or a dining room table. Check the main centres Yellow Pages listings for 'house lifting'. One Auckland company, Andrews Housemovers lists stock on www.andrewshousemovers.co.nz. The property section of newspapers and the real estate websites often list houses for removal.

One company, www.qbay.co.nz started advertising houses for removal from Northland down to Otago.

Check with the Local Council First. Before you buy that section, check with the town planning department to see what restrictions apply and whether you may need both building and resource consent.

Cost. While a relocated house can appear to be cheaper than building a new one, often the house will need extensive renovation. And removal costs are likely to increase with stricter legislation, which currently requires the removal company to obtain permits from the utilities companies and roading authority. Once on the new site, the house will need to be fixed to its new foundations, re-piled and no doubt, rewired.

* * *

TIMESHARE

If you thought timeshare had disappeared in the 1980s along with *Dynasty* style big hair and shoulder pads, think again as the timeshare touts are back. Now referred to as 'holiday ownership' or 'vacation clubs', nothing has changed as you still won't 'own' anything. The drawbacks of timeshare are the same in New Zealand as anywhere else. It will never be 'home', as you may only spend two weeks a year in it. In fact, it's just like renting an apartment except that you don't have to book it and are guaranteed a holiday every year. It's difficult to see how timeshare will appeal to internet-savvy millennials, who prefer to use last-minute accommodation websites.

There are high setup costs and running costs to consider. If you paid ten thousand dollars for a 50-year timeshare lease, plus on-going costs, your annual week's holiday might cost $157 per night. If you're prepared to make your booking at the last minute, you could make that $10,000 work for you by investing it. Not only would you gain interest on your investment, but you could also beat that $157 rate, without the hassle of owning a timeshare that you may struggle to sell on.

Consumer NZ offers some great tips on the purchase

of timeshare. Buy second-hand, they suggest, it's much better value. They also recommend buying from a member of the New Zealand Holiday Ownership Council. This organisation has a code of practice which allows purchasers a five-day cooling-off period during which you can ask for your money back in full, whether the timeshare is new or second-hand.

Useful Addresses

New Zealand Holiday Ownership Council: PO Box 1648, Christchurch; 03 377 5888; www.nzhoc.org. nz; e-mail enquiries@ nzhoc.org.nz.

Commerce Commission: 44-52 The Terrace, PO Box 2351, Wellington 6011; 04 924 3600; fax 924 3700; www.comcom.govt.nz

The Commerce Commission is the regulatory body for consumer affairs and has offices in Auckland and Christchurch. If the timeshare company that you're dealing with isn't a member of the Holiday Ownership Council, then a quick call to the Commerce Commission for advice could save you considerable cost and heartache.

* * *

FARMS AND VINEYARDS

Anyone contemplating giving up the farming life in the UK or Ireland, in exchange for one in New Zealand, may be pleased with the relative lack of red tape. But with minimal regulation comes a corresponding lack of any safety net. With no farming subsidies available, farmers are at the mercy of the market and the exchange rate for their living, as most of their income comes from exports.

While living off the land can be an immensely reward-ing life, farmers can't control the weather. All it takes for a crop farmer to lose their entire vegetable or fruit crop is a freak storm at the wrong time of year. And hill country farmers regularly lose a large number of their lambs during late snowfalls. Owning a winery is a dream for many city folk, but they should have a second income. These delicate fruits are fickle, labour-intensive and extremely susceptible to frost. In a major grape growing region like Marlborough, commercial growers spend thousands of dollars hiring helicopters, which hover over the grapes on frosty nights, blowing warm air on the vines to prevent frost damage. Some developers have advertised properties within a grape growing area where the individual owners have the oppor-tunity for a shared ownership scheme in a winery, presum-ably with certain rights on drinking the merchandise. If you want the benefits of life among the vines without the responsibilities, this may be the perfect solution.

Overseas Investment Office. The Overseas Investment Office – part of Land Information New Zealand is the regulatory body that oversees the purchase of large blocks of 'sensitive' land – trophy property such as iconic sheep stations or large coastal blocks. As this is now assessed on a case-by-case, anyone interested in acquiring land larger in size than an ordinary residential property, should check with their solicitor and the Overseas Investment Office first at www.linz.govt.nz.

Lifestyle Blocks or Small Holdings. Lifestyle blocks of three to four hectares are becoming increasingly popular with jaded city dwellers who want to plant grapes, graze alpacas or take up some other form of hobby farming. Some may be dismissive of 'town-ies' wanting to get back to nature, but subdividing unproductive farmland into lifestyle blocks has made some farmers very comfortable in their retirement.

* * *

ECO HOUSING

For a nation selling itself to the rest as the world as 'clean and green', it's surprising that so few housing projects in New Zealand deliver on that promise. One notable exception is the Earthsong Eco-Neighbourhood in Waitakere, West Auckland. The Earth song Eco Neighbourhood has around 50 homes but in surroundings that include four acres of organic orchard and an area of native bush. The architect designed houses are made of rammed earth.

The principles behind Earthsong includes permaculture – or 'edible landscaping' as they call it. Solar heating and rainwater tanks are designed to save owners a considerable amount on their energy bills. There is an aspect to co-housing to the project – with some shared facilities such as office space and a library, but the individual homes are fully self-contained. They're built in a cluster of terraced houses, rather than as freestanding detached houses. Owners of such properties must be prepared to contribute to the eco-community in a way that is outlined in their promotional literature.

Earthsong Eco-Neighbourhood 09 832 5558; www.earth-song.org.nz; email info@earthsong.org.nz. If you don't want to buy into the community aspect of living in such a development but are keen to build an environmentally sustainable house, you can, of course, have an architect build one for you. For more information contact: *Passive*

House Institute New Zealand, 021 993 413;www.phinz.org.nz; email enquiries@phinz.org.nz

RENTING A HOME IN NEW ZEALAND

CHAPTER SUMMARY

Reasons to rent. Find out what it's like to live in a community before you buy a house there. Renting gives you the freedom to try out a new lifestyle before you buy into it.

Renting first may save you money in the long-term if you're not sure where you want to settle. It's more cost effective to rent for six months than it is to buy and have to sell again if you change your mind. You can walk away at the end of a tenancy without the worry of having to sell quickly. Rental prices and availability can fluctuate, depending on the time of year.

Check broadband internet speeds. Don't assume that a serviced apartment will come with fast broadband.

Fewer property listings at holiday time in January. Property listings are scarce in the first two weeks of January when estate agents are on their annual holidays at the beach.

Consider hiring a relocation consultant. Paying

someone else to find you a selection of properties to choose from can allow you to get on with all the other aspects of moving to a new country.

The deposit. Tenants can be asked to pay anything up to four weeks deposit.

The deposit is held by a government agency and not by the landlord.

Short-term Accommodation. The biggest selection of short-term apartments is in Auckland, Wellington and Christchurch. In smaller towns try motels or accommodation websites.

Holiday lets. Holiday lets in holiday hotspots can be booked up as much as a year in advance for the January holidays.

House sitting. House and pet sitting as an alternative to short-term renting can be a great cost-effective option for house hunters. House sitting allows prospective homeowners the chance to meet the locals.

* * *

WHY RENT?

Renting short-term in selected areas around the country gives prospective buyers an opportunity to try out a lifestyle before they buy into it. Many buyers coming to New Zealand hope to live differently from the way they did back home. But it's not uncommon to feel apprehensive about such a change. Instead of spending the weekends on DIY, renting leaves you and the family time to explore your new surroundings and community.

Renting gives you flexibility. Try out a different lifestyle to find if you're suited to it. And if, not, you can move on, ready for the next challenge. And when the time comes to make that all-important decision to buy, you'll have narrowed down your choices.

SHORT-TERM RENTALS

Because short-term fully furnished apartments in Auckland, Wellington and Christchurch are marketed to corporate tenants, it can be hard to find anything larger than two bedrooms. Deals can be negotiated at better rates for a longer term. Your money will stretch further in the South Island's largest city, Christchurch. For around 20% less, you'll have more space and even an extra bedroom.

Three bedroom apartments, although scarce, do exist but the options for family-style lodgings may have to be a motel or motor lodge. For families that want more privacy than a motel or a motor lodge, try an accommodation website.

ACCOMMODATION WEBSITES

Airbnb and Bookabach, two companies that allow private landlords to rent out rooms or entire houses to tourists and visitors, have proved popular with New Zealanders looking to make money out of their homes. But be aware that these sites don't offer the same guarantees as hotels or motels. Check that the photographs have the Airbnb watermark, which proves they are of real accommodation and not a scam. Be aware that scammers trawl these sites and that payment should always be made through the official site and not via email with the host. Check the price of nearby hotels first, before you book. Sometimes it can be just as cheap to book a last minute room elsewhere.

Holiday Lets

If you're looking to rent short-term in a holiday area, avoid January when rates are at their peak. While you'll find a good mixture of apartments and family-size accommodation in the Bay of Plenty, the Bay of Islands and Nelson, the best places get booked out at least six months ahead because Christmas and the main summer holiday break come at the same time. If you can leave it until February or even March, the days are still long and the weather is at its best. Not only will you have the pick of the accommodation, but also you'll pay a lot less than at peak times.

The traditional bach or crib (if you're in Southland and Otago) may not offer much in the way of facilities, but the location, close or right next to a beach is hard to beat.

Queenstown, the only year-round destination gets busy on weekends during the ski season with domestic visitors and fills up with overseas tourists the rest of the year. There are short-term fully furnished rentals available to suit most budgets. Prospective house hunters might get better rates if they're prepared to rent away from the main centre of town.

* * *

OTHER ACCOMMODATION

Motels

In smaller towns, the only fully furnished options may be motor lodges and motels. Motels catering for business travellers offer a better standard than those aimed at families.

The Qualmark system has a reasonable rating system, although why a motel on a main road with drab furnishings that happens to have a Jacuzzi-style plastic bath, should be awarded more stars than one with well-appointed rooms on a quiet street, is difficult to fathom.

Hotels

Hotel chains can be found in Auckland, Wellington and Christchurch and in the popular tourist resorts. Look out for special deals out of season. In smaller towns, a 'hotel' might be a 'pub' with a few rooms to let. Just make sure yours isn't over the bar as it can get lively at weekends, especially in the winter months when a rugby game is on.

Upmarket Backpackers

The children of baby boomers refuse to rough it the way their parents did and now expect modern facilities. While still catering for gap year students prepared to sleep in a dorm, they're responding to the needs of families and those individuals who wouldn't dream of sharing a bathroom with a stranger. Double rooms with ensuite facilities are cheaper than hotels and motels. Many travellers who could afford to stay elsewhere find the friendly, personal welcome and the chance to meet fellow travellers much more preferable than a bland corporate hotel.

Farmstays

Handy for the house hunter in rural areas, the farmstay can introduce those looking to move to the country to the reality of a country life.

Bed and Breakfast Accommodation

Bed and Breakfast (Homestay) accommodation caters for all budgets. Prices depend on location but in rural areas in the off-season, discounted rates on luxury accommodation can be good value.

Useful Websites

www.aatravel.co.nz The site of the Automobile Association gives driving related advice, including maps and driving distances as well as the listings for budget to luxury lodgings.

www.accommodationnz.co.nz Homestays and farm-stays www.jasons.co.nz/motels-motor-*lodges* is a handy guide for tourers.

www.airbnb.co.nz The global crowd-sourcing plat-form for short-term lets.

www.bookabach.co.nz The site to book the traditional New Zealand beach house.

www.nzholidayhomes.co.nz This company says they do more than provide contact details and can assist clients with more personal advice on the area and amenities.

www.holidayhouses.co.nz A good selection of holiday homes on this site covering both islands.

www.jasons.co.nz The Jasons site offers other useful travel related information as well as listings for all types of places to stay.

www.tourism.net.nz There's a great deal more on offer on this site than listings of where to find a bed for a night. You could be seriously distracted from your house-buying trip by the spas, fishing lodges and other attractions.

www.truenz.co.nz/farmstays Farmstays from North-land to Southland.

www.homestay.co.nz Bed and breakfast lodgings as well as farmstays.

*www.wotif.com.*A last-minute accommodation specialist. Offers great deals if you're prepared to delay booking in advance. Good rates in the off-season.

* * *

LONG-TERM RENTALS

Properties for let for six months or more are generally unfurnished. You could struggle to find suitable furnished accommodation in the same location for a longer length of time. If you're based in an apartment block and are prepared to move within the building, there may be a similar apartment available when your short-term lease runs out.

Rental Furniture. In the main centres renting furniture and appliances is one option but it isn't cheap. The hire of the furniture package can be more expensive than the rent. Prices, though, do drop the longer the hire period.

How to Find Rental Properties

Wednesdays and Saturdays are the most popular days for real estate agents to advertise their rental properties in the main daily regional newspapers. In areas of high demand, because the best rental property turns over quickly, many estate agents don't bother listing in the paper or online. Larger agencies will fax or email you a rental list but in small towns, they may not even have a list. National real estate agency chains such as Harcourts, LJ Hooker and Ray White list rental properties on their websites. Trade Me also lists rental properties for all price brackets.

Relocation Consultants

Many would-be renters from abroad struggle with finding suitable rental properties, particularly if they don't have rental references or have pets. A relocation specialist who knows the best areas for your budget can save weeks of your time by lining up suitable properties and taking you to see them. It's a service that you pay for, but in the end, a consultant could save you money by negotiating a lower rent, or a break clause in the contract, in case your employer decides to relocate you before the end of the tenancy. A consultant will also connect the utilities and can also help with finding suitable schools for your children, if you opt to use that part of the service. A consultant can also arrange a short-term furniture package, while you wait for your effects to be shipped, so that you don't have to go into short-term accommodation.

Elite Executive Services is a global relocation company that will assist you in all your relocation needs, whether you are moving to New Zealand from the UK, the USA, Asia or anywhere else in the world.

International office: Suite 42, 296 Bay Road, Cheltenham, Victoria, Australia, 3192 Tel: +61 1300 762 388 Fax: + 61 (0) 3 9583 5488   email: relocations@eliteexecutive-services.com.au www.eliteexecutiveservices.com.au

* * *

TENANCY AGREEMENTS

Periodic Tenancy

A periodic tenancy has no fixed date for the end of the tenancy and is suitable for tenants (and landlords) who want to rent for a short term. A tenant must give 21 days notice in writing and a landlord must give 90 days notice. This kind of tenancy would be most suitable for house hunters or anyone needing somewhere to live on a temporary basis, while they wait for the completion or settlement date on their new house.

Fixed Term Tenancy

Apart from those landlords looking to sell a property, or those letting their main home short-term, landlords renting out unfurnished property prefer to let for a fixed term of six months or more. The legal minimum for a fixed term is a month, but landlords of unfurnished properties prefer not to let a property for less than six months because of the wear and tear caused by moving furniture in and out. In a fixed term tenancy, the agreement can only be ended on the date specified in the lease, unless by mutual consent, or by a ruling from the Tenancy Tribunal.

TENANCY LAWS AND YOU

Renting a property is relatively hassle and risk-free in New Zealand. Tenancies are regulated by a hands-on government agency that mediates between tenant and landlord. If a deposit or bond against damages is requested by the landlord, any payment must be lodged with the Tenancy Services Centre within three weeks. Landlords can't invest the tenant's deposit, nor can they claim that the tenant caused damage to a property and then withhold a large chunk of the deposit for repairs.

Tenancy Services acts as a low-cost mediator in case of disputes between landlord and tenant. In addition to the mediation service, there's a help line, general tenancy information, copies of the Residential Tenancies Act and information on the Tenancy Tribunal – the final arbitrator for disputes between landlord and tenant.

Making an Application

The tenant makes an application to rent a property by completing a pre-tenancy application form. Tenants should bring with them a valid form of photo ID such as a passport or driver's licence. To allow the agent or landlord to carry out a credit check, prospective tenants can be asked to provide details of their previous address and why they left it. Telephone contact details of two referees, one of whom must be able to provide a reference about credit worthiness is required. Anyone employed in New Zealand will be asked to confirm salary details or submit a bank statement showing proof of income.

Should the application be successful, a prospective tenant should find out how much money they will be expected to have with them when they sign the tenancy agreement. This could total as much as six weeks rent plus one week's letting fee plus 15% GST (Goods and Services Tax). New arrivals who have only recently opened bank accounts should alert their branch that they will need to organise a relatively large amount of money at short notice. Rental agents will request a bank cheque, cash or a transfer by electronic banking.

A written tenancy agreement will need to be completed and signed by the landlord and tenant before the start of the tenancy. Conditions can be written in that you both agree to. A landlord is entitled to limit the number of people who are allowed to live in the house or apartment.

At the start of the tenancy, ensure that a property inspection report is carried out and that all the chattels are listed. Tenants are advised to take photographs of the interior of a property before they move, as a visual back up to the inspection report, should any disputes arise over the condition of the property at the end of the tenancy. The report lists the condition of each room and is valid when signed off by both tenant and landlord. Both parties should keep a copy so that renters can be sure that they get their deposit back at the end of the tenancy. Ensure that the meters are read (including the water meter if there is one).

A CHECKLIST FOR TENANTS:

Connect the telephone and utilities. New account holders are generally asked to provide photo ID.

If the property has a water meter the bill will go to the landlord who will charge the tenant for metered water. Landlords pay for wastewater charges. If the water charge is taken out of general rates, then the landlord pays for water usage.

Organise a mail redirection.

Find out from the local council the day of rubbish and recycling collection.

Take out contents insurance and make sure this includes tenant liability.

Contact Tenancy Services after three weeks if they haven't confirmed that your bond has been lodged with them.

SUMMARY OF A TENANCY AGREEMENT

The Tenant's Responsibilities

A tenant must pay the rent on time.

Any damage caused by the tenant is their responsibility to organise repairs and pay for.

Tenants must not make any alterations without the landlord's written consent.

A tenant must make sure that the property is used mainly for residential purposes.

The care and maintenance of a garden can sometimes cause problems. Landlords like to make it the tenant's responsibility to mow any lawn and ensure that the grass is regularly cut, unless stated otherwise in the lease. If a garden is extensively planted then the tenant can't reasonably be expected to take care of it.

Tenants must allow the landlord to enter the premises and consent must not be unreasonably withheld, although they don't have to allow this if they haven't had 24 hours notice.

Tenants are required to notify the landlord if repairs are needed. They are not permitted to withhold rent if they cannot get repairs done. In that event they should seek advice from Tenancy Services https://tenancy.govt.nz.

Tenants aren't permitted to change the locks without the landlord's permission.

In the case of a periodic tenancy, a tenant must give 21 days written notice that they are to vacate the premises.

Tenants are required to leave the property in the same condition that they found it. It should be clean and tidy and all the rubbish must be removed. If the carpets were professionally cleaned before the start of the tenancy, then the same must be done before you hand back the property. Agents have got wise to tenants saving money and cleaning the carpets themselves. They can stipulate in the lease that tenants need to produce a receipt from a carpet cleaning company as proof that the work has been carried out to the required standard.

Landlord's Responsibilities

A landlord can't ask the tenant to pay more than two weeks rent in advance, nor can they ask for more than four weeks rent as a bond against damages.

A landlord can't ask for key money unless the Tenancy Tribunal has agreed to this and they would only do this in special circumstances, for example, if the landlord supplied a lawnmower with the property and asked for a small sum of money as deposit.

A landlord must lodge the bond paid to them with the Tenancy Services Centre within 23 working days.

A landlord can't enter the premises without either giving notice or gaining the tenant's consent.

A landlord must give the tenant 24 hours notice for repairs and 48 hours notice for an inspection.

As soon as any problems arise with a tenancy, the landlord and tenant should try to negotiate to sort out any issues. If the two parties fail to reach agreement, then contact Tenancy Services.

Termination of Contract. The landlord is entitled to apply to the Tenancy Tribunal if the rent is in arrears for more than 21 days.

Explanation of 'Address for Service'. An 'Address for Service' must be provided by landlord and tenant on the Tenancy Agreement.

For an 'Address for Service' to be legal it must be a physical street address, as if an application is made to the Tenancy Tribunal, legal documents cannot be sent to a post office box number.

If the address changes, it's important to inform Tenancy Services. Tenants need to do this to ensure that the bond is returned to them, as soon after the completion of the tenancy as possible.

Letting Fees

If you find a rental property through an agent, it's the tenant rather than the landlord that pays the agent's letting fee, which is one week's rent plus GST at 15%. If a property manager shows you a house or apartment there is no letting fee payable. Only a registered agent with the words MREINZ after their name is entitled to charge a letting fee. Private landlords have been known to take advantage of tenants from abroad by charging a fee and then pleading ignorance when they're pulled up for it. It's clearly stated in the Residential Tenancies Act 1986 that only registered agents acting in an official capacity, (that is letting someone else's house) can charge the fee.

Discrimination

The Human Rights Act 1993 stipulates that a landlord may not discriminate against a person because of their colour, race, ethnic or national origin, sex, marital status, age, religious or ethical belief, because they have children or because they are unemployed. A tenant who has grounds to believe they have been discriminated against can take the matter to the Tenancy Tribunal or the Human Rights Commission.

There is no legal requirement in New Zealand for either electrical or gas appliance safety checks, although there is provision in the Residential Tenancies Act that landlords have a duty to comply with health and safety standards. It is the landlord's responsibility to ensure that for safety reasons a chimney is clean before the start of the tenancy. In 2016 new compliance laws for landlords were brought in requiring smoke alarms and insulation for rental properties.

FEES, CONTRACTS AND CONVEYANCING

CHAPTER SUMMARY

Buying at auction. Attend as many auctions as possible to become familiar with this popular way to sell property.

Employ an agent to bid on your behalf if you don't trust yourself not to get carried away in the heat of the moment.

Only if it is the house of your dreams and you are prepared to risk paying over the odds, should you consider making a pre-auction offer.

New Zealand has outlawed 'dummy' bidding, although vendor bidding is still permitted.

Valuation. A valuation is sometimes the only way to gauge the correct price to bid.

Offers are legal and binding. Only serious buyers should consider making an offer on a property, as the written offer they sign is a legal and binding contract. Before you sign anything, have your solicitor check the contract for you first. Direct the agent to the last page of the Sales and Purchase agreement, which recommends both parties seek professional advice before signing.

Negotiated settlements – signing and counter-signing. Agents try to get both parties to reach a settlement on the day the offer is made.

Conditional contracts. Conditions in a contract are a buyer's safety net. Changing your mind is not a valid reason for backing out of a signed contract.

* * *

THE THREE WAYS TO BUY PROPERTY IN NEW ZEALAND

Buying property in New Zealand was, until relatively recently, a straightforward process, similar to the way that property is bought in Scotland. There is no gazumping, nor are buyers reliant on other parties in a buying chain to complete their sales on the same day. And from the outset, the buyer would know if the house was in the right price range by the advertised asking price. The buyer would put in an offer and then the agent would negotiate between the vendor and the buyer until an agreement was reached. The only properties that went to auction were mortgagee sales, unusual properties, or those that were hard to sell.

Now, buying at auction is as common as negotiating a price. For international buyers, who have never purchased at auction, it can seem an intimidating way to buy a house. But at least there is transparency at auction, whereas a house sold by tender is a guessing game for interested buyers. But whether you buy at auction, tender, or negotiate a price where there is no price tag, by paying for a valuation, the buyer can be sure that they are paying the right price.

Capital Value (CV) and Land Value (LV). Local authorities use a system to determine the rating value of property – referred to as the CV and the LV. They're a very basic valuation – carried out by a council officer, who uses a combination of a visual assessment from the street, as well as details held on the LIM of any improvements. The Council valuation takes into account what other houses in the area have been sold for. Properties are re-evaluated every three years, and you should only use the CV, or LV, as a yardstick. It neither replaces the valuation, nor is it an accurate measure of a property's market value.

Buying at Auction

While discretion over financial affairs is an aspect of the British character, New Zealanders (and Australians) are willing to conduct their house sale and purchase in a public auction room. Some British people may recoil in horror at the very idea.

To generate maximum interest in a sale, the agent may prefer to hold the auction on site at the weekend, to attract as many potential buyers as possible. Some auctions take place during the week, in the agent's office. An auction held on a weekend is a forum open to all comers, including those who have no interest in bidding – from curious neighbours, Sunday drivers on an outing, and most importantly for potential overseas buyers, those looking to see how the auction process is conducted.

Auctions are run in a relaxed fashion and once you're familiar with the process, you'll be far more confident about bidding if you've attended a few first. Fans of the auction process say that it's the most transparent of selling techniques and reveals the true value of a property. After all, a property is only worth what someone will pay for it. The counterargument is that it is a process designed to intimidate buyers. Many buyers would rather buy a property that has a set price and make an offer on that. If their offer is accepted, then and only then do they pay for a builder's report and valuation. When a property is sold at auction, buyers have to pay upfront for services that may be useless, if they are then outbid.

Agents love auctions, as it gives them a set date to work towards to collect their commission. Vendors with an unrealistic price expectation can find the process a humbling experience. Both agents and auctioneers love the emotive atmosphere that potential buyers bring to the auction. It is in both their interests to ensure there is an element of excitement in the auction process. Auctioneers use sales techniques to raise the emotions during the auction. Slick operators, they are adept at pitching one buyer against another and can easily spot a novice. But you can prepare yourself for such tactics. Don't get carried away by an over-enthusiastic auctioneer.

If you find the whole process too nerve-wracking, you can always nominate a professional to bid on your behalf. If you set the upper limit before the auction starts, then the agent bidding for you has to work within those defined boundaries.

Pre-auction Bids. You should register your interest as a potential bidder for a property with the vendor's agent before the auction, but on no account should you reveal what you believe the property to be worth. Once an agent knows that you're interested, don't be persuaded to put in a pre-auction bid, unless you have your heart set on this property, are prepared to take both a risk and pay over the odds. There's no guarantee that the vendor will accept your bid and may have been advised by the agent to wait until auction day.

All a pre-auction bid does is expose the potential buyer into disclosing how much they're prepared to bid. That information can be used against the buyer by the vendor's agent, to set a price for the reserve. If the reserve has already been set, it could lead to the auction being pulled forward.

If you made your best offer, thinking this would secure the house, you'll be in for a shock, as the auctioneer will open the bidding with that price. You'll just have to hope that nobody else bids if you've made your best offer. If another buyer bids against you, then either you'll end up paying more than you wanted to secure the property, or you may on this occasion, have to walk away.

A Pre-Auction Checklist

Contact a registered valuer to get a valuation on the property to see if it's within your price range.

Arrange for a builder to carry out a building inspection.

Contact a solicitor to check the title and to attend to all the other legal matters that are involved in the purchase process.

Ask the solicitor to take you through the auction documents so that you understand the sales conditions. These include the date and amount of deposit, the possession date and when the balance of the purchase price has to be paid.

If you have a pre-purchase approval of an amount from your mortgage lender, then you should notify them that this is the property you are going to be bidding for. Buying by auction is unconditional and all the finance has to be in place before you bid.

Take a bank cheque for the deposit to the auction. Know in advance how much you can afford for the deposit as you'll need to fill in the amount yourself once your bid has been accepted. Once this happens, you agree to purchase the property and are required to sign the contract. If you change your mind, you will still have to pay the deposit, usually 10% of the purchase price.

VENDOR BIDS

The law changed in 2013 to outlaw dummy bidding. Vendor bidding is still permitted, provided the following three conditions have been met: There is a reserve price, the reserve price has not been reached and the bid is identified by the auctioneer as a vendor bid.

Subject to reserve. The seller, in consultation with their agent, sets the reserve price. Once this reserve has been reached, the auctioneer announces that the property is officially on the market.

Passed in. When a property fails to reach its reserve price, it's passed in. A period of intense negotiation follows, where the highest bidder is given the first option to purchase the property at the seller's reserve price. If this process fails to secure the sale, the second highest bidder can approach the seller's agent and the process is repeated. Agents will do their utmost to broker a deal satisfactory to both parties and secure a sale on the day. If they fail, then the property will go back on the market. The reserve price will be put on it as the sale price and the property will then become 'subject to negotiation'.

Tender

The advantage for the seller of a tender is that it is conducted in private. The drawback is that the entire system is so discreet, especially with a closed tender, that the buyer has to go in blind, neither knowing the price expectation of the seller, nor what the other buyers are prepared to pay. The buyer fills out a written offer, which can include conditions and then has to wait until the day the tender closes. The seller may choose an unconditional offer, even if it's not the highest price. If you're going to attach conditions to your offer, then suggest the minimum number of days needed, to tempt the vendor to choose you over another bidder. Because the buyer has to do much more research first, as well as have their builder's report and valuation carried out, before putting in a tender, this puts off all but the keenest buyers. Buyers prepared to take a risk bide their time, to see whether or not the tender process has been successful. They will then make their offer if the house fails to sell this way, before it goes on to the open market.

By Negotiation

This system will be the most familiar to UK buyers. The speed at which property transactions are conducted in New Zealand can come as a shock, especially for anyone who has been stuck in a seemingly endless property chain. It is vital for prospective buyers to be certain that the property they are going to offer to purchase, is the one that they intend to buy.

All offers are made in writing and are legally binding, once they've been signed by the buyer and countersigned by the vendor. It's the real estate agent who initiates the contractual process between buyer and seller, not the solicitors. Agents do have to undergo a training course and become a member of the Real Estate Institute of New Zealand to be legally permitted to do this. The document you will be asked to sign is called the Agreement for Sale and Purchase of Real Estate. The main points are summarised below.

You should, of course, go through this document with your lawyer, but knowing what your obligations are before you sign, allows you to organise what needs to be done, in order to meet the deadlines imposed. You should, in any case, alert your lawyer that you intend to make an offer on a property, so that they have time to explain which conditions you should add to the contract and the exact wording to use.

The vendor's agent may try to put the pressure on you early on in the proceedings, by setting an unrealistic time frame for you to complete all your paperwork. Before you make an offer, it's worth asking the local council how long they're currently taking to process the local searches or Land Information Memorandum (LIM). When an agent suggests five working days for all reports to be completed, make a counter offer of ten. If the agent then tells you that there are back-up offers, then call their bluff and request to see them. This may do the trick and buy you the required time.

Summary of Main Points of the Sales and Purchase Agreement

Page 1 – The front page of the document contains the important information, with the date of the agreement, the names and addresses of vendor and purchaser and the address of the property.

Estate. The choices are: fee simple (for a freehold property), leasehold, cross-lease (where a property has been subdivided from one site), or unit title (usually refers to an apartment).

Legal description. This is the information held by the council, which shows the land area and the reference number of the property on the district plan. This is the aspect of the contract that your lawyer will be paying close attention to ensure that what is being described is correct.

Purchase price. In a negotiated settlement, the purchase price is the most common part of the contract that is countersigned by each party, until they reach an agreement. The first step is that the buyer nominates a purchase price. This isn't the final price that is to be paid, as the vendor will countersign the agreement with his or her own price. In a model negotiated settlement, the buyer will write the price $500,000 on the contract and put their signature on it. The vendor (who may have a higher price in mind) will cross out and sign against the buyer's figure and write $570,000 on the contract. The buyer will then cross out the new figure and sign it and meet the vendor half way with $535,000 and sign it. The vendor will agree on the figure and sign their name next to the new figure of $535,000.

Deposit. Each agency works on a percentage figure of the purchase price as a deposit, as the notes with the contract don't stipulate what percentage this has to be. The deposit can be as low as 5% of the purchase price.

Possession. Possession is the equivalent to the completion date in an English contract. Again, this is another part of the contract that may require negotiation, especially if the seller hasn't yet found somewhere else to live.

Conditions. This is the key area of the contract that a buyer should be familiar with. The only time you should enter into an unconditional sale is if you buy a house through auction. You should satisfy yourself that you've checked out all the risks associated with buying the property before you sign. Otherwise you risk losing your deposit.

Additional Clauses

The clauses you want to add to a conditional contract are: A clause that states that the purchase is subject to finance. Even if you have a mortgage offer from the bank, this clause allows time to complete the paperwork on this particular property. You may want to add an additional one, stating that the property is subject to a valuation.

Many prospective buyers don't believe that a valuation is necessary once they have put in their offer. The outlay of a few hundred dollars for a valuation could potentially save you thousands.

A clause that states that the purchase is subject to a builder's report, or a building inspection. The building inspector may recommend that you commission an engineer's report. These two professionals undertake similar work to the structural surveyor in the UK.

One important clause to add is that the purchase is subject to solicitor's approval. This general wording allows the solicitor to carry out the local searches and obtain the Land Information Memorandum (LIM) from the council and ensure that there is nothing untoward with any aspect of the property. The LIM reveals what work has been carried out on the property and whether or not a building consent was granted for that work.

All of these clauses are extremely important for the purchaser to consider adding to their offer to purchase. Your solicitor will advise you of the exact wording. Additional clauses may be included, such as a clause relating to the checking that chattels such as dishwashers and ovens are in full working order. If the property is highly desirable and there are a number of interested parties, the purchaser has to try to minimise the number of clauses, or else reduce the time allowed to get the reports back, so that their contract appears enticing to the seller.

The clause that relates to OIA Consent refers to the Overseas Investment Authority and as stated in **Chapter 6, What Type of Property to Buy,** this only applies to the purchase of large areas of iconic or 'sensitive' property. The centre pages of the Sales and Purchase Agreement explain in detail what the terms used in the document mean. But the important information is on the first and last pages.

Agents can't be expected to give overseas buyers any special assistance in helping them understand the contract, but if you encounter one who tries to rush you through the process, ask for an adjournment and call your lawyer. Every buyer should read through the last page of the Agreement. If there's anything there that you don't understand that needs further explanation, then this is the point that you should assert your rights and request that you take the contract to your solicitor.

Signing and Countersigning

Contracts can be signed and countersigned a number of times until agreement is reached. Agents will work long into the night, driving between the two parties to negotiate and try to secure a sale. While negotiation over purchase price is the most common reason for contracts to be countersigned by the vendor, another can be agreeing on a settlement date that suits both parties. If buyers require a long settlement date, because they have a house to sell first, they should check this out with the vendor's agent, before making the offer.

A vendor of an expensive property may trade a long settlement date, in return for an increased purchase price. While their investment is tied up, waiting for you to settle, they're prevented from investing their money and earning what can be considerable interest on it.

Pre Settlement Inspection. You are entitled to check

that the property that you are buying is in the same condition as when you agreed to buy it. Do this as close to
settlement date as possible and when the house has been
vacated by the previous owners. You should inspect for
any damage caused by moving, checking to see that all the
chattels on the chattels list are still there and that they're in
working order. Make sure too that no rubbish has been left
in the garage, or in the attic, or other storage areas. If there
are any problems or discrepancies you should contact your
solicitor immediately, who will then contact the sellers and
ask for any outstanding matters to be attended to urgently,
prior to settlement.

Title Search

Your solicitor will search the title to find out if there are
interests, such as rights of way and easements that can affect
the future use of your property. You should also ask your
solicitor to explain in practical terms what they can mean,
especially if you want to extend. If the property you intend
to buy is in an established area, where all the adjoining sites
have houses on them already, it is less likely that there will
be any need for the local council to take up their easement
rights. Your solicitor can always find out if they're planning
to upgrade any drains that pass underneath your property
in the near future.

If your property adjoins an empty section, then sooner
or later it's bound to be developed. And you could be in for
a nasty shock when you receive a letter from the council,
stating that your neighbours have the right to dig up part of
your garden to connect drains. Even though councils have
a statutory requirement to ensure that all work has to be
made good afterwards, you're the one that will have to put
up with the disruption and inconvenience.

Freehold Title. A freehold title allows you the same
rights as buying freehold in the UK.

Leasehold. The lessor owns the land on which the building is situated and the lessee pays the lessor ground rent. Leasehold can take different forms and you should seek legal opinion first, before you make your offer. The most restrictive lease is a non-renewable fixed-term. Renewable leases, which can be taken out for a designated number of years, are subject to increases in ground rent. Ground rent is calculated as a percentage of land value. You should budget at least 5% of land value, although the percentage will be clearly stated in the lease contract.

Freehold Cross Lease. When land is subdivided and where townhouses or terrace houses are built on a site, the owners of the townhouses each own a part of the freehold and are tenants-in- common. No property owner can do anything with the land without the others permission. Each homeowner leases their houses from each other on identical terms such as 999 years.

Unit Title. When buying an apartment in a block, your apartment may be either freehold or leasehold, depending on whether the apartment owners own the land collectively, or if this is owned by a third party. For example, the apartments in the Princes Wharf development on Auckland's waterfront are leasehold. If the block you are buying into is freehold then it will have a body corporate, an organisation set up to manage and maintain the development. Each apartment pays a fee each year to the body corporate for maintaining common areas. The more facilities on site, the higher the body corporate fees. There will often be rules and regulations that restrict various activities at night-time, including running washing machines and vacuum cleaners; whether pet ownership is permitted, and where you can dry laundry.

Council Matters

Your solicitor should examine the Land Information Memorandum (LIM) held by the local council to check that everything is in order. But you can check out not just the LIM but also the property file by going to the local council and requesting to see this. Many councils now charge for this service. The property file may contain important information not on the LIM, that relates to the building, as well as resource consents and correspondence.

The LIM will contain information on features of the land and can alert homebuyers as to whether the property they are about to buy could be on land subject to: erosion, subsidence, alluvion (silt from flooding), flooding, and whether or not, prior to the development for residential use, there were contaminants or hazards stored on the site. The LIM will also detail any protected trees. A protected tree can require resource consent, even for pruning. Trees don't have to be all that large, or special, to be protected. The removal of a tree without permission, either native or exotic, in an area where resource consent is required, will result in a large fine. Some councils provide LIMs via their websites, which can speed up the process considerably. The cost of a LIM varies between councils and whether or not you need it urgently. For a non-urgent LIM, it's a statutory requirement that these are processed within ten working days.

Solicitors charges – allow $1000

For an urgent LIM – allow $270

Building inspection – allow $1000

Valuation – allow $300

Mortgage related costs – $300

Engineer's report (for steep sites) – $450

You should keep money aside for the other miscellaneous costs once you move, such as upgrading the locks, putting in electrical sockets and plumbing in appliances.

Useful Websites

www.finda.co.nz Whether you need a lawyer or a registered valuer, this site helps you sort through the listings of the professionals you will need to employ for your property transaction.

www.yellowpages.co.nz This site is specific to a particular location so that you can source professionals working in the area you intend to buy.

www.qv.co.nz Quotable Value is a company that provides both on-line valuations (the basic information for which you no longer have to pay for) and links to registered valuers. *www.homes.co.nz* is a website that provides valuation estimates for properties that you are looking to purchase.

PART IV

WHAT HAPPENS NEXT
SERVICES

MAKING THE MOVE
BUILDING OR RENOVATING
MAKING MONEY FROM YOUR PROPERTY

SERVICES

CHAPTER SUMMARY

Cost. It can be very expensive to get mains services for telephone and electricity to isolated rural properties.

Electricity. Electricity is no longer cheap in New Zealand, compared with the rest of the world. **Plugs.** New Zealand plugs have three flat pins like Australia's. Appliances work in both countries, with no adaptor needed.

Heating. New Zealand houses can be damp and cold. You may need to upgrade the heating. There are still far too few homes with central heating. A dehumidifier or a ventilation system is one way to ensure your house remains warm and dry in the winter.

Gas. Mains gas is only available in the North Island. In the South Island, you'll need to use bottled gas.

Water. If you don't have access to a mains water supply, have the roof water tested by a laboratory to see if it is safe to drink.

Buying in water. Droughts are common in the eastern part of the country, and you may need to buy in water.

Service connections. Organising service connections is simply a matter of proving your identity and that you can afford to pay for the services required. The utility providers ask for standard information from applicants, including personal details as well as those that relate to the house. For renters, this will be the name of your landlord and letting agent. New customers needing a landline connection are required to provide a copy of photo ID such as a passport.

Rural areas. In rural areas, it can be very expensive to get connected to mains electricity and telephone services. There may be no mains sewer or water supply, services that city dwellers take for granted. They still need regular maintenance, which you will have to undertake at your expense.

* * *

ELECTRICITY

Electricity is generated in New Zealand from a combination of gas, coal, hydro, geothermal resources and increasingly, wind generation. Since deregulation in 1999, the private sector generates around 40% of the country's electricity. The government still retains control of the transmission company, Transpower.

As well as allowing the private sector to generate electricity, deregulation allowed electricity consumers to switch supplier. You can find out which electricity company offers the best deal in your area by logging on to the Powerswitch website: www.powerswitch.org.nz. The site provides a good comparison of electricity prices in your area. In the areas that don't yet have a competitor for you to switch to, the site offers advice on how to save money with your current supplier.

Meters are supposed to be read at least three times a year, although consumers are obliged to pay an estimated bill if the meter hasn't been read. Ring in with your own meter reading, if the company allows this. You can pay your bill electronically or with a credit card, or in person at any New Zealand Post Shop. A discount incentive scheme may be available if you pay by direct debit.

Arranging a Contract over the Telephone or Internet. Most suppliers have a separate department for clients that are moving house. Check with your estate agent that the meters have been read and that the previous owners have paid up. As well as the address of the property, you may need to supply the meter number.

Meters. Because meters are installed outside the property and the meter reader has to come on to the land to read it, you need to inform the electricity company if you own a dog.

Power Supply and Plugs. New Zealand's power supply is 230/240 volts, 50Hz and electrical sockets take a three-pin type of plug (not the same as the UK one). British appliances will work with an adaptor, North American equipment requires a transformer as well as an adaptor, but Australian appliances can just be plugged in.

Electrical Safety. As a precaution, when buying an old house, you should ask a qualified electrician to check that the wiring meets current standards. There is no mandatory safety inspection required, even when renting out a house, so it is up to you to ensure that the wiring is safe. It is very easy to overload circuits in old villas – all it takes is too many appliances run off the same circuit all being used at once. While the occasional fuse blow out is understandable in older houses, if it occurs on a regular basis, then it's a sure sign that all is not well and time to call a registered electrician.

Bulbs. Both bayonet and screw fitting bulbs are in use

in New Zealand homes, although bayonet fittings are more common in older houses. New Zealand is lagging behind the rest of the world in energy efficiency, as incandescent light bulbs are still in use.

Rural Properties. You have to have deep pockets to get a rural section connected, especially if the house is going to be further than 400 metres from an existing transformer. If it's within that distance and close to the road boundary, then it may be just cabling that is required.

Although the costs of getting services to the gate have to be paid upfront by the owner of the land, before you purchase it, it can cost them $25,000 per km for new power lines and $5000 for a transformer and high voltage extension. To make it economic to subdivide land, the cost is going to have to be passed on. And it doesn't stop there. Although some savings can be made if all the services (power, telephone and water) can be run in the same trench, you could still be paying around $10,000.

Heating

Some New Zealanders are cold weather deniers, pretending that winter doesn't exist. Older people who were brought up tough, think nothing of putting on an extra sweater when it gets cold in winter, rather than acknowledge that it's the house itself that's the problem. It's hardly surprising then that New Zealand homes are colder and damper than those in many other countries. There is increasing evidence that these damp and cold homes are contributory factors to the 800,000 cases of asthma and respiratory illness – one of the highest rates in the world. Poorly insulated houses contribute to the problem.

New Zealand's system for heating houses is different (and some would say inferior) to the combination boiler with radiators in every room. Some houses have a system that can be pre-set. The more expensive type of portable oil fired radiators operate on timer switches, but this still won't give complete coverage of the whole house, in the way that fixed radiators do.

Modern houses with tiled floors and bathrooms are particularly cold in winter, although some may have under-floor heating. The trend for open plan living has made houses even colder, as they become even harder to heat. A form of gas central heating is available, but the system blows hot air and the house needs to be well ventilated. Individually controlled gas fires are an option, but should never be used in bedrooms because of the risk of carbon monoxide poisoning. You'll need alternative heating in these rooms to keep warm in winter.

There are some other steps that homeowners can take to make their homes warmer. These include putting in ceiling insulation, as well as under floor insulation, which can be installed underneath wooden houses, providing there is a big enough crawl space to allow access. Fortunately, winter in New Zealand is short and it's only cold for four months of the year unless you live in Canterbury, Otago and Southland.

Dehumidifiers. A dehumidifier can be useful in winter, particularly in houses that don't get much sun. Many home-owners have theirs running permanently in the coldest part of the house (usually the south-east corner). Make sure the dehumidifier you buy is one with a decent sized water container, as it's a chore to empty it more than once a day.

Ventilation Systems. There are two types: (a) a heat recovery ventilation system uses a heat exchanger where air is pumped in from the outdoors and stale air is pumped outdoors, and (b) forced air ventilation that blows dry air from the roof space around the house. How much such a system costs will depend on the size of the house, but it could be as much as $8000.

GAS

The gas fields are concentrated off the central North Island coast. Mains gas is supplied to over 50 towns and cities in the North Island. The mains gas pipeline doesn't extend across the Cook Strait and South Islanders have to rely on electricity or bottled liquid petroleum gas (LPG) for their supplies.

There are a number of companies that supply both electricity and gas. Consolidating your gas and electricity with one supplier may save you money and you'll only have one bill. Meter reading and payment methods operate in a similar way to the electricity companies. The Consumer NZ website www.consumer.org.nz allows you to compare the best deals for natural gas in your area.

Don't bother searching inside the house for anything as compact as a combination-boiler. The gas hot water cylinder is too big to go inside and will be attached to the outside of the house. The gas supply for the heating will feed into the house separately. Only registered technicians are permitted to carry out installation and maintenance of mains gas appliances.

There is no statutory requirement for regular gas safety checks to be carried out, but all gas appliances, especially un-flued portable gas heaters should be checked for wear and tear on a regular basis. The room must be well-ventilated while using these appliances.

Bottled Gas

Bottled gas can be used for heating, hot water and cooking but this needs to be organised with a supplier. The cost varies from region to region. The gas bottles will connect to the outside of the house and a registered gas technician will need to install this.

PORTABLE CABINET LPG HEATERS

Used as a way of heating a remote rural bach, portable LPG room heaters (with the gas cylinder integral to the appliance) have been banned from sale in Australia based on their previous poor safety history. New Zealand has yet to follow suit.

The *Energy Safety Service*, a division of the Ministry of Economic Development at *www.energysafety.co.nz* has a list of safety tips for their use, one of which is to carry out regular leak tests and to ventilate the room. They advise that an LPG service agent should service the appliance once a year.

* * *

WATER

The mains water supply and wastewater is under the control of the local authority, which may have a separate company that runs this side of council business. In the larger cities, water is metered and a separate bill will be sent out over and above the rates.

Turning off the Water. Ask the agent to show you where the stopcock is situated, so that you know where to turn the water off in an emergency. It's usually in front of the house, under a manhole cover in the pavement.

In rural Canterbury and Marlborough and other eastern parts of the country, drought conditions and water restrictions are a regular feature of late summer. If you live on a small holding or a lifestyle block with crops or stock, there'll be times when you run out of water and may need to buy it in. The costs include delivery and could cost you several hundred dollars.

New Zealand mains water is world class and only those

on tank supplies should spend their money buying bottled water. Some people think roof or rain water to be better for them, but a Massey University study has proven otherwise. From the sample of 450, 30 percent contained enough bacteria to make the average person ill.

Unless you buy a house with a new water tank or have a new one installed, (which will cost anything between $3000 to $5000) you should have the water quality tested by a Ministry of Health approved laboratory. Don't take the vendor's assurances that their roof water is safe to drink, just because it hasn't made them ill. Immunity can build up to unsafe drinking water.

Householders are advised to inspect the tank for holes, to clean out the tank as well as the gutters and have their water tested regularly.

Waste Water or a Resource for Recycling?

Many rural properties will have a septic tank installed. You should have this checked, as many older systems still in use were badly designed or incorrectly sited. It is up to the property owner to ensure that the septic tank works properly and doesn't pollute the environment. One of the problems with septic tanks is that they don't suit our modern lifestyle, especially appliances such dishwashers and washing machines, which pump large amounts of water into the system. Toxic household chemicals can also cause septic tanks to fail. One solution is to add an aerobic sand filter to the outlet of a conventional septic tank.

If you need to put in a replacement septic tank, or install a new one, seek advice from a plumbing and drainage inspector at your local council. An engineer who has experience in their design must design any new system. Soil conditions, the size of the section, the number of people in the household and other factors, such as ground water levels and whether or not the site is sloping, will all determine whether or not your property is suitable. The cost of putting in a new septic tank, if the property is sited near natural water (a lake or a river), including tank and installation could be as much as $20,000.

The septic tank may have been a revolutionary invention in the nineteenth century, but when building from scratch, should homeowners be looking at a more up-to-date system and one with better 'green' credentials? Consider a composting toilet with a separate system for collecting and recycling grey water from washing.

Installing a Solar Hot Water System

Depending on the size of your house, installing a solar hot water system will cost between $10,000 to $13,000. This is both environmentally sustainable and can halve your energy bills in the long-term.

Fire Prevention in Rural Areas

Fire warnings are regularly issued over summer. In forested areas this may include a total fire ban. Fire prevention measures outdoors include storing firewood and flammable items away from the house and clearing the property of any rubbish. Fit the house with smoke alarms (testing them at the start and end of daylight saving), keep a fire blanket in the kitchen and have the wiring in the house checked to ensure that it complies with current safety regulations.

SECURITY

There's no point in installing an expensive alarm system if the front door can be operated by one easily copied key. Make friends with your neighbours and let them know when you are going to be away. Security sensor lights around the outside of the house are a good idea. Because the wind, or even a spider in the system can trigger an alarm, an unmonitored alarm ringing in suburbia might not be investigated. Providing your property is not too remote and difficult to get to, a monitored alarm system may be your best option.

You can leave windows open during summer without attracting burglars if you install window locks. When going away, leave security lights on and use timer switches so that lights and radios can come on in the evening. As well as cancelling the newspaper, ensure that you arrange for a neighbour to collect your post as well as clear out all the junk mail. An overflowing letterbox can be spotted from any passing car.

Home Insurance. Check the small print in your insurance contract to see how long you are allowed to leave your property unoccupied.

House Sitters

A house sitter could be the ideal solution to ensure that your house is occupied and cared for. The company will undertake reference checks. If you live in a remote region, or have a large garden to care for, or a large and boisterous dog, it may take longer to find a sitter. One enticement would be to offer to pay for some or all of the sitter's power bill.

STAFF/CLEANERS

Buying a cleaning franchise is one of the ways that many new immigrants who came in under the old General Skills category were able to make a living. With New Zealand's low unemployment rate, locals aren't interested in doing these kinds of jobs. This may be the only way you'll find a cleaner in wealthier areas. Expect to pay $60 per hour plus 15% GST. If you hire directly, the minimum wage is $15.25 per hour.

Finding a Gardener. There are plenty of garden maintenance companies that will weed and tidy your garden, as well as mow the lawn, but they won't necessarily know about plant care. Ask your local garden centre, or get a personal recommendation for a good local gardener who can assist with lawn care or propagation.

Hard landscaping and garden design are best left to specialist companies, who will be able to advise you on what resource consents are needed to carry out the work.

Caretaker. You may find it easier to employ a property maintenance company that will provide a cleaner and caretaker who will come in for a few hours each week. The prices of such services vary but expect to pay at least $60 per hour plus GST (12.5%).

MAKING THE MOVE

CHAPTER SUMMARY

Preparing for the move. Start clearing out attics and garden sheds well in advance of the packers arriving.

Cars. Whether you have to pay import duty on a used car you bring in depends on your visa.

Removals. The firm you choose should be up-to-date with the latest bio-security requirements in New Zealand.

Pets. Only dogs and cats are permitted to be imported into the country.

Because of respiratory problems that can increase during air travel, there are restrictions placed on shipping snub-nosed dogs.

Get your pet accustomed to sleeping in their shipping container well before they fly.

* * *

REMOVALS

What to Take with You to New Zealand

What to bring with you will depend on whether you are financing the move yourself, or if an employer will be picking up the bill for the removal of your household effects. If you are the one who is paying to ship furniture, the major cost could be the insurance (see the comment from the Taylor family, below). You will, of course, want to take antique furniture or other valuable items and personal effects. Items that are worn should be sold off, or donated to charity and replaced in New Zealand.

If you've recently purchased an expensive television, it may be worthwhile taking it, even if the shipping company advises against it. It really isn't worthwhile taking wardrobes, unless they are heirloom pieces. New Zealanders regard them as old-fashioned and prefer to have them built-in.

Clearing out unwanted items from home should be tackled as far in advance as possible – especially attics and garden sheds. Put aside all the equipment that will need to be scrubbed and disinfected together, as this will ensure that they don't get forgotten.

Removal Firms

There are a number of large companies that specialise in international removals. Choosing a firm will be dependent on such factors as cost and delivery time. The shortest and most direct route will be the most expensive, but you should be careful about opting for the alternative. The container will otherwise go on a circuitous route, or it may be left sitting on the quayside, waiting to be loaded. The less time your effects spend in a container, the better, as otherwise, you could find that your household goods are damp when you come to unpack them.

Then there is the consideration about what arrangements have been made for your temporary furnished accommodation. Companies that move their staff to New Zealand expect to have to pay short-term accommodation for up for a month, to allow for delivery of furniture.

As well as factoring in cost and speed of delivery, choose a firm that is both knowledgeable about your destination and is up to date on New Zealand's strict bio-security laws, which are among the world's toughest. Biosecurity New Zealand has to ensure that unwanted insect pests don't get into the country and will look out for certain types of wooden furniture, particularly cane, which could be harbouring insect larvae. You'll need to note them, as well as any outdoor equipment, as these will be inspected on arrival. There are strict rules regarding the need to disinfect hiking boots, camping equipment, gardening tools, plant pots or any other items (including shoes) that may have been in contact with soil.

Whether you do your own packing depends on whether you are taking fine furniture and antiques, as you won't be able to claim against insurance, if you pack these yourself and they break. Most firms have a special service for valuables, where they are bubble wrapped and covered in corrugated cardboard. However, if your belongings only contain a few delicate or precious items, one way of cutting costs is to buy your own packing materials wholesale, doing all your own packing and then shipping everything in your own container, provided by a specialist freight forwarder. You can save a few hundred pounds this way.

As anyone who has moved long distance before will know, it will be delicate items such as fine china or glassware that gets broken. Because of the high excess charges it won't be worth claiming on the insurance. And you can bet that the chain store glassware will survive the trip but the Waterford crystal won't.

The Taylor family who moved from Devon to New Zealand in 2002 had this to say:

> We read the information for immigrants given to us by the New Zealand immigration people (very useful pack with video) which advised against taking televisions. Only the really expensive ones from the UK seem to work in New Zealand. We were surprised that all the furniture from our four-bedroom house managed to fit into a twenty-foot container. We did take our fridge and freezer as they were brand new – even though some removal firms suggest you don't – in case they get damaged in transit. It can be tempting to take everything but only do that if your goods still fit the container. It's not worth paying extra for a bigger container to take a few more worn out beds and mattresses.
>
> We took a risk on the insurance and decided that for the price it wasn't worth it. Of course, the ship could have gone down, but we knew of another family who moved a valuable book collection and ended up paying £17,000 just for their insurance. We would advise anyone moving to go for an insulated container rather than a metal one as there is less condensation. The last thing you want to find when you unpack is that clothes and bedding have gone mouldy. We didn't pay extra for the insulated container – it was just that there was slightly less internal volume due to the extra layer of insulation.

Removal firms and freight forwarders that ship to New Zealand:

Allied Pickfords: www.pickfords.co.uk (UK). www.alliedpickfords.com (USA).

Crown Worldwide Movers: www.crownworldwide.com.

Robinsons International Moving Services: www.robin-sonsrelo.com.

Importing a Car or Motorcycle

Whether you are exempt from paying duty on an imported used car depends upon a number of factors. If you are coming into the country for the first time and hold a permanent residency visa then you won't have to pay tax, providing you can prove that you have owned the car for at least twelve months, that it is for personal use and that the vehicle won't be sold within two years. A Deed of Covenant, which you have to sign, stipulates that if you do sell within two years you agree to pay the tax owing on it.

Everyone else, including returning New Zealanders, are liable to pay Goods & Services Tax (GST). GST must be paid regardless of how long you have owned the vehicle and however long you have been away from New Zealand. The importer must show proof of purchase, preferably an original receipt and produce the overseas registration papers. Although there is a depreciation allowance granted for tax assessment, providing that the vehicle has been owned for a minimum of three months the cost of shipping and marine insurance premiums is included in the GST calculation.

Owners of classic cars should be aware that all vehicles that have been registered outside New Zealand after December 1981 must have a Statement of Compliance from the manufacturer to confirm that it meets New Zealand standards. Information on standards can be found on the Land Transport Safety Authority website at www.ltsa.govt.nz. Find out first, before you go to the expense of shipping that your car will be allowed out on New Zealand roads.

Used cars made in South East Asia are relatively cheap to buy and parts are readily available. It could be worth your while bringing in a late model, high-performance European car as these are expensive to replace. Make sure that the make and model are available in New Zealand, otherwise spare parts, servicing and repairs could be a problem.

Registering a Foreign Vehicle in New Zealand

The New Zealand equivalent of an MOT is a warrant of fitness or WOF. The WOF is carried out at testing stations or approved garages. As well as a WOF you will need to pay for registration, new licence plates and vehicle licensing. The cost of licensing depends on the size of the engine. The vehicle licensing fee includes an Accident Compensation levy. Cars that are six years old or older require a new warrant of fitness every six months.

* * *

IMPORTING PETS

Pets are members of the family and it's only natural that you will want to bring your pets to New Zealand with you. With very few exceptions, only dogs and cats are allowed to be imported. There are restrictions on certain breeds of dog deemed dangerous, which are banned by the government as well as the airlines. Some airlines place restrictions on certain breeds of snub-nosed dog because of animal welfare concerns – these breeds are prone to increased respiratory problems when stressed. Dogs entering New Zealand must be nine months or older to travel and no more than 42 days pregnant.

While there is no official upper age limit for pets to travel, they do have to be given a clean bill of health from the vet first. An elderly dog or cat travelling from Australia should cope with a shorter journey time, but it's a different matter if travelling from the UK or the US. You should consider carefully whether or not it might be kinder to leave an elderly, nervous dog behind with friends or relatives, rather than subject him to a long journey of up to 25 hours in a travelling crate. Although, as one economy passenger remarked, his dog probably had more legroom than he did.

The airlines say that it is a safe way for pets to travel, as according to estimates, a million pets a year are transported by air from which only 30 deaths or injuries occur. Most of these fatalities are preventable and due to over sedation. Vets advise against this, because there's no way to judge how your pet will react to the potentially dangerous combination of sedatives and high altitude. Pet travelling crates contain water and this is checked at the stopover en route to New Zealand, but pets are unsupervised during their flight. Pets should only be given a light meal before they fly. They are not fed again until they reach their destination.

From Australia there is no quarantine and information on the testing and documentation necessary can be obtained from your vet. If travelling from the United Kingdom, Norway, Sweden, Singapore or Hawaii, check with the Ministry of Primary Industries (MPI) whether your pet will need an import permit. No quarantine is necessary but a series of tests, injections and procedures, including microchipping are required for dogs before the animal is allowed to be imported. Pets travelling from the USA have to undergo 30 days quarantine. You should check with your vet before the microchip is implanted that it can, in fact, be read by New Zealand scanners.

Import and Export Permits

There are three different import permits issued by the Ministry of Primary Industries (MPI), depending on which country you are coming from. If you're coming from a country where quarantine is required, the import permit will not be issued until you have confirmation from an MPI approved quarantine facility that a booking has been received for your pet. As well as an import certificate you'll need an export certificate issued by the ministry of agriculture in your own country.

The New Zealand government, as well as a number of airlines that transport dogs, have singled out four dog breeds that they will not fly, nor allow into the country. They are the Togo Argentinos, the Fila Brazileiros, the American Pit Bull Terrier and Japanese Tosas. These include cross-breeds.

Check with a pet transport company regarding the latest regulations concerning the transportation of snub-nosed dog breeds, as a number of airlines refuse to carry Bulldogs, Pugs and Pekinese for animal welfare reasons, as they suffer from respiratory problems that increase with stress.

Many airlines will now only accept pets to fly as unaccompanied cargo through a specialist shipper, as airlines claim that too many amateur shippers fail to fill out the accompanying paperwork correctly.

How Much Will it Cost to Import a Pet? Your best friend isn't going to travel cheaply, particularly if he is a medium to large dog. If travelling from the UK allow £400 for vet costs and £1200 for the travel. The import permit will set you back NZ$220.74; then there's the cost of shipping. If coming from a country that requires your dog to be quarantined for a month, this will cost around NZ$1500 to $3000.

Preparing your Pet for the Journey. You can minimise the stress on your dog by getting him used to sleeping in a travelling container, well in advance before he is due to travel. Ask your pet shipper to loan you a regulation container. Start training him by putting his favourite toy in there. You may have to coax him in there using food treats, and ensure that you keep the door to the pet cage open.

The goal is to have your pet become so familiar with his container he will want to sleep in there.

Animals on long haul flights will be placed in the animal hold, at the front of the plane, which is pressurised and heated during the journey. Animals are usually last to be loaded and first to be off-loaded. Make a specific request to your pet shipper that your pet is hand loaded and off-loaded. If you have a choice of refuelling stops, choose the one with the better climate. From North America, the connection from Los Angeles or San Francisco should be direct. Pets may not fly from parts of North America during the summer months because of extreme temperatures. The same conditions may apply during periods of extreme cold.

Useful Addresses and Websites:

Ministry for Primary Industries www.mpi.govt.nz. Website for the government department in charge of the importation of live animals into New Zealand. Follow the link to: Steps to Importing Cats and Dogs.

Defra, Animal Welfare Division: www.defra.gov. uk. Although primarily the site for the Pet Travel Scheme (PETS), there are excellent tips on preparing your pet for a long journey.

Independent Pet and Animal Transportation Association Inc: www.ipata.org.

A membership organisation not affiliated to the airlines with a directory of members as well as advice on shipping pets.

Pet Shippers from the UK.

Airpets: Stanwell Moor, Middlesex (01753-685571 www.airpets.com. Based at Heathrow they can arrange pick-up, delivery and quarantine and vet services.

Skymaster Air Cargo Ltd: 7, 308, Cargo Centre, Manchester Airport M90 5PZ; 0161-436 2190; www.skymaster.co.uk. Skymaster, based at Manchester Airport, can arrange collection, flight bookings, as well as kennelling and veterinary procedures and supply of IATA-approved pet carriers.

From the USA.

JetPets: 9111 Falmouth Ave, Playa del Rey, CA 90293-8617;(310-823- 8901; www.jetpets.com for all pet transportation from the Los Angeles area.

BUILDING OR RENOVATING

CHAPTER SUMMARY

Building and resource consent. It is the property owner's responsibility to apply for building and resource consents and to ensure that a code of compliance is issued on completion. Incorporating sustainable building design into your house plans will save you money in reduced power bills as well as being better for the environment.

Pools. All new pools including spa pools are required by law to be fenced.

Gardens. There are at least three different climate zones in New Zealand and climate as well as soil type will determine what you can plant.

Public gardens. Public gardens are a good place to find ideas for your garden.

Tree trimming. Some local councils require resource consents for tree trimming, as well as removal and the rules are strictly enforced, particularly for native trees.

Invasive plant species. Your garden centre will advise you on what to plant as some plant species have become invasive.

* * *

THE HIDDEN COSTS OF RENOVATION

Restoring a previously neglected house can be satisfying and a good restoration should increase value. An old house that retains some original features with modern additions, such as a good quality kitchen and bathrooms is ideal. This will not only make the house very comfortable to live in but will be appealing to buyers, should you ever need to sell.

It's too easy to get carried away with a renovation unless you keep to a budget. And always build in a 10% contingency for any unexpected repairs. Adopting the ad-hoc approach to restoration, doing the essential work as soon as you move in and then waiting to have the rest done when you can afford it, may result in budget creep unless you're careful. Be wary of over-capitalising on installing new state of the art kitchens and bathrooms. Do so for reasons of comfort, aesthetics and enjoyment, but don't expect to make your money back when you sell.

As the kitchen will be the most expensive room to renovate, be prepared to pay from $15,000 to $60,000 plus. There is no IKEA in New Zealand so your options for a cheaper, flatpack DIY kitchen are limited. Revamping the existing kitchen with a new bench top, drawers and doors will cost you at least $5000. Choose granite for the bench top and the budget rises accordingly. One downside of renovating is that the shiny new restoration can show up the rest of the house. When choosing tiles, slate costs around $125 per square metre, while timber flooring costs from $90 per square metre. The second most expensive room to renovate will be the bathroom. New Zealanders have developed a taste for expensive European bath and tapware. A basic bathroom renovation will cost from $10,000. To move plumbing will add to this cost.

If you are handy with a paintbrush or good at tiling and plan to undertake your own decorating, New Zealand is awash with DIY stores. New Zealanders are known for their enthusiasm for renovation, but as Helen Davies points out in **Chapter 13 Case Histories**, paint is expensive. Some stores, (try Bunnings or Mitre 10) offer videos and booklets demonstrating how to tackle certain jobs. As the going rate for any contractor in Auckland and Wellington is from $45-65 per hour, you could save yourself money in the process.

As anyone who has ever bought a house from a DIY electrician or plumber will know, there are some jobs that amateurs should never be allowed to touch. As well as placing restrictions on some plumbing, electrical and gas work, from 2009 certain building work was restricted to licensed builders. Only those who have the qualifications and ability to carry out the work are permitted to become licensed. Some restricted building work may be carried out by amateurs who are supervised by a licensed building practitioner.

* * *

BUILDING AND RESOURCE CONSENTS

Whether it is for alteration, building from new, or removing or relocating existing buildings, it's the property owner's responsibility to get a building consent. The Building Act 2004 states that some of the work that needs consent includes:

Alterations. This includes moving a load-bearing wall.

Demolition or Relocation. Relocating or demolishing an existing building.

Decks above 1.5 metres. Anything under this height is not deemed a safety risk and does not require consent.

Retaining Walls. Any retaining wall higher than 1.5m above ground level or any retaining wall that retains a driveway, even if it is under this height.

Fences. A substantial fence made out of concrete or a fence over two metres high.

Change of building use. This might include converting a garage into an extra room.

Swimming Pools and Spa Pools. Even putting in a spa pool requires resource consent, (see section on pools below).

Certain jobs will require you to get what is known as Resource Consent. In Auckland for example, you need resource consent just to trim even a small exotic tree (native trees having greater protection). Some councils check building consent applications to see if a resource consent is required as well. At the end of the building job it's the homeowner's responsibility to ensure that the building consent has been carried out to the specifications required and to apply for a code compliance certificate.

* * *

CHOOSING THE RIGHT TEAM

Any tradesperson that you select for a renovation or building job should be properly qualified and belong to a professional trade organisation. Ask to see their work and to talk to their previous customers. Ask too if the work comes with any guarantee. Key personnel in the team – the architect, project manager and lead builder need to understand what you're trying to achieve. The project manager should assist you with a contingency plan in case you can't afford to get all the work done in one go.

Be wary of the cheapest quote as there's no guarantee that the job will be done to your exacting standards. Whoever you choose has to have the right insurance, including public liability. If something goes wrong and you use an unregistered tradesperson without insurance, you won't receive a cent in compensation.

Builders can belong to one of two trade organisations – the New Zealand Certified Builders Association (NZCB) or the Registered Master Builders Federation. Both organisations require their members to have a recognised building qualification and to have worked in the building industry for some years. They both operate a code of conduct and provide guarantees of workmanship.

If the job is substantial and requires a complete re-design, then you will want to employ an architect. The architect's design has the potential to add value to your house so make sure you visit examples of their work first. Some months before you plan to start your project, collect newspaper cuttings of new houses that you admire. The property section in the weekend edition of the *New Zealand Herald* and the *Property Press* often feature the names and details of architects and builders in their editorial. The specialist publications, *Urbis* and *Architecture New Zealand* (both published by AGM Publishing) feature the best of recent New Zealand architectural design. Glossy monthly magazines, available at newsagents include *NZ House and Garden* and *Home New Zealand*. The latter features an annual Home of the Year Award.

If you are undertaking a restoration of an old building make sure that the architect you employ doesn't just want to rip out the whole interior and start again. So many old houses have had the character stripped out of them and all that is left of the original is the front of the house.

Building an Eco-friendly House. The Building Research Association of New Zealand (BRANZ) operate a Green Home Scheme which offers those building a house, as well as existing homeowners, a method of assessing how new homes rate on key environmental issues. Good design can make a home more energy efficient and more comfortable to live in. The principles behind eco-housing mean that the materials chosen are less toxic than conventional building materials, that they use passive solar energy where possible and incorporate systems to recycle wastewater.

Useful Contacts and Websites

BRANZ www.branz.co.nz. Great website that supplies not only contacts for eco-building with local councils, but offers advice on all matters relating to building.

Certified Builders Association (CBANZ): www.nzcb.nz.

Electrical Workers Registration Board (EWRB): www.ewrb.govt.nz.

Plumbers, Gasfitters and Drainlayers Board: www.pgdb.co.nz.

Registered Master Builders of New Zealand: www.masterbuilder.org.nz

* * *

POOLS

At the height of summer, where better to relax than around the pool in your garden? As well as enhancing the look and value of your property, having a pool is a convenient way of entertaining friends and family. Sadly, though, around five New Zealand children a year die in domestic swimming pools and these fatalities prompted a change in the law relating to pool fencing. By law, all domestic swimming pools and spa pools must be fenced off. As well as complying with the legislation in the Fencing of Swimming Pools Act, the fence has to comply with the New Zealand Building Code. Information on the building code can be found on the Ministry of Business, Innovation and Employment's website at www.building.govt.nz.

New Regulations Cover Existing Pools. An unfenced pool could provide too much of a temptation to the neighbours' children, not to mention pets and wildlife and it is the pool owner's responsibility to ensure their pool is safe. Since 2002 lockable spa pool covers were no longer compliant. If the house you are buying or have bought has an existing pool, this should be inspected carefully by a building inspector. A badly maintained pool with cracks or other signs of poor maintenance could be more of a liability than an asset.

The guidelines on pool fencing in brief are:

Height. The pool fence must be at least 1.2m high from the ground.

Gaps. As well as not being climbable, there are regulations regarding gaps between the vertical bars as well as under the fence.

Boundary Fencing. It's not advisable to include a

boundary fence as part of a pool fence. If a neighbour's children put a structure next to the fence, they could climb over and your fence would no longer comply with the regulations.

Lockable Gate. Gates must be the sort that close and latch automatically.

Pool fencing around the immediate pool area. The fencing can't extend to lawn areas, children's play areas or the whole garden. Only certain equipment relating to the pool is allowed in the immediate area.

Building a New Pool. You will need a building consent for putting in either a spa or pool. You should include drawings that show where you intend to put the fencing, as well as a plan of the immediate pool area. Your local council may also require that you need a resource consent.

* * *

GARDENS

If you adore everything to do with gardens and gardening, New Zealand is the place to indulge your passion. If you've lived in a climate of freezing winters and hot, sultry summers, you will marvel at the range of plants the New Zealand gardener can grow. In the upper part of the North Island and parts of Nelson and Golden Bay, you are only limited by your imagination in what you can plant in the garden.

Visit Public Gardens for Inspiration. Before you plant up, visit a local public garden. In every town and city up and down the country, you can find public displays of plants and flowers.

Auckland's Regional Botanical Gardens are out of town in Manukau City. The Domain and Myers Park in the city centre have fine displays of herbaceous borders and magnificent trees. The Domain has a Winter Garden and a fernery. Hamilton Gardens, as well as incorporating a fine display of roses, has a series of themed landscaped garden rooms from around the world that should inspire any amateur gardener.

Further south, Wellington Botanical Gardens makes the most of its hilly site. In Christchurch, as well as the roses and English style planting, the gardens incorporate a variety of native plant species. And in the Dunedin public gardens, azaleas are a feature.

If you are in New Zealand during spring (September-November), it's worth detouring to New Plymouth just to visit Pukeiti. At the foot of Mount Taranaki, this garden has one of the world's most beautiful backdrops in which to see rhododendron and azaleas, incorporated into a native bush setting.

New Zealand gardening style has finally stepped out of the shadow of its colonial past and has forged a new identity. The New Zealand garden at the Chelsea Flower Show won a coveted gold medal in 2004. This proved to New Zealand gardeners that with imaginative planting you don't have to sacrifice colour to have a native garden.

Billed as the Southern Hemisphere's version of the Chelsea event, the annual Ellerslie Flower Show, held at Auckland's Regional Botanical Gardens in November, is the gardening event of the year. Unlike at Chelsea, the show gardens at Ellerslie have been designed with the home gardener in mind.

You can buy a simple testing kit from the local garden centre to find out what kind of soil you have. In addition to testing the soil, work out which areas you need to plant and how much sun, wind and exposure your site will get. By then you'll have a better idea of the kind of look you want to create. Draw a plan of the garden, or employ a professional garden designer to do this.

Trends come and go in garden design. Currently, sub-tropical 'easy-care' gardening is 'in' and labour-intensive cottage gardens are 'out.' Gardens landscaped by professional garden companies tend to look the same, no matter what the season. Combining sub-tropical, native, as well as deciduous plants adds year-round interest.

Even sub-tropical gardens require frequent watering. Given that New Zealand has long and warm summers, many gardeners install an automatic watering system. This allows them to go away for their summer holidays, knowing that the garden won't shrivel up in their absence. The alternative is to plant a drought-resistant garden or to use plenty of mulch. Mulch is a New Zealand gardener's best friend – retaining moisture as well as suppressing weeds. Container gardens can be a chore to water too. Even if you only have a small courtyard, fewer, larger containers, rather than many small pots will be kinder to the plants as their roots won't bake or dry out as much in the hot sun.

While Northern Hemisphere gardeners get a chance to pack away the gardening gloves and retreat to the sofa with next year's seed catalogues in winter, in New Zealand's North Island, mowing and weeding are year round activities.

The Kitchen Garden

You don't need much room to create a kitchen garden – even tomatoes can be grown in a pot but if you do have some space, imagine the satisfaction you'll get from picking your own produce. Whether you want a grapefruit for breakfast, or lemons for the evening gin and tonics, all you'll have to do is walk across the back lawn to get them. In the sub-tropical kitchen garden, how about growing figs, limes or avocados?

Problem Plant Species. That combination of abundant rain and warm sunshine, which makes gardens so lush, has had a few unfortunate side effects. The early settlers who brought gorse with them (to remind them of Scotland) weren't to know that this plant would one day become one of New Zealand's most difficult plant pests to eradicate.

Rebecca, who arrived from the UK, relates this story:

I asked at an Auckland garden centre for a Jasmine plant, only to have the checkout operator make an announcement for someone to come to the desk. A rather hairy long-shorted, socks and shoes type stormed down the aisle. When I enquired about Jasmine, he became quite animated and told me off for asking for such a noxious weed, which is banned in this region.

Jasmine fans shouldn't be too dismayed as there is a less invasive alternative to the pink variety, which smothers the forest once it gets into the wild. One country's flower is another's pest plant and millions of dollars are spent each year on getting rid of pest plants and the list is increasing all the time. To do your bit for the environment requires a re-think on what to grow in your garden. You only need to go out into the wilderness to see what damage some introduced plant species have had on parts of the eco-system.

To assist you in what to plant and what to remove, contact your local council. They should give you further information on which introduced plants threaten native communities. Each gardening region of the country – northern, central and southern, has its own particular problem plant species. The invasive plant pests that are a problem throughout the country include: Climbing asparagus (Asparagus scandens), Japanese honeysuckle (Lonicera japonica), Banana passionfruit (Passiflora mollissima & P. mixta), Chinese Ladder Fern (Nephrolepis cordifolia), Periwinkle (Vinca major), Cotoneaster (Cotoneaster glaucohphyllus,

C. franchetti), Pampas (Cortaderia selloana, C. jubata), German ivy (Senecio mikaniodides), Chinese privet (Ligustrum sinense).

Garden centres have to be up to date with the regulations as they are banned from selling or propagating pest plants. The list of banned species is regularly reviewed.

There has been a resurgence in interest in planting native plants in gardens. But because the habitats of native plants are localised, it's best to check with a native plant nursery first as to which species will suit your soil and site. A New Zealand native plant, the Renga Renga lily makes excellent ground cover and is a much better alternative to the clump-forming and ubiquitous Agapanthus, which has been declared an invasive species in Auckland and is banned from sale in the region.

If you live on the coast the sight of a Pohutukawa (known as the New Zealand Christmas tree) in flower is enough to make a returning ex-pat's eyes mist over. The small to medium size Kowhai tree is a brilliant yellow and like the Pohutukawa is beloved of nectar-feeders such as the white-throated tui. Native species are versatile and look great combined with sub-tropical plants such as cycads or even desert plants like succulents, all of which grow well in the Northern region. Further south, native plant species look wonderful within a setting of Rhododendron or Azaleas.

Insects and Other Pests in the Garden. Mosquitoes are prevalent nearly everywhere, but the common species is only really active at dawn and dusk. While there are plants that help to keep insects away, there are a number of measures you can take to prevent them from taking residence in the first place. Birdbaths, plant saucers, or as little as an inch of rainwater in a watering can may be all that it takes to provide the ideal breeding ground for mosquitoes to thrive. Washing out all such containers with disinfectant will minimise their presence, as will keeping away greenery from the outside of the house. Herbs and plants such as basil, rosemary, lavender and lemon verbena are said to keep insects away.

New Zealand's creepy crawlies are relatively benign and there are no snakes. You might suffer a few painful bites but there is nothing out there that can kill you – unless you suffer from severe allergies. Possums can be a nuisance in suburban gardens, especially when they climb on the roof. It can sound as though someone is breaking in, but it will just be a possum or two taking a shortcut to get to your fruit trees. Cute they might be but with over 90 million brush-tail possums, these native Australians are wreaking havoc on the habitats of a number of highly endangered native bird species.

Books and Magazines for New Zealand Gardeners

A Guide to the Identification of New Zealand Common Weeds in Colour, E.A, Pritchard.

Complete New Zealand Gardener, Geoff Bryant and Eion Scarrow; a practical guide (with good photographs) to all aspects of gardening in New Zealand from assessing your site and climate to information on plants as well as techniques for caring for the garden.

Landscape: Gardens by New Zealand's Top Designers, Rosemary Thody. Creative inspiration for your garden.

Organic Gardening for New Zealand Gardeners, Random House.

Plant Me Instead, NZ Dept of Conservation. A

helpful guide of what to plant instead of invasive species. *100 Best New Zealand Native Plants for Gardens,* Fiona Eadie.

Subtropical Plants for New Zealand Gardens, Jacqueline Sparrow & Gil Hanly.

Yates Garden Guide, Anon. Full of practical tips.

Protected Trees

Some councils have strict controls over trees of a certain spread and height. You may require Resource Consent even to trim them. These trees are listed in the District Plan. Your solicitor should bring the details of any protected trees on your property to your attention during the purchasing process. The rules governing native trees are even stricter. Trying to surreptitiously lop off a branch of a Pohutukawa, when you think no one is looking may backfire on you.

One East Auckland resident put in a Resource Consent application to trim a Liquid Amber tree. After four months with no response, she rang Auckland Council and got a verbal agreement to trim the tree. When the tree surgeon had done his job a neighbour rang the council, alleging breach of Resource Consent. A council officer came round immediately and gave the owner a stern warning, denying that any consent had been given, nor taking any responsibility for failing to respond to the application in a timely manner.

MAKING MONEY FROM YOUR PROPERTY

CHAPTER SUMMARY

Running a bed and breakfast business. Bed and Breakfast income should be regarded as a supplement rather than a main income.

Running a Home Business. New Zealand is a nation of small businesses where 86% of people are employed in firms employing five or fewer. One of the challenges of running a business from home is not to become socially isolated and to remain connected with other business people doing something similar.

There is government advice available for those wanting to start up new businesses.

Advertising your holiday home. You'll need to advertise your holiday home or bach on a website to reach your target market.

Selling On. Give your house a makeover before you put it on the market.

The high cost of commission. Agents' commission is high in New Zealand.

Agents may be forced to lower their fees in the future because of increasing competition from internet marketing.

* * *

B&B

Offering bed and breakfast or a room on Airbnb is one way to supplement your income, although many property owners in popular tourist spots do this not just to make money, but as a way of meeting people. Owners of bed and breakfast accommodation say it's labour-intensive. There is the laundry change as well as cleaning, answering queries, taking the bookings and the fact that you don't get a lie-in, even on a Sunday morning.

To be listed on a website, hosts should contact their local council as well as their mortgage and insurance providers first, to ensure compliance. Then there is the website's terms and conditions about safety, including the requirement to provide fire and smoke alarms.

Good photographs of the property are essential. Airbnb charges for official photography, but it's worth paying for, as the Airbnb watermark on the photos proves to potential guests that the listing is real. How much you can charge will depend entirely on where your house is situated. Prices start at around $60 per head.

B & B is offered by a mixture of overseas residents, empty nesters, as well as the active retired. If you specialise in a particular cuisine, or cook with organic produce, it's a good idea to include this in your advertising. Remember too that you will be reviewed on such sites as TripAdvisor so make sure you have the sort of personality that could cope with a negative review. It's not advisable to get into a dialogue with a reviewer.

* * *

RUNNING A BUSINESS FROM YOUR PROPERTY

You can run a business from home, providing that your visa allows you to do so. Because the nature of work has changed in the digital age, running a home office is perfectly acceptable, even if you are ordinarily resident for tax purposes in another country.

Useful Contacts

Joining the local branch of a membership organisation such as the American Chamber of Commerce, for those involved in trade between New Zealand, the USA and the Asia-Pacific region, gives new residents the opportunity to link in and build up a network of business contacts. Whether you join for the presentations and guest seminars, or the networking events or even the golf tournaments, organisations such as these provide great networking opportunities. (www.amcham.nz).

New Zealand is an economy of small businesses. 86% of registered businesses employ fewer than five people. The key challenge is isolation – 'not having people around to bounce ideas off.' (source Business Mentors website). Business Mentors New Zealand is a registered charity and provides free mentors to small businesses. They can be contacted at www.businessmentors.org.nz. Whether you live in Christchurch, Wellington or Hamilton, there will be a local Chamber of Commerce for you to join. The Auckland Chamber of Commerce (www.aucklandchamber.co.nz) offers training and mentoring, seminars and discount schemes on insurance, petrol, vehicles and financial services.

Given that New Zealand is a nation of small business

owners, there's a great deal of good (free) advice offered to anyone running a business. The National Library of New Zealand's Te Puna Web Directory has links to all the regional economic development agencies, the Chambers of Commerce, as well as the Small Business Enterprise Centres of New Zealand (community-based organisations located in rural areas).

Those involved in the creative industries should go to www.creativehq.co.nz (an initiative for those in the Wellington region) and read the inspiring stories. Creative HQ helps Wellington based creative entrepreneurs with infrastructure and business support. One of its success stories, Virtual Katy, a sound-editing software package was developed by the *Lord of the Rings* sound effects editor and secured $2 million in venture capital.

Whatever your business, trade or idea, bear in mind too that there are only just over four and a half million people in the entire country and that some businesses require a certain critical mass to be viable. Artists, writers, web designers, or IT professionals have the luxury of being based anywhere they choose and can take their pick from New Zealand's finest locations.

While it could be useful to live in an urban cluster of other creatives who might use your services, if your business is one that needs a strong local client base – for example a medical therapist or a masseuse, you will, of course need to do the research to find out if the population is big enough to sustain another local practitioner. Business people who need to be close to clients or customers don't have to be based in Auckland, especially as median property prices are now so high. The regional centres with good transport links could suit you just as well.

Doing Business with New Zealanders

The New Zealand business community has an air of informality about it that may delight, vex or just plain irritate you and it becomes more informal, the further away you go from the main centres. There's no standing on ceremony and certainly less of the deference than you would find in the UK or the USA. Introductions are carried out on first name terms.

Because the Christmas and the summer holiday are combined into one break, you will have to get used to the entire nation shutting up shop from lunchtime on Christmas Eve and not re-opening again until the second or third week of January. Trying to conduct business (unless you're in the retail trade) is a waste of time. Many business people resign themselves to the shutdown and join the throng at the beach – where they are as likely to meet their peers, all off on their summer holidays, as they are down at the local Chamber of Commerce.

Business owners should note that the standard office hours in New Zealand are 8.30am until 5.00pm Monday to Friday, although many owner-operators and other business owners work longer.

Tax and Finance for Businesses

You should seek professional advice from an accountant who will advise you on all tax matters involved with running your business – whether or not you should be registered for GST (Goods and Services Tax), or whether it's advantageous to set up a limited liability company if you're a sole trader. Registering for GST (like being VAT registered) requires regular administration, which can be done using a software package.

Advantages and Disadvantages of Working from Home

Advantages:

You don't have to rent business premises.

You don't need to hire office space or professional rooms.

Working from home can be so convenient that you can never get away from it.

You don't have to waste time sitting in traffic commuting.

You can work any hours you want.

Say goodbye to office politics.

Disadvantages:

Visitors and callers who find you are at home may not understand that you are working.

Sole traders may no longer have any administrative support staff.

Social isolation and no one to bounce ideas off, or consult when work isn't going so well.

* * *

RENTING OUT YOUR PROPERTY

With the cost of coastal retreats rocketing skywards and demand increasing, you might want to consider renting your holiday home. You should get a good return in the peak season of January.

Bach and holiday home owners still have to pay rates and maintenance on top of any mortgage payments. Any income you make could be spent on upgrading the property later if it needs it. An occupied property will deter thieves. If you're going to rent there are many ways that you can make your property more desirable.

Suggestions for Renting Out a Property

Clean, tidy well-equipped kitchen

Clean, tidy bathroom

Allow pets. New Zealand isn't as pet-friendly as the UK or Europe and many pet owners find going away difficult as they can't get anywhere to stay.

Provide some recreational kit such as bikes, kayaks, golf clubs, and board games for wet weather.

Marketing Your Property

You can market a holiday property informally through friends, family and work contacts. But these networks only go so far. To reach a wider market, you'll need to plan a marketing campaign. That might cost you a few hundred dollars, but that could be offset against tax.

If you're going to advertise in the print media, it's important that your advertisement stands out from the rest. If you take pets and the other holiday homes in the area make no mention of this, you may even get repeat business from grateful pet owners.

Build a Website. If you aren't sure what to include on your website check out the competition on-line. Good photographs and a virtual tour – showing every room including kitchens, bathrooms and the outside area are a much better indication of what the house looks like than written description. Holidaymakers want to see what the specification is, what the cooking facilities are like, whether cooking is done by electricity or gas, whether the appliances are new or old and whether the furniture is of a good standard. If a holidaymaker is booking your place because of its proximity to the beach, the accuracy of the information relating to that is crucial. Distances need to be exact, rather than approximate, including how far it is to local shops, the petrol station, and the nearest supermarket.

Advertise on Other Websites. Websites advertising baches and holiday homes have multiplied in recent years. Check the terms and conditions carefully. Some charge an annual fee to advertise or others, such as Airbnb, charge a percentage on each booking. Check what others are charging and what facilities they have compared with yours. Make sure you set your rates competitively. Your place doesn't have to be an architectural statement with a lap pool – provided the price reflects that.

Websites merely bring your property to the attention of a wider market – they aren't management agencies. Once a provisional booking has been made through a website the rest is up to the owner. A professional booking system with updated availability is very important. Provide a mobile phone number so that you can be reached in the daytime as well as the evening. Return emails and calls promptly. If you are targeting international visitors, a quarter of your potential market, you must be able to take credit card bookings.

Marketing to Satisfied Customers. Repeat business should be the aim of every holiday homeowner, so don't forget to ask guests to sign the visitors' book so that you can stay in touch. You could offer some kind of loyalty or discount scheme for regulars. An email or two during the year with what's going on in the area will remind your former guests of their holiday and could be enough to persuade them to re-book.

Using a Property Manager. You could be paying up to 25% of the income from the property to a property manager in return for a total management service including finding tenants, organising key collection, supervising cleaning and linen change between tenancies, ensuring that the grounds are maintained, checking on wear and tear and finding tradesmen to carry out regular maintenance. Good service is vital in this business and when things do go wrong (as they invariably do with houses) there needs to be someone close by to sort out any problems. Property management charges can be offset against tax.

Before you buy a property it could be worth talking to a property manager from a different agency, to get an unbiased opinion of occupancy rates and how much you could charge. The location is crucial, as holiday home occupancy is seasonal and that season could be as short as twelve weeks in some areas.

* * *

SELLING ON

New Zealanders can, on average, expect to stay in one property for seven years. But as life sometimes takes an unexpected turn, you could find that you need to sell up. As Helen Davies points out in **Chapter 13, Case Histories**, marketing and real estate commission are very expensive. But although most New Zealanders grumble about these high costs, the majority of houses are still sold through an agent.

The average agent's commission is around 4% (expensive enough as it is), but this is only for the agent's services and excludes the marketing fee. The agent commission is paid solely by the seller. For a $600,000 house, you'll be paying a commission of around $24,000. Add on $3500 for marketing. For that, you get a sign outside your house with colour photographs, colour advertising in the property press and on real estate websites such as TradeMe.

Anyone who has ever tried to sell a house without an agent will know that this can be time- consuming. Many of those who do end up trying to sell privately may be those who have bought recently and who may be too stretched to afford the commission. With the success of TradeMe, where agents also list their properties for sale, the site has increased its fees to private sellers. It operates a sliding scale, but for a house priced over $500,000 you would be charged $399 for the listing with up to 20 photographs. For a feature advertisement you could be paying a further $400. It still works out cheaper than going through an agent, but they do of course run Open Homes and conduct the negotiation with buyers.

If you have enough time to wait until spring to sell your house that will be a bonus, but if you need to sell it immediately, then you should invite three local agents in the area to give you a market appraisal. You may not get an exact price but a guide price – 'in the region of'. Ask the three agents for the costs of marketing, their commission and the different prices for selling by negotiation, at auction or through a tender. Ask them to show you their figures of the current percentage of successful sales by auction. Ask every agent for a list of what needs doing to the property to prepare it for sale.

Cleaning, Grooming and Staging

Your house and garden have to look their best before you put them on the market. The house should ideally be recently painted (outside as well as inside), as even a wide-angle lens can't hide a grubby exterior. If you can't afford to paint the exterior, then arrange for an external house cleaner to water blast with a chemical wash or a high-pressure hose to clean the dirt off the outside. Buyers prefer neutral décor as it makes it easier for them to imagine their furniture against a plain background. Not everyone likes colour, so Spanish white (the New Zealand answer to Britain's Magnolia) is a safe option.

One homeowner in Hamilton was told to make some cosmetic changes to a recently renovated house. The house had been freshly painted and a brand new kitchen had been installed. The bathroom was the only room that hadn't been done up and was the least inviting room in the house. A café curtain and a plant gave this room the lift it needed.

The helpful agent pointed out that the house lacked 'street appeal'. With the assistance of a local gardener, a plan was drawn up to soften the view to the front of the house with appropriate planting. Two conifers in pots were placed by the front door to provide more of a welcome. Total spend including garden labour – less than $400. It took 24 hours to sell this house to a cash buyer, who made an unconditional offer at the asking price.

As well as attending to all the tidying up, cleaning and painting needed, expensive houses are often 'staged'. The owner's furniture is removed and replaced with a furniture package from a home staging company so that potential buyers don't get distracted by the owner's taste.

Asking Price

Attend 'Open Homes' of similar houses in your local area to check out the competition for price, presentation and length of time needed to market a property. Assess the agents' valuations. Take the average of the three sales figures and use that as your asking price. The agent may of course decline to put an asking price on the property and let the market decide. But whichever strategy you choose, setting too high an asking price could hamper rather than help the marketing campaign.

As well as knowing the median house price in your area, you should check how many days on average houses take to sell. Make sure that the agent gets feedback from potential buyers and whether there's anything that might be putting them off. Cosmetic redecoration will not offset a more serious problem such as a boundary dispute with a neighbour, or poor access. Boundary disputes need to be clarified and addressed with a solicitor and poor access needs to be addressed. If there is an ongoing boundary dispute with neighbours and this isn't disclosed to the buyer, there could be legal repercussions.

CASE HISTORIES

SANDRO AND LAURA

Sandro and Laura came to New Zealand and ran a bed and breakfast business in the Nelson region. Originally from Liguria in Italy, they moved from a country that some would say has an enviable lifestyle – a rich cultural heritage, wonderful cuisine and climate to match, making it the ideal place to settle. But as Sandro and Laura point out, to earn a living in Italy these days, the majority of Italians have to base themselves in the bigger cities.

Many New Zealanders dream of buying a place in the Italian countryside – yet you've come to New Zealand. What was it that attracted you to the country and the Nelson region as a place to live? We decided to migrate to New Zealand in order to have a better lifestyle. The Italian countryside is beautiful but very difficult for the average Italian to settle there – houses are very expensive and there are no jobs. The Italians have to stay in the big cities in order to have a job but the lifestyle in the bigger cities is terrible. We thought New Zealand was a quiet, friendly and safe place. We chose Nelson because of the nice climate, similar to the one we had in our region of origin, Liguria.

What was different about buying a house in New Zealand compared to Italy? When we moved here the houses in NZ were far cheaper compared to the Italian ones. They are probably still cheaper but not that cheap!

How did you find adjusting to New Zealand life compared to where you lived before? We took a while to adjust to the New Zealand lifestyle. In particular, it was difficult for Laura – being a city girl. But the friendly environment made it easy to adapt.

What do you miss from home – regional cuisine, cultural life perhaps? Of course, we miss the Italian culture and the beautiful art-filled cities. We don't miss the cooking much because we like cooking and we do a lot ourselves. We like to eat organic food; we try to make as much by hand as possible such as bread, cakes, panforte, jams as well as vegetarian and healthy recipes. And the New Zealand lifestyle helps us a lot in achieving this.

How did you find getting residence in New Zealand? Getting residence in New Zealand was quite difficult with the points system. There was a lot of bureaucracy and paperwork. But we were successful in the end.

Do you have any advice for others planning to do the same thing? Always try to work out the good and bad expectations that you have. Try to figure out how much you will miss family and friends before deciding to move and don't think that here is paradise anyway! New Zealand appears 'green' on the surface but living here we are discovering that it is not that green and we decided to go organic precisely because we found that there is genetic modification and horticultural spraying. A lot of foreigners think that New Zealand is the last resort in good living, and it could be in theory, but stupid governments don't only exist in Europe and North America, unfortunately!

HELEN DAVIES

Helen Davies moved with her family to a rural area just north of Auckland where the trees and greenery remind her of Wales.

What was it about New Zealand that first attracted you to live there? We were attracted by the lifestyle but it turned out that where we wanted to buy we weren't able to afford. We wanted to live in Coatesville in the country. We didn't want to go coastal and we realised the price difference. In the suburbs you can get a house for $400-$500,000 – around here it's in the millions. We live in an area where you have to buy 5.5 acres. It's the price of the land.

Cost of living. I knew what food and electricity cost as we'd done our research. There are hidden costs: things that are imported – which are cheaper in the UK. Although meat is cheaper here and the fruit and veg quality is much better. You change the way you eat. Petrol is cheaper. You still have to have your WOF (MOT) done twice. If you worked it all out it would probably be the same. I would say that because you're taxed higher in your wage anyway, that it's the same.

You're taxed on every dollar you earn.

On there being no NHS in New Zealand. I used to work for the NHS so to me the NHS was a brilliant service. I find it an absolute pain to have to pay for the doctor. It's $28 for the children and $40 for me. People run the NHS down but it's a fantastic service.

How difficult was it to get into the country? Paul did his Certificate in Business Studies, which had to be verified from Swansea College and then the qualifications had to be assessed by NZQA (New Zealand Qualifications Authority). We used the Emigration Group to help us. They were really good as we were both working full-time and didn't have time. They filled in the forms, although you pay for it (£3000). Paul got a job through a contact who was setting up a sales office in Auckland making wood burning stoves.

Look see visit. I thought I'd done my research. We came out three months before we moved and had a look around for a couple of weeks in the Auckland area as this is where Paul's job was going to be. Of course that was in the boom and houses were going like hot potatoes. We were looking to rent and rent out here (in the rural Coatesville/Riverhead area) and it was really expensive – $600 to $700 per week. We realised we'd really struggle to pay that level of rent for a long period of time on Paul's salary. We were in a Catch 22 situation as houses to buy were expensive as well. We were bringing the children – they didn't want to move to NZ and we wanted to make it as pleasurable for them as possible and we wanted them to be settled in the countryside. As well as rent being so expensive there were very few properties for rent to choose from. By then we'd sold our place in the UK.

On buying a house sight unseen over the internet. When

313

we went home (to Wales) we bought a house over the internet. We were faxed a contract which we didn't know, nor was it explained to us that what we were signing we couldn't back out of. We had signed an unconditional contract with no valuation, builder's report or any conditions in the contract. We had done our own research and had heard of Leaky Building Syndrome so there was a concern about that.

What happened when they arrived. The house we bought had an electricity pylon right opposite it and this house that was supposed to be completely done up wasn't and we had to do it ourselves. (As well as that the Davies' found out that half of their front garden belonged to the local council).

On buying a house in New Zealand. You can buy a house in a day here. It's too easy to buy a house in New Zealand compared with the UK. In the UK the solicitor checks everything and asks for different reports. In New Zealand it's different. I would totally avoid buying a house at auction, as you still have to pay for LIMS up front and then you could still lose out, especially if the agent says the house is going to go for a certain amount and then it goes over that. Buying a house in New Zealand is a minefield.

On home maintenance and renovation. Tradesmen cost a fortune and paint is much more expensive than in the UK.

On selling a house in New Zealand. The cost of all the advertising and the commission is huge. It cost £250 to sell the old house – compared with $30,000 for the house here.

On living in New Zealand. Auckland is not the rest of New Zealand. We came here as my husband's job was in Auckland. Property is more expensive in Auckland and we didn't realise how bad the traffic was. Paul spends three hours a day in traffic. But compared with Swansea, Auckland is a nice city. It's clean and close to the water. It has the lifestyle – the outdoor way of life, lots of people have boats and it's a nicer environment. The UK is overpopulated. There's more space and freedom to do things. They go out in all weather, though. When my son was taking part in a school event we didn't think it was going to happen as it was raining so hard, so when a friend rang and asked where we were and I said it would probably be cancelled, she told us that, 'no, you're in New Zealand now'.

Advice for house buyers. Always go and see a property for yourself rather than relying on what the agent tells you. Or if you know someone with a camcorder send them out. Talk to lots of agents as compared with the UK, agents are very pushy. One we dealt with would ring us in the middle of the night when we were in the UK.

What are the main differences you've found about living in New Zealand compared with living in Wales? People are more laid-back which is mostly a good thing but sometimes can be a bit frustrating. They don't have villages, which we found really strange. We wanted to be in a community but with space around us. That's why we came to the countryside. When you come down East Coast Bays road you see a sea of roofs. You think, you didn't come to New Zealand for that. You don't build behind each other in the UK and sell off your back garden.

What do you miss? The only thing I really miss is the language because we speak Welsh. My children went to an all-Welsh school so English was a foreign language and now my son finds it difficult to speak Welsh and we haven't even been here a year. Welsh is my first language. We obviously miss our family and we feel guilty about taking our children away from the grandparents. Both sets have been out. You do miss family and friends. The culture as well. Both my husband and I have strong Welsh roots. Ffion, my daughter, sings.

MIKE COLE

Mike Cole and his family moved to New Zealand in 2003. He set up his own business and now runs his own company BritsNZ which helps people with advice and guidance on moving to New Zealand.

You've started a brand new business in the past two years, which must be stressful enough – yet you've managed to have a house built as well. Why did you choose to build from scratch rather than buy a house? Here in NZ buying a property is relatively straightforward (compared to the UK anyway) and although we went to many Open Homes, we never quite found what we were truly looking for and nothing really grabbed us. You know that sort of feeling you get when you walk in somewhere and it feels right. This could probably be put down to us just being somewhat fussy, but also as there is quite a 'culture' difference between NZ and UK. Building looked a more attractive way of getting back into the property market, as it allowed us to be creative. Coming from the south-east of the UK it was something we could never have done there and so there was also an element of doing it because we could!

How long did it take to find the right section to build on? We were guided by friends who were building also and so we opted to look in the same area and because at that time the section was well priced. Of course, before we moved in the friends sold and moved elsewhere. From getting to NZ in October, I think we eventually settled on the section the following April.

What do people need to look out for when buying a section? The list is long. It needs to be primarily north facing and needs to able to capture the sun most of the day, particularly in winter. Ideally, it should be a flat section and have no fill in it, that is, the section is all original, natural ground. Usually, if there is fill on the section, you will have to drive wooden piles, which simply adds to the costs. It should be well draining and you need to be aware of the water table and of course what is around it – bush, houses, industry, etc! You also need to feel comfortable in the neighbourhood and have an eye for what else is being built in the area. For instance, is the area going to suit your plans and give you a ready re-sale value?

What was it about Taranaki and New Plymouth that was so special that made you want live there? Initially we had met the Mayor at an Emigrate show. He is a charismatic character and he and the video we saw of the area stuck in our minds. When we were job searching, we remembered these things and therefore targeted the area and hey presto, up popped the job we needed to get into NZ. But apart from that, we are surrounded by stunning scenery, great rivers and surf beaches and a totally awesome mountain so what's not to like? We have a great climate which means warm, but not oppressive summers and mild winters. Plus there are all the facilities we need locally.

The only downside to the area is that it is a little cut off – three hours north or south to the next largest town and this does give the people an introverted attitude. They are absolutely great and have helped us no end, but they are slow to accept change!

How did you go about finding the right team to build the house – architects, builders and other trades people? We took our time and asked as many local people as possible, which of course threw up many different opinions, but we gradually found the same names cropping up both positively and negatively and made decisions based on that. One thing that does surprise (and worry us to a degree), is that too many people come over here and want everything in a hurry. They are supposedly coming for the rest of their lives, so why do they need to make these key decisions so quickly? They certainly would not have made a house buying decision that quickly in the UK. As a consequence, most people will move two or three times in the space of the first 12/18 months, something very few people do in the UK. People need to be encouraged to take their time and get into their new environment and find where is comfortable for them.

What kind of red tape did you encounter along the way? To be honest not much red tape at all. The purchase of the section was slowed as we used a solicitor, as we had not seen a land purchase contract before and although we were assured it was a standard contract and could be dealt with via the selling agent, we opted for caution. Plans went through the Council process with next to no problems and the council inspections of the build as it progressed threw up no oddities.

We did, however, discover that we had not understood just where our boundaries were and ended up having to build a retaining wall around two sides to provide us with the full size of what we had purchased, so that caught us out somewhat!

What were some of the highs and the lows of the building process? Highs – seeing our ideas appear as a plan, getting those plans through Council with next to no changes, then seeing the slab being created and poured and then seeing the house flat-packed waiting to be turned into our home and of course watching it being built!

Lows – in reality I think the only low was hassle with a flooring contractor, who caused us no end of problems because of some pretty shoddy service and because, even after ten months our slab was still too wet to apply some floor coverings!

Where did you live while the house was being built and how did the family cope? We initially stayed in a motel for the first month (which was a godsend as our motel owner took us under her wing and helped us enormously). We then rented two different properties from the same landlord, staying 18 months in one place and six months in another, so making life pretty simple for us. As we were in rented accommodation and had all our own stuff around us, the family coped pretty well. The first rental was no more than twelve minutes from the city centre, but was considered rural, whilst the second was in town itself.

You were in the house in time for Christmas 2005 – how did that feel? It was a great relief for my wife to at last have somewhere that was her own. She'd not had a home of her own for about five years. We had rented in the UK before coming to NZ due to work problems and the need to be mobile. In reality it did help when we wanted to come to NZ, as we only needed to give notice and leave, whereas so many people are struggling to sell and that is affecting their migration plans! It was great to be in our home that we had created in time for Christmas.

What advice would you give to anyone else who was contemplating having a house built in New Zealand? Take your time and don't stop asking people who is good and as importantly, who is not and go to those, who on balance, seem to be mentioned positively the most often. Never stop asking questions and remember your designer works for you, so if you want something in the house make sure to demand it. Once you have your plans, go and sit with them on the section and try and imagine what it will look like – even peg it out so you get a feel for size etc and go and see your friends and let them have a say. They may have some good ideas too! Once you have your builder on board, make sure you have a fixed price contract and go and see progress regularly and befriend the guys working on the house. Tea and cakes are always welcomed by builders – and do NOT forget the roof shout! (Free drinks for the team when the roof goes on). If you have a budget, make sure there is plenty of slack in it because you will definitely want things changed as it goes up and you see your plan taking actual shape.

It's such a big step moving half way across the world – and you and your family had your fair share of heartaches just to get accepted into New Zealand. What do you think is the secret to a successful relocation? Knowing what you want to achieve and not being distracted from it no matter what. You have to have a complete focus on what you want to do, and you must live the process 24/7. We were once asked what our contingency plan was if NZ did not happen – the answer was that there was no contingency plan. We were going to get to NZ. You also have to change your attitude once in your new country. You are 'Johnny foreigner' and you have to make every effort to get out into the community and speak with people and find out things. Never pass up any opportunity or invite and always be willing to listen and learn. And NEVER, NEVER, NEVER say 'we didn't do it like that at home', that will not endear you to anyone. We have found that Kiwis respond very positively to people who make an effort whereas if you hold back, they will not come forward.

Also, dream the dream. Individually think what you

want your new life to be like before you leave the UK. Write it down and share and compare it with your partner etc and periodically go back and revisit it and amend and refine, as you want. Take it with you on the flight and read it as you take-off and as you land in your new country and make it happen.

Be prepared for settling into NZ to be more expensive than you currently perceive it will be. Nearly everyone we have surveyed (for our trips back to the UK whether Poms or returning Kiwis) have commented that it cost more than they thought it would.

Finally, tell your family and friends your plans early. Accept that there will be those who will be upset, but over time you will need their help and support, so get the anguish out the way early and by the time you come to leave they should be there to support you. You know why you are doing this and if once explained, people can't accept it, that is their problem, not yours.

Oh and one last thing, whatever else you do, do NOT let anyone, friend or family, come to the airport to see you off. It will be emotional enough but saying goodbye at the departure gate is just too distressing, particularly when you have a 24+ hour flight ahead of you!

* * *

BIBLIOGRAPHY

Alpers, Antony, *Maori Myths and Tribal Legends.* (1964) Even though Alpers sources date back to Victorian England, he is a fine storyteller and researcher.

Automobile Association, *Regional Guides. Bed & Breakfast Book New Zealand*

Bryant, G. and Scarrow E., *The Complete New Zealand Gardener*

King, Michael, *The Penguin History of New Zealand*

Lonely Planet, *Lonely Planet New Zealand*

Magazines: Cuisine, Listener, Metro, Property Press

Newspapers: *New Zealand Herald*

Taylor, Paul, *Naked Eye Wonders: A Short Guide to the Stars as Seen from Aotearoa New Zealand*

Rough Guides, *The Rough Guide to New Zealand*

Shaw, P., *A History of New Zealand Architecture*

Shaw, P. and Hallett, P., *Spanish Mission Hastings – Styles of Five Decades*

FURTHER READING

Barbara Anderson – *Long Hot Summer*

Defies the stereotype that New Zealand fiction is gloomy. Has a fine wit and gift for comic observation in this story of a holiday at the beach and a clash of cultures.

Fergus Barrowman (ed) – *The Picador Book of Contemporary New Zealand Fiction*

Eleanor Catton – *The Luminaries*

Janet Frame – *Faces in the Water, Owls Do Cry*.

Maurice Gee – *Plumb Trilogy*

Keri Hulme – *The Bone People*

Witi Ihimaera – *The Whale Rider*

Lloyd Jones – *The Book of Fame*. The tale of the first All Black tour of England.

Elizabeth Knox – *The Vintner's Luck* – an imaginative and evocative book set amongst the vineyards in France written by a contemporary New Zealand writer.

Katherine Mansfield – *The Garden Party and Other Stories*.

Noel Virtue – *The Redemption of Elsdon Bird*

NEW ZEALAND ON SCREEN

An Angel at My Table, The Piano Jane Campion's adaptation of Janet Frame's autobiography and the tale of a Scottish mute mail-order bride.

Top of the Lake, Jane Campion's television thriller series set in Queenstown.

Boy and *Hunt for the Wilderpeople,* Taika Waititi – comedy-drama.

Frontier of Dreams – documentary series broadcast on TV One,

Heavenly Creatures, Lord of the Rings and The Hobbit Peter Jackson. The New Zealand director who put Wellington on the map.

No 2 - Toa Fraser. A comedy set in Auckland's Polynesian community which won the Audience Award at the 2006 Sundance Film Festival.

Once Were Warriors, Lee Tamahori. As hard-hitting as Cathy Come Home comes this tragic tale set in modern South Auckland.

Scarfies, Robert Sarkies. Dunedin university students get up to no good.

The Navigator, Vigil, Vincent Ward. Two films from one of

New Zealand's most acclaimed art house directors.

The World's Fastest Indian – Roger Donaldson. The tale of Southland motorcycling legend Burt Munro.

Utu, Geoff Murphy A tale of revenge set in the 1800s.

Whale Rider, Niki Caro. Set in rural Gisborne, the story of a girl destined for leadership.

INDEX

Accident Compensation
Commission   57, 182, 191, 192
Accommodation   231-234
Airlines   31-34
Apartments   215-217
Art Deco   212
Auckland   108-114
Auctions   247-250

Bach   10,44,95
Banks   181-188, 188-189
Bay of Plenty   93, 125-131
Builders   287, 299
Building Consents   285, 287, 290

Californian Bungalow   95, 213
Case Histories   310-321
Christchurch   91, 93-94, 162-167
Climate   10, 29, 30
Coromandel Peninsula   120-125
Contracts   179, 245, 246, 255
Conveyancing   245
Crime   29-30
Currency   188-189

Doctors	55-57
Driving	36-39
Eco-Housing	228-229
Economy	181, 185-186
Education	46-55
Electricity	263-266
Embassies & Consulates	87-88
Estate Agents	199-201
Farms	226-228
Finance	181-189
Fire Prevention	271
Food and Drink	41-46
Gardens	292-298
Gas	268-269
Geographical Information	26-29
Getting There	5, 31-35
Gisborne	131-135
Government	22-26
Hawke's Bay	135-139
Health	55-57
Heating	208, 263, 266-267
History	13-24
Home Businesses	299, 301-302
House and Land Packages	217-218
Importing Currency	188-189
Immigration	72-88
Importing Vehicles	275, 279-280
Insurance	195-196
Internet	6, 40, 64

Kauri	11, 96, 98, 104
Kerikeri	10, 101, 106
Land Purchase	217-218
Leaky Building Syndrome	218-223
Lawyers	245, 249, 251-252, 254
Lifestyle Blocks	227-228
Local Authorities	194-195, 234
Manawatu	143-148
Maori Mythology	11-13
Maori Vocabulary	67-68
Marlborough	156-158
Media	62-65
Monolithic Cladding	96, 218-223
Mortgages	186-188
Nelson	10, 30, 159-162
New Houses	217-218, 316-320
Newspapers	62-63
Northland	101-108
Offshore Banking	190
Old Houses	94-99 104, 210-213
Open Homes	197 202-203
Otago	171-175
Pets	280-284
Political History	17-24
Population	6, 21
Post	39
Proportional	
Representation (MMP)	25-26
Property Seminars	197-202
Public Holidays	68-69

Radio	63-64
Relocation Consultants	230, 237
Removals	275-279
Renovation	285-290
Renting	230-244
Residency	72-88
Rural Properties	264 & 266
Sales & Purchase Agreements	252-255
Schools & Education	6, 46-55
Security	271-272
Selling On	299, 307-308
Shopping	59-62
Southland	175-178
State Houses	211
Style of Housing	210-213
Surveys (Building Inspections)	249, 254
Swimming Pools	288, 291-292
Tax	60, 191-193
Telephone	40-41
Television	64-65
Tenancy Laws	238
Tender Process	247, 250-251
Timeshare	225-226
Travel Agents	35
Treaty of Waitangi	5, 18-19
Trusts	190-191
Universities	54-55
VAT (GST)	60
Villas	207, 210-11
Vineyards	45-46, 323

Waikato	115-120
Wairarapa	148, 152-153
Wanganui	143-148
Water	263, 269-271
Weatherboard	210-211
Wellington	148-154
West Coast	168-170
Wills	195
Work Permits	82-83

ABOUT THE AUTHOR

Alison Ripley Cubitt is an author, columnist, memoirist, novelist, screenwriter and short story writer. She has been published by Daydreams Dandelion Press, Endeavour Press, Vacation Works and Writers News.

She has lived and worked in Australia, Malaysia, New Zealand and the UK. For the past fifteen years she has helped over 100 relocation clients in Auckland and Melbourne find their perfect home.

For more information and future publications:

Hop over to her website at
http://www.lambertnagle.com

You can sign up for her mailing list here:
http://www.lambertnagle.com/newsletter

Facebook page:
https://www.facebook.com/alisonripleycubittwriter

Connect with her on Twitter:
https://twitter.com/lambertnagle

ALSO BY
ALISON RIPLEY CUBITT

BOOKS

Castles in the Air: A Family Memoir of Love and Loss, 2015

Buying a House in New Zealand (first edition), 2006

Retiring to Australia and New Zealand (with Deborah Penrith), 2006

Revolution Earth (with Sean Cubitt), writing as Lambert Nagle, 2013

SHORT STORIES

Blue Silk Dress appears in Mosaics 2: A Collection of Independent Women 2016

Contained, (as Lambert Nagle) in *Capital Crimes*, 2015

ACKNOWLEDGEMENTS

Special thanks are due to the contributors for their generosity in sharing their case histories: Helen Davies, Laura Totis and Sandro Lionello and Mike Cole. Thanks to Rebecca Russell for sharing her anecdote with me and to Eden Sharp and Karen Bali from Write On Hants for encouraging me to write this second edition.

The author and publisher believe that the information and accuracy of this book was correct at the time of going to press. Readers are strongly urged to check the most up-to-date information regarding exchange rates and regulations as these can alter.